DAS SYNAGOGEN PROJEKT

Zum Wiederaufbau
von Synagogen in Deutschland

On the Reconstruction
of Synagogues in Germany

THE SYNAGOGUE PROJECT

Das Synagogen-Projekt
The Synagogue Project

Herausgeber
 Editors
 Jörg Springer
 Manuel Aust

Inhalt
Contents

9		Zum Synagogen-Projekt
		On the Synagogue Project
		Monika Grütters
11		Neue Synagogen
		New synagogues in Hamburg & Berlin
		Jörg Springer
19		Salomon Korn im Gespräch mit
		in conversation with
		Jörg Springer
31		Mario Marcus & Dekel Peretz im Gespräch mit
		in conversation with
		Andreas Fuchs & Ivan Reimann
45		Synagoge Fraenkelufer
		Fraenkelufer Synagogue
87		Edward van Voolen im Gespräch mit
		in conversation with
		Ivan Reimann & Gesine Weinmiller
101		Roger Diener im Gespräch mit
		in conversation with
		Jörg Springer
115		Tempel Poolstraße
		Temple Poolstraße
141		Franz-Josef Höing & Philipp Stricharz im Gespräch mit
		in conversation with
		Wolfgang Lorch, Ivan Reimann,
		Jörg Springer & Gesine Weinmiller
153		Mirjam Wenzel im Gespräch mit
		in conversation with
		Wolfgang Lorch & Jörg Springer
171		Synagoge Bornplatz
		Bornplatz Synagogue
217		Appendix

Zum Synagogen-Projekt
On the Synagogue Project
Monika Grütters

Im vergangenen Jahr haben wir 1700 Jahre jüdisches Leben in Deutschland gefeiert. Dieses Datum hat viele Gelegenheiten geboten, vom beachtlichen Beitrag des Judentums zum kulturellen Reichtum, aber auch zu Fortschritt und Entwicklung unseres Landes zu erfahren – sei es in Wirtschaft oder Wissenschaft, Philosophie oder Physik, Malerei, Musik oder Architektur.

Das Festjahr hat uns auch vor Augen geführt, dass nach der Barbarei des Nationalsozialismus Deutschland wieder Heimat jüdischen Lebens geworden ist. Dieses Wiederaufblühen jüdischer Kultur ist das größte Geschenk in der deutschen Nachkriegsgeschichte. Ein Geschenk ist auch das Vertrauen, das Jüdinnen und Juden in Deutschland setzen: das Vertrauen darauf, hier sowohl willkommen als auch sicher zu sein; das Vertrauen darauf, dass jüdisches Leben sich in Deutschland frei entfalten kann. Dieses Vertrauen nicht zu enttäuschen, ist Verantwortung des Staates, der Gesellschaft und jedes einzelnen in unserem Land. Umso beschämender ist es, welch erschreckendes Ausmaß Hass und Gewalt gegenüber Jüdinnen und Juden in Deutschland wieder angenommen haben. Diesen schlimmen Entwicklungen müssen wir alle gemeinsam entschlossen entgegentreten.

Das Synagogen-Projekt trägt seinen Teil dazu bei: Studierende und ihre Professorinnen und Professoren haben Entwürfe vorgelegt, die die zerstörten Synagogen in Hamburg und Berlin in neuem Glanz und alter Schönheit rekonstruieren. Damit zeigt das Projekt jüdisches Leben als inspirierenden Teil deutscher Geschichte und Gegenwart. Das ist ein wichtiger und unverzichtbarer Beitrag auch zur Antisemitismusprävention. Denn wo Menschen begreifen, wie stark europäische Kunst und Kultur, Wissenschaft und Wirtschaft von Jüdinnen und Juden geprägt sind, wie stark jüdische Kultur Teil unserer europäischen Kultur ist, wird die giftige Saat antisemitischer Hetze nicht aufgehen. Dieses Wissen wächst auch und gerade im Angesicht des baukulturellen Erbes.

Ich bin überzeugt: Das Engagement der Aufrechten ist auch heute unverzichtbar. Deshalb unterstütze ich das Synagogen-Projekt, damit die wiederaufgebauten Synagogen erneut zum Zentrum jüdischen Lebens in Hamburg und Berlin – und auch Orte der Begegnung mit jüdischem Leben in Deutschland – werden.

Es ist vorbildlich, mit welchem Eifer und wie intensiv sich die Teilnehmerinnen und Teilnehmer an diesem Projekt mit jüdischer Kultur, mit der Liturgie und mit dem jüdischen Alltag auseinandergesetzt haben. Ihre Offenheit, ihre Neugier und ihr Engagement sind ein wichtiges Signal weit über die Projektarbeit hinaus. Dafür bin ich dankbar.

Last year, we celebrated 1,700 years of Jewish life in Germany. The landmark date offered numerous opportunities to appreciate the impressive contributions made by Jewish people to the cultural wealth of the German nation, and also to our country's advancement and national development—whether in the spheres of economics or science, philosophy or physics, in painting, music, or architecture.

This celebratory year has heightened our awareness of the fact that, even after the barbarity of National Socialism, Germany has again become a home for Jewish life. This renaissance of Jewish culture is the greatest blessing of German postwar history. Also a blessing is the trust that Jews have placed in Germany: the confidence that they are both welcome and safe, that Jewish life can develop freely here. To avoid betraying this trust is the responsibility of the government, of society, and of every individual throughout this country. All the more shameful, therefore, are the alarming dimensions of the growing phenomenon of hate and violence against Jews in Germany. We must join together, all of us, to confront these appalling developments with the firmest resolve.

The Synagogue Project is doing its part: students and their professors have presented designs for the reconstruction of the destroyed synagogues in Hamburg and Berlin with new splendor and in all of their former glory. The project thereby highlights Jewish life as an inspiring aspect of German history and of the German present. It also makes a vital and essential contribution to the prevention of anti-Semitism. For when people understand just how profoundly European art and culture, science and commerce, have been shaped by the Jewish people, and the degree to which Jewish culture is an integral part of European civilization, the poisonous seeds of anti-Semitic agitation can hardly flourish. And such an understanding is nourished as well and in particular by an awareness of our architectural heritage.

I am convinced that today, as well, the engagement of decent people is imperative. Which is why I am supporting the Synagogue Project, in the hope that the reconstructed synagogues again become centers of Jewish life in Hamburg and Berlin—and, at the same time, places of encounter with Jewish life in Germany.

With exemplary zeal, enthusiasm, and intensity, the project participants have turned their attention toward Jewish culture, ranging from liturgical matters to the rhythms of everyday life. Far beyond their work on the project itself, their openness, curiosity, and commitment send an important signal. And for that I am grateful.

Neue Synagogen
New synagogues
in Hamburg & Berlin
Jörg Springer

Das Synagogen-Projekt leistet mit architektonischen Entwürfen – erarbeitet an vier deutschen Universitäten – einen anschaulichen Beitrag zu der mit großer Intensität geführten Debatte um den Wiederaufbau von zerstörten Synagogen in Deutschland. Ergänzt durch eine Reihe von Gesprächen begeben sich die Arbeiten der Studierenden in Zeichnungen und atmosphärisch dichten, perspektivischen Darstellungen auf die Suche nach einem heute angemessenen baulichen Ausdruck jüdischen Lebens in deutschen Großstädten.

Streit um die Rekonstruktionen

Im Februar 2020 beschloss die Hamburger Bürgerschaft einstimmig den Wiederaufbau der 1938 in der Reichspogromnacht von Hamburger Bürgern zerstörten und im Folgejahr – auf Kosten der jüdischen Gemeinde – vollständig geschleiften Hauptsynagoge am Bornplatz [→ Abb.1&3].[1] Mit der «Wiederherstellung des sichtbarsten Wahrzeichens jüdischen Lebens in Hamburg»[2] soll die stetig wachsende jüdische Gemeinde eine angemessene Präsenz in der Stadt erhalten und nicht zuletzt soll auch ein Zeichen gegen neonazistische Tendenzen in Deutschland gesetzt werden. Bereits seit Längerem gibt es auch in Berlin Bestrebungen, die ebenfalls 1938 in Brand gesetzte und später abgerissene, große Synagoge am Fraenkelufer wiederaufzubauen [→ Abb.2].

Als Reaktion auf den Beschluss der Hamburger Bürgerschaft entbrannte um die Wiederherstellung der Synagoge am Bornplatz ein Streit, der mit großer Intensität öffentlich und überregional in der Presse geführt wurde. Die Kontroverse entzündete sich an der Absicht der jüdischen Gemeinde, die 1906 durch den Architekten Semmy Engel in einem romanisierenden Historismus errichtete Hauptsynagoge – wenngleich auch nur in ihren äußeren Formen – dem historischen Vorbild

Through an ensemble of architectural designs developed at four German universities, the Synagogue Project has made a salient contribution to the debate—pursued with great intensity—concerning the reconstruction of destroyed synagogues in Germany. Supplemented by a series of discussions, the student projects—presented here through drawings and atmospherically dense, perspectival renderings—engage in a search for an appropriate contemporary architectural expression for Jewish life in Germany's metropolises.

The controversy concerning the reconstructions

In February of 2020, the Hamburg Bürgerschaft (Parliament) unanimously adopted a resolution for the reconstruction of the city's former main synagogue, located on Bornplatz [→ Figs.1&3].[1] The synagogue was destroyed by the citizens of Hamburg during Kristallnacht in 1938, and was completely demolished the following year, the costs being borne entirely by the Jewish community. With the "restoration of the most visible landmark of Jewish life in Hamburg," the steadily growing Jewish community would

1
Abbruch Bornplatzsynagoge,
Hamburg,
Foto: um 1939
Demolition of the
Bornplatz Synagogue,
Hamburg,
photo: ca. 1939

2
Ruine der Synagoge
am Fraenkelufer,
Berlin,
Foto: um 1958/59
Ruins of the
synagogue on
Fraenkelufer,
Berlin,
photo: ca. 1958/59

entsprechend originalgetreu wiederherzustellen. Tatsächlich wäre eine derartige, mehr oder weniger getreue Rekonstruktion einer zerstörten Synagoge ein Novum in der kurzen Geschichte der Synagogenbauten in Deutschland seit 1945.[3]

Wenig überraschend verlief die Debatte zunächst entlang der bekannten Argumentationslinien aus anderen Rekonstruktionsdiskursen, wie sie etwa in Berlin zum Stadtschloss oder in Frankfurt zu den wieder aufgebauten Häusern am Römer geführt wurden. Doch eine derartige Verengung auf denkmaltheoretische Aspekte oder bestenfalls auf Fragen nach dem angemessenen Umgang mit den Zeugnissen der Geschichte greift hier zu kurz.

Ein anderes, mit einer neuen Bedeutung aufgeladenes Verständnis der künftigen, rekonstruierten Synagoge scheint schon früh in der Argumentation der jüdischen Gemeinde in Hamburg auf. Nach Vorstand Philipp Stricharz sei «dem Versuch der Nazis, die jüdische Kultur auszurotten, vernünftig damit zu begegnen, dass man das Judentum in seiner damaligen Erscheinung wieder sichtbar macht – sonst hätte Hitler mit seiner Auslöschungspolitik ja gewonnen».[4]

Einem solcherart symbolhaften Verständnis der wiederaufgebauten Synagoge entgegenzuhalten, «dass dadurch das Resultat verbrecherischer Handlungen unsichtbar gemacht und die Erinnerung an dieses Verbrechen erschwert»[5] werde, ginge an dieser ernstzunehmenden und ja auch schon im Beschluss der Bürgerschaft angedeuteten Intention des Wiederaufbaus vorbei. Und man wird auch kaum behaupten wollen, die Verfechter eines Wiederaufbaus strebten nach einem «Symbol für eine konservative Wende, die das Gedenken hinter sich lassen wolle»[6].

Der etwas holzschnittartige Streit für und wider eine Rekonstruktion der historischen Gestalt der Bornplatzsynagoge führt hier offensichtlich nicht weiter. Es lohnt aber dennoch, die alten Bauten und ihre Architekturen selbst in den Blick zu nehmen. Wie die meisten der um die Jahrhundertwende errichteten Synagogen waren auch die beiden Häuser in Hamburg und in Berlin gebauter Ausdruck eines Selbstverständnisses der jüdischen Gemeinden, die sich im ausgehenden 19. und im frühen 20. Jahrhundert als Teil der deutschen Gesellschaft verstanden. Die Verwendung von zur Zeit der Erbauung als «deutsch» konnotierten Stilformen und die Übernahme christlicher Bau- und Raumformen brachten die Zugehörigkeit der Gemeinden zu Nation und Stadtgesellschaft für alle sichtbar zum Ausdruck. Eine zuversichtliche Perspektive, die doch nur kurze Zeit später mit der Zerstörung der Synagogen durch deutsche Mitbürger tragisch scheiterte.

Damit erscheint allerdings auch die Wiederherstellung derselben architektonischen Bildprogramme heute, über 80 Jahre später, höchst fragwürdig. Diesen Einwand vorwegnehmend stellt Hanno Rauterberg – durchaus bedenkenswert – in der ZEIT fest, dass die Wiedererrichtung einer Synagoge im neoromanischen Stil im heutigen Kontext der Stadt nicht in der gleichen Weise als Ausdruck der Assimilation verstanden würde: «Heute wäre es anders. Heute würde eine Rekonstruktion höchst seltsam wirken, ein Fremdkörper, gerade im nüchternen Hamburg. Sie fügte sich nicht den Üblichkeiten der deutschen Erinnerungskultur mit ihrer Rhetorik der Brüche und Wunden. Und bewiese gerade darin einen Eigensinn, den man niemandem, erst recht nicht der jüdischen Gemeinde, absprechen sollte.»[7] Das ist zwar ein schöner Gedanke, aber ich habe doch große Zweifel, dass diese sympathische Qualität des «höchst Seltsamen» eines rekonstruierten

now acquire a commensurate presence in the city, and, not least of all, a clear statement would be made against neo-Nazi tendencies in Germany. In Berlin, as well, efforts have been underway for some time to rebuild the large synagogue on Fraenkelufer, also destroyed by arson in 1938, and later demolished [→ Fig. 2].

A dispute erupted—conducted with great intensity publicly across the nation as well as in the media—concerning the reconstruction of the synagogue on Bornplatz in Hamburg immediately after the resolution was adopted by the Bürgerschaft. The source of the controversy was the intention on the part of the Jewish community in Hamburg to rebuild the historic main synagogue—originally erected in 1906 by the architect Semmy Engel in a Romanesque historicist style—as a faithful reconstruction, albeit only with regard to its external form. And in fact, such a more-or-less faithful reconstruction of a destroyed synagogue would set a precedent in the brief history of synagogue building in Germany since 1945.[3]

Initially, at least, and unsurprisingly, the debate ran along argumentative tracks familiar from other discussions concerning architectural reconstructions: for example the City Palace in Berlin or the recreated buildings at the Frankfurter Römer. In this case, however, such a narrow focus on theoretical aspects related to the preservation of historic monuments, or at most to questions concerning the appropriate treatment of historical evidence, would clearly fall far short.

A very different understanding of the future reconstructed synagogue, one charged with new meaning, emerged early on in the debates within the Jewish community in Hamburg. According to first chair Philipp Stricharz, it was a question of "countering the attempt by the Nazis to eradicate Jewish culture by making Judaism as visible, once again, as it formerly was—otherwise, Hitler will have succeeded with his policy of extermination."[4]

To argue against such a symbolic understanding of the synagogue reconstruction by claiming that "this approach would render criminal acts invisible and make it more difficult to preserve the memory of these atrocities"[5] overlooks the seriousness of the intention behind the planned reconstruction, as expressed as well by the resolution adopted by the Bürgerschaft. Nor can it reasonably be claimed that the advocates of reconstruction strove to produce a "symbol of a conservative turn that leaves commemorative functions far behind."[6]

Clearly, such broad-brush arguments for or against the historically faithful reconstruction of the Bornplatz Synagogue will lead nowhere. Still, it would certainly be useful to take a closer look for ourselves at these old buildings and their architectural features. Like most of the synagogues erected around the turn of the twentieth century, those in Hamburg and Berlin were built expressions of the self-understanding of the Jewish communities, which during the late nineteenth and early twentieth centuries regarded themselves as a part of German society. The use of stylistic forms that were connoted as "German" at that time, and the adoption of Christian architectural and spatial forms, amounted to the visible expression of the membership of the communities in the nation and in urban society. An optimistic perspective, and one that ended tragically not long afterward with the destruction of the synagogues by the fellow citizens of the German Jews.

And for this reason, a reconstruction of the same architectural and iconographic program today, more than eighty years later, seems highly questionable. Anticipating this very

3
Bornplatzsynagoge, Hamburg, Postkarte: 1908
The Bornplatz Synagogue, Hamburg, postcard: 1908
—
Semmy Engel & Ernst Friedheim
1906

Bauwerks tatsächlich so wahrgenommen würde. Zu vertraut sind uns derartige Architekturen des Historismus heute noch – auch in Hamburg.

Suche nach dem angemessenen Ausdruck

Jenseits allzu bekannter Rekonstruktionsdebatten ist damit in diesem besonderen Fall zuallererst die Frage nach einem heute angemessenen baulichen Ausdruck jüdischen Selbstverständnisses in Deutschland angesprochen. Sich dabei allein darauf zurückzuziehen, das Judentum in seiner damaligen Erscheinung sichtbar zu machen, griffe wohl doch zu kurz. Beschränkte sich der Wieder-Neubau der Synagogen doch dann allein auf eine an unwiederbringlich Zerstörtes erinnernde Memorialarchitektur.

Dennoch ist auch heute noch jeder Neubau einer Synagoge in Deutschland selbstverständlich zugleich auch ein Beitrag zur Erinnerungskultur. Aber zuallererst wird die neue Synagoge die neue Heimat einer jüdischen Gemeinde sein, Raum für künftiges jüdisches Leben in der Stadt. Dieser in die Zukunft gerichteten Dimension einen architektonischen Ausdruck zu geben, ohne die Erinnerung an das Menschheitsverbrechen zu verdecken, das ist die Aufgabe, der wir uns gemeinsam mit den Studierenden gestellt haben.

Es ist eine Recherche, eine Suche, die sich mit den Mitteln des architektonischen Entwurfs, in Form von Zeichnungen und atmosphärisch dichten, perspektivischen Darstellungen den möglichen Ausdrucksformen einer neu – oder wieder – zu errichtenden Synagoge annähert. Die Ergebnisse dieser Suche sind so individuell, wie die Autoren der einzelnen Projekte, sie erzählen auch von den Persönlichkeiten der Studierenden, von ihrer je eigenen Sicht auf diese besondere Aufgabe. Gegenüber dem oft um Wahrnehmbarkeit bemühten, zugespitzten Textbeitrag haben die architektonischen Entwürfe den Vorteil des Anschaulichen auf ihrer Seite. Sie können differenzierter, vielschichtiger «argumentieren» und auch das Mehrdeutige, sogar das Widersprüchliche als eine besondere Qualität zulassen – vielleicht eine durchaus wünschenswerte Eigenschaft für den Neubau einer Synagoge in unserer Zeit.

Neben den beiden großen zerstörten Synagogen, deren Wiederaufbau diskutiert wird, haben wir auch die noch erhaltenen Fragmente des Tempels in der Hamburger Poolstraße in den Blick genommen. Der Israelitische Tempel [→ Abb. 4] in einem Hinterhof war Mitte des 19. Jahrhunderts der erste Neubau einer liberalen Synagoge. Gerade weil sich die Aufgabe an diesem lange vernachlässigten Ort mit den ruinösen historischen Bauteilen anders darstellt, war die Auseinandersetzung mit dieser besonderen Situation für das Verständnis der beiden großen Wiederaufbau-Projekte wichtig.

Das Synagogen-Projekt versteht sich als Beitrag zu einem Diskurs, dessen Bedeutung über die einzelnen Bauprojekte in Berlin und in Hamburg hinausreicht. Die architektonischen Projekte der Studierenden sind in diesem Sinne Momentaufnahmen unseres gemeinsamen Nachdenkens. Manches sähe heute gewiss anders aus. Aber gerade weil sich die Entwürfe von Anfang an als Diskursbeiträge (und eben nicht als zu realisierende Projekte) verstanden haben, konnten sie die Grenzen des Vorstellbaren ausloten.

objection, Hanno Rauterberg observed—in a way well worth pondering—in *DIE ZEIT* that, in the contemporary urban context, the reconstruction of a synagogue in the neo-Romanesque style cannot be understood as an expression of assimilation in the same way as formerly: "Today, it would be different. Today, a reconstruction would make an impression of extreme strangeness, would be a foreign body, all the more so in austere Hamburg. It would be inconsistent with the conventions of German commemorative culture, with its rhetoric of ruptures and wounds. And precisely this aspect displays an obstinacy that should not be denied to anyone, especially not the Jewish community."[7] A nice sentiment, but I seriously doubt that the congenial quality of "extreme strangeness" would actually be perceived in a reconstructed building in this way. Up to the present, such historicist architecture remains far too familiar for that—in Hamburg as well.

The search for an appropriate form of expression

Paramount in this particular instance, beyond the all-too-familiar debates concerning historical reconstruction, is the question of an appropriate contemporary architectural expression of Jewish self-understanding in Germany. A simple reversion to the notion of endowing Judaism in Germany with its former appearance falls short of what is needed. It would mean restricting synagogue reconstruction to a memorializing architecture designed to remind us of what has been irretrievably lost.

At the same time, self-evidently, every synagogue construction in Germany today is also a contribution to the culture of remembrance. But first and foremost, a new synagogue is a new home for a Jewish community, a space for future Jewish life in the city. To give this future-oriented dimension a suitable architectural expression, without at the same time obscuring the memory of crimes against humanity: this is the task we set ourselves together with our students.

It was a question of an investigation, a search, of employing the resources of architectural design, in the form of drawings and atmospherically dense, perspectival representations, to circumnavigate the possible forms of expression of a newly constructed or a reconstructed synagogue. The results of the search are as individual as the authors of the individual projects, and they tell us much about the personalities of the participating students, about their distinctive approaches toward this exceptional assignment. In contrast to the often rather pointed textual contributions, with their effort toward incisiveness, the architectural designs enjoy the advantage of vividness, concreteness. They are capable of "arguing" in a more differentiated, complex way, and are capable of integrating the ambiguous, even the contradictory as a specific quality—perhaps a thoroughly desirable attribute when it comes to constructing a new synagogue in our era.

Alongside the two major destroyed synagogues whose reconstructions were then under discussion, we also took up the surviving fragments of the temple on Poolstraße in Hamburg. In the mid-nineteenth century, the Israelite Temple [→ Fig. 4], which occupied a rear courtyard, was the first new building for a liberal synagogue. And precisely because the assignment at this long neglected site, with its ruinous historic architectural elements, was so different, it was productive for our understanding of the two major reconstruction projects.

Sichtbarkeit und Erinnern

Ergänzt werden die Entwürfe durch eine Reihe persönlicher Gespräche. Vertreter der jüdischen Gemeinden, aus Hamburg Philipp Stricharz, aus Berlin Dekel Peretz und Mario Marcus, sowie Hamburgs Oberbaudirektor Franz-Josef Höing vermitteln als unmittelbar Beteiligte ihre Sicht auf die anstehenden Wiederaufbauten. Mit Mirjam Wenzel, Direktorin des Jüdischen Museums in Frankfurt, Salomon Korn, Architekt und vormals Vizepräsident des Zentralrats der Juden in Deutschland sowie dem Rabbiner Edward van Voolen und dem Schweizer Architekten Roger Diener kommen weitere Stimmen von außen zu Wort und diskutieren Vergangenheit und Zukunft der Synagogen in deutschen Städten als Orte religiösen jüdischen Lebens und jüdischer Kultur.

Die Gespräche, alle geführt, als die architektonischen Entwürfe der Studierenden bereits vorlagen, unterscheiden sich von den zumeist sehr entschieden formulierten Diskursbeiträgen für und wider eine Rekonstruktion der zerstörten Synagogen. So wie erst die Bandbreite der in diesem Buch gezeigten architektonischen Entwürfe die Potenziale, oft aber auch die Grenzen der verschiedenen «Denkfiguren» anschaulich und für den Diskurs relevant macht, so ist auch der Charakter der Gespräche ein gemeinsam suchender. Dennoch werden die unterschiedlichen Perspektiven und die je eigenen Positionen der Gesprächspartner sichtbar.

Deutlich geworden ist, dass sich die Bedingungen eines Neu- oder Wiederaufbaus von Synagogen in Deutschland heute in mindestens zweifacher Hinsicht sowohl von den Synagogen der Jahrhundertwende als auch von den Neubauten der Nachkriegszeit unterscheiden: Anders als noch um die Jahrhundertwende soll die Synagoge heute nicht mehr in der

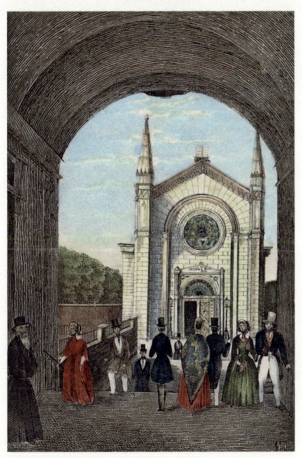

4
Tempel Poolstraße, Hamburg, kolorierter Stich: 1859
The Temple on Poolstraße, Hamburg, colored engraving: 1859
—
Johann Hinrich Klees-Wülbern
1844

The Synagogue Project was conceived as a contribution to a discussion whose significance goes beyond the individual building projects in Berlin and Hamburg. In this sense, the student projects provide snapshots of our collective reflections. Today, to be sure, some things would look different. But precisely because the designs were conceived from the very beginning as contributions to an ongoing discussion (and not intended for practical realization), they were able to explore the very limits of the conceivable.

Visibility and memory

The designs are supplemented by a series of personal conversations. The direct participants were Philipp Stricharz from Hamburg and Dekel Peretz and Mario Marcus from Berlin as representatives of the Jewish communities, along with Hamburg's chief building director Franz-Josef Höing, all of whom shared their perspectives of the pending reconstructions. With Mirjam Wenzel, director of the Jewish Museum in Frankfurt, Salomon Korn, an architect and the former vice president of the Central Council of the Jews in Germany, as well as Rabbi Edward van Voolen and the Swiss architect Roger Diener, additional voices from the outside made themselves heard, discussing the past and the future of synagogues in German cities as places of religious life and of Jewish culture.

These conversations, all conducted after the student projects had reached completion, are very different from the usual contributions to the discussions for or against reconstructions of destroyed synagogues, which are for the most part formulated with notable firmness and resolve. And just as it is only the spectrum of the architectural designs presented in this volume which make the potential—but also the limits—of the various "figures of thought" vivid and relevant for the discussion, the tenor of these conversations is one of shared searching. Coming to the fore, nonetheless, are the diverse perspectives and individual positions of the discussion partners.

It has become clear that, today, the conditions governing the construction or reconstruction of synagogues in Germany must be distinguished in at least two respects from the situation at the turn of the twentieth century, and from that of the postwar era: today, in contrast to the turn of the century, the synagogue is no longer primarily a space of prayer; instead, it is the focal point of a multifarious community life. The prayer hall may be the most important space, but it no longer dominates the synagogue with the same exclusivity that still characterized the older buildings. And today, in contrast to—and in a certain relationship of tension with—most of the new synagogue buildings erected in Germany after World War II, which also expressed the insecurity of Jewish life in Germany at that time, the declared aim of the new buildings is precisely the renewed presence and visibility of the synagogue in the city—both from the perspective of the Jewish communities, as well as from the point of view of urban society. The synagogue is meant to show that Jews are present in the city, and must hence "argue with force and visibility."[8]

At the start of the twentieth century, the two large (and later destroyed) synagogues in Berlin and Hamburg served as built symbols of the mutually beneficial cohabitation of Jews and non-Jews in major German cities. Today, "the desire to refer back to a glorious German Jewish culture [. . .] is an expression of the rediscovery of tradition"[9] within the Jewish

Hauptsache Gebetsraum sein, sie ist vielmehr Mittelpunkt eines vielfältigen Gemeindelebens, der Gebetsraum mag hier der bedeutendste Raum sein, er dominiert die Synagoge wohl aber nicht mehr mit derselben Ausschließlichkeit, die noch die alten Bauten prägte. In einem gewissen Spannungsverhältnis dazu und anders als bei den meisten in der Nachkriegszeit in Deutschland errichteten Neubauten, in denen auch die Unsicherheit jüdischen Lebens in Deutschland zum Ausdruck kam, sind heute Präsenz und Sichtbarkeit der Synagoge in der Stadt erklärte Anliegen der Neubauten – sowohl aus der Perspektive der jüdischen Gemeinden als auch aus der Sicht der Stadtgesellschaften. Die Synagoge soll zeigen, dass Jüdinnen und Juden in der Stadt präsent sind, sie «sollte mit Kraft und Sichtbarkeit argumentieren»[8].

Die beiden großen zerstörten Synagogen in Berlin und in Hamburg standen am Beginn des 20. Jahrhunderts als gebaute Symbole für das einander befruchtende Zusammenleben von Juden und Nicht-Juden in deutschen Großstädten. Heute ist «der Wunsch, sich auf die bedeutende und prachtvolle deutsch-jüdische Kultur zurückzubeziehen, [...] Ausdruck einer Wiederentdeckung von Tradition»[9] in den jüdischen Gemeinden. Dass die Hoffnungen dieser Zeit einst in so furchtbarer Weise zerstört wurden, mag das Wiederaufführen der historischen Bauformen heute fragwürdig erscheinen lassen. Dennoch ist der in die Zukunft gerichtete Optimismus dieser Position zu bewundern.

Nach wie vor ist der Neubau einer Synagoge in Deutschland keine Selbstverständlichkeit. Auch wenn das Erinnern an die Shoah nicht Aufgabe der jüdischen Gemeinden und ihrer Gotteshäuser sein kann, so ist diese Erinnerung doch immer gegenwärtig. Der Neubau einer Synagoge in Deutschland wird diese Erinnerung unausweichlich – auch – zu seinem Thema machen müssen. «Das Erinnern ist eine Aufgabe beider Seiten»,[10] wie Salomon Korn es im Gespräch formuliert hat. Vielleicht ist als zeichenhaft Sichtbares das Portative, Provisorische, die gebaute Erinnerung an das Stiftzelt [→ Abb. 5] auch heute noch ein ureigener und ein auch im Wissen um die Geschichte angemessener Aspekt des architektonischen Ausdrucks einer Synagoge in Deutschland.

communities. That the hopes of those years were destroyed in such a hideous way tends to make the revival of historical building forms seem highly questionable today. Nevertheless, the future-oriented optimism of this position is admirable.

As earlier, the building of a new synagogue in Germany cannot be taken for granted. And while the memorializing of the Shoah is hardly a task to be shouldered by the Jewish communities and their places of worship, its memory nonetheless remains ever-present. Inevitably, the construction of a new synagogue in Germany cannot avoid involvement with this theme. "Memory is a task for both sides,"[10] as Salomon Korn put it in his discussion. Today as well, perhaps, the emblematically visible, the built reminder of the portable, the provisional structure of the tabernacle, [→ Fig. 5] remains a characteristic and—also in awareness of history—fitting aspect of the architectural expression of a synagogue in Germany.

5
Darstellung des Stiftzelts
Depiction of the Tabernacle
—
Aus dem Buch/ From the book:
The Works of Josephus, 1683

1 Heute nach dem letzten Oberrabbiner Joseph-Carlebach-Platz genannt.
2 Aus dem fraktionsübergreifenden Antrag an die Bürgerschaft der Freien und Hansestadt Hamburg vom 29.01.2020.
3 Ausnahme ist die Synagoge in Herford, die 2010 wieder in ihrer 1938 zerstörten äußeren Gestalt aufgebaut wurde. Der Innenraum ist neu gestaltet und hat, anders als früher, keine Frauenempore mehr.
4 Philipp Stricharz, Vorstand der jüdischen Gemeinde Hamburg, zit. nach Till Briegleb: *Jetzt erst recht*, in: Süddeutsche Zeitung, 13.02.2020.
5 Miriam Rürup, Moshe Zimmermann u. a.: *Für einen breiten, offenen Diskurs über den Wiederaufbau der Bornplatzsynagoge*, Offener Brief, Februar 2021.
6 Miriam Rürup, seinerzeit Direktorin des Instituts für die Geschichte der deutschen Juden in Hamburg, zit. nach Till Briegleb: *Jetzt erst recht*, in: Süddeutsche Zeitung, 13.02.2020.
7 Hanno Rauterberg: *Wie modern muß eine neue Synagoge sein?*, in: Die Zeit, 09/2020, 20.02.2020.
8 Philipp Stricharz im Gespräch, siehe S. 141–151.
9 Mirjam Wenzel im Gespräch, siehe S. 153–169.
10 Salomon Korn im Gespräch, siehe S. 19–29.

Salomon Korn
im Gespräch mit
in conversation with
Jörg Springer

Salomon Korn ist der Architekt des Jüdischen Gemeindezentrums in Frankfurt am Main. Sein Satz zur Eröffnung 1986 «Wer ein Haus baut, will bleiben, und wer bleiben will, erhofft sich Sicherheit» ist auch heute – leider – noch aktuell. Das neue Haus war seinerzeit ein Zeichen und so war es auch gemeint. Salomon Korn hat sich zudem auch in zahlreichen Artikeln und mehreren Büchern sehr grundsätzlich mit den Möglichkeiten (und mit den Grenzen) von Denkmalen und dem Erinnern gewidmeten Architekturen auseinandergesetzt. Dass er sich in der Debatte um die Wiederaufbauten in Hamburg und in Berlin bisher noch nicht zu Wort gemeldet hat, kann kaum heißen, dass er zum Diskutierten keine eigene Position hätte.

JS Die Debatte um die in Hamburg und in Berlin geplanten Rekonstruktionen zerstörter Synagogen hat uns als Architekten zunächst als eine grundsätzliche architektonische Frage interessiert. Die Diskussion zeigt, dass eine Reihe der bekannten Argumente, wie wir sie aus anderen Rekonstruktionsdebatten kennen, in diesen besonderen Fällen des Wiederaufbaus von Synagogen nicht zu greifen scheinen. Uns schien in dem Wunsch nach Rekonstruktion auch ein Verlangen nach Sichtbarkeit, nach Zeichenhaftigkeit des Gebauten zum Ausdruck zu kommen – vielleicht auch gepaart mit einer gewissen Skepsis gegenüber zeitgenössischen Architekturen. Die Rekonstruktionsfrage ist hier also offensichtlich im Kern eine Frage nach der angemessenen Baugestalt – eine architektonische Frage. Vielleicht lohnt es sich zurückzublicken?

Wäre es nicht eine doppelte Demütigung, Synagogen in nicht-originären Stilen zu rekonstruieren?

SK In den Jahrzehnten des 19. Jahrhunderts, als sich die Emanzipation der Jüdinnen und Juden langsam andeutete, gab es von jüdischer Seite keinen Baustil, auf den man sich berufen konnte oder in Anbetracht dessen man sich fragen konnte: «In welchem Style sollen wir bauen?» Man hatte schlichtweg in den vergangenen Jahrtausenden keine eigene architektonische Haltung entwickeln können, da man in der Diaspora lebte. Das

Salomon Korn is the architect of the Jewish Community Center in Frankfurt am Main. A statement he made when it was inaugurated in 1986 remains germane today—regrettably: "Whoever builds a house wants to stay, and whoever wants to stay, hopes for safety." When new, the building served as a symbol, and was intended as such. In numerous articles and a number of books, Korn has also offered essential reflections on the possibilities and limits of memorials and of architecture devoted to memory. That he has yet to express himself on the debate about synagogue reconstructions in Hamburg and Berlin by no means implies that he has no position on the issue.

JS To begin with, the architects among us were interested in the debates about the planned reconstructions of destroyed synagogues in Hamburg and Berlin as a fundamental architectural question. The discussion suggests that when it comes to rebuilding synagogues, a series of familiar arguments—ones recognizable from earlier debates on architectural reconstructions—seem beside the point. For us, the desire for reconstructions also seemed to express a yearning for visibility, for architecture to possess a symbolic character—perhaps also coupled with a degree of skepticism regarding contemporary architecture. Here, evidently, the question of reconstruction is also essentially a question of the appropriate building style—an architectural question. Perhaps a backward look might be helpful?

Wouldn't it be a double indignity to reconstruct synagogues in non-authentic styles?

SK During the decades of the nineteenth century when the emancipation of the Jews slowly progressed, there was no building style, from the Jewish perspective, that could be invoked, or in relation to which one could pose the question: "In which style should we build?" Having lived in the Diaspora during the previous millennium, they had simply been unable to evolve an independent architectural attitude. The problem for Jews was hence also a problem of the relevant point of reference: to remain with the Orient, where the roots of Jews were

Problem für Jüdinnen und Juden war daher auch die Frage nach dem Bezugspunkt: Sollte man sich an den Orient halten, wo man die eigenen Wurzeln vermutete? Oder sollte man auf das deutsche Mittelalter als chronologische Vergangenheit, die man ebenso durchlaufen hatte, Bezug nehmen? Daher entbrannte im 19. Jahrhundert eine Diskussion, ob man im morgenländischen oder im christlichen Stil bauen sollte. Ersterer hatte den Vorzug, dass er auf den unmittelbaren Ursprung der Jüdinnen und Juden hinwies – allerdings sah man ihm damit auch von außen sofort an, dass er fremdartig war und nicht unmittelbar zur deutschen Geschichte gehörte. Das war der Nachteil. Wenn man dagegen christliche Baustile kopierte, also die Neogotik oder Neoromanik bemühte, entstand das Problem, dass man Dinge nachbildete, mit denen man nichts direkt zu tun hatte. Das heißt, die Juden waren im 19. Jahrhundert in einer Zwickmühle: Wenn sie christliche Stile für ihre Synagogen imitierten, dann wurde ihnen vorgehalten, dass diese eben nicht originär jüdisch waren – und wenn sie in neo-islamischen Stilen bauten, dann hatte man gewissermaßen das Bewusstsein des Fremden und Andersartigen in der Architektur nach außen getragen, was dementsprechend für viele Jüdinnen und Juden auch keine Lösung war. Gottfried Semper hat bei der Synagoge in Dresden versucht, beide Strömungen zu verbinden [→ Abb. 1 & 2]. So wies sein Gebäude im Inneren die neo-islamischen Stilelemente auf, in der äußeren Anmutung zeigte man dagegen neoromanischen Stil. Das war keine schlechte Kombination – aber es änderte auch nichts an dem ganz grundsätzlichen Problem, dass Juden in Stilen bauten, die ihnen schlichtweg nicht zugehörig waren. Aus diesem Konflikt konnte man sich erst befreien, als sich zu Beginn des 20. Jahrhunderts die moderne Architektur und das Bauhaus ankündigten. Da entstanden dann die ersten Synagogen, die tatsächlich neu, originär und originell waren – hier hatte man endlich angefangen, das Zeitalter des synagogalen Eklektizismus hinter sich zu lassen. Mit dem Wissen um diese Geschichte muss man sich daher aber auch fragen: Wenn es schon für die Juden des 19. Jahrhunderts eine Demütigung war, nicht in einem eigenen Stil bauen zu können, ist dann der Umstand, dass wir heute Synagogen aus dieser Zeit in ebendiesen nicht-originären Stilen rekonstruieren, nicht eine doppelte Demütigung? Ich meine, was haben die Jüdinnen und Juden von heute mit den Maßgaben zu tun, die im 19. Jahrhundert wesentlich waren? Damals wollte man zeigen, dass man zumindest so deutsch wie die Deutschen war, wenn nicht sogar noch deutscher.

JS Dieser Umstand, dass es tatsächlich die Gemeinde selbst ist, die den expliziten Wunsch nach Rekonstruktion äußert, hat uns erstaunt und gewundert. Daher haben wir uns auch zunächst einmal gefragt, woher dieses Bedürfnis nach einem Wiederaufbau eigentlich überhaupt kommt und was mögliche Beweggründe für diese Entscheidung sein könnten.

thought to reside? Or should the primary reference be the German Middle Ages, a chronological past through which Jews, too, after all, had lived? In the nineteenth century, this ignited a discussion about whether to build in an Oriental or a Christian style. The first option had the advantage of pointing directly toward the geographic origins of the Jewish people—although in external appearance, such a building was immediately recognizable as foreign, as not really belonging to German history. That was the disadvantage. If you instead copied Christian building styles, having recourse to neo-Gothic or neo-Romanesque styles, the problem was that you were now imitating things with which you had no real connection. In the nineteenth century, consequently, Jews faced a dilemma: if they imitated Christian styles for their synagogues, they were criticized because these were not intrinsically Jewish; if they built in neo-Islamic styles, there was a sense of having imported the foreign, the different, into architecture from outside, which for many Jews did not appear to be a solution. In the synagogue in Dresden, Gottfried Semper attempted to unite both tendencies [→ Figs. 1 & 2]. The building's interior displayed neo-Islamic stylistic elements, while its exterior appearance was in a contrasting neo-Romanesque style. Not a bad combination—but it altered nothing concerning the basic problem that Jews were building in styles that simply did not belong to them. Only in the early twentieth century, with the emergence of modernist architecture and the Bauhaus, did liberation from this conflict become possible. Now, the first synagogues could be constructed that were genuinely new, authentic, and original—finally, a real attempt was made to leave the era of eclecticism in synagogue building behind. In awareness of this history, however, we have to ask ourselves: if it was already an indignity for Jews in the nineteenth century to build in a style that was not their own, isn't the circumstance that, today, we're reconstructing synagogues from that era in the very same non-authentic styles not actually a kind of double indignity? What I mean to say is: what do today's Jews have to do with standards that were essential in the nineteenth century? Back then, Jews wished to demonstrate that they were at least as German as Germans, if not more so.

JS We, too, were surprised, even amazed that it's actually the community itself that is expressing the explicit desire for reconstructions. This led us to ask ourselves: what is the origin of this need for reconstructions? What other possible motives might exist for such a decision?

You are reconstructing a building with whose past you have no real connection

SK These questions are justified. In particular because, historically, the Jews who live in Germany today have absolutely no connection with the German Jews of the nineteenth century. This means you are reconstructing a building with whose past you have no real connection. Viewed historically, you're actually creating a kind of stage scenery.

1
Alte Synagoge, Dresden, Foto: undatiert
Dresden's old synagogue, photo: undated
—
Gottfried Semper 1840 (zerstört/destroyed 1938)

Man rekonstruiert ein Gebäude, zu dessen Vergangenheit man gar keinen Bezug hat

SK Die Fragen sind berechtigt. Vor allem, weil die Juden, die heute in Deutschland leben, in ihrer Geschichte gar nichts mehr mit diesem deutschen Judentum des 19. Jahrhunderts zu tun haben. Das heißt, sie rekonstruieren ein Gebäude, zu dessen Vergangenheit sie gar keinen Bezug haben. Historisch gesehen ist es also eigentlich ein Kulissenbau.

JS Genau, es wäre ein Neuaufbau. Dafür spricht auch, dass sowohl in Hamburg als auch in Berlin überlegt wurde, zwar die Fassade wiederherzustellen, aber das Gebäudeinnere komplett losgelöst davon zu behandeln. In Hamburg wäre ein solches Vorhaben natürlich besonders schwierig, weil die Bornplatzsynagoge ein Zentralbau ist, dessen innere Raumkonstitution eng mit der äußeren Gestalt des Hauses zusammenhängt.

SK Aber die Frage bleibt doch: Was haben heutige Gemeinden davon, wenn sie einen Stil aus einer konfliktreichen Periode des Synagogenbaus nehmen und reproduzieren? Einen Stil, mit dem sie rein chronologisch gar nichts mehr zu tun haben – es sei denn, die Gemeinde Hamburg würde in ihrer Mehrzahl aus Nachfahren deutscher Jüdinnen und Juden bestehen. Aber das ist nicht der Fall. Deswegen ist es doppelt fraglich, sich für eine Rekonstruktion zu entscheiden.

JS Mirjam Wenzel, mit der wir auch sehr intensiv über diese Themen gesprochen haben, hat vermutet, dass die Hamburger Gemeinde möglicherweise an eine als bedeutend und groß empfundene Tradition jüdischen Lebens in Deutschland anknüpfen möchte und diese eben im ersten Drittel des 20. Jahrhunderts sieht.

SK Ja, aber diese Tradition war in der Zeit, in der die Synagoge gebaut wurde, mehr als ambivalent – und eine solche jetzt in eine Zeit, in der jene Ambivalenz nicht mehr existiert, herüberzuretten, ergibt für mich keinen Sinn.

JS Aus meiner Sicht spielt hierbei vor allem der Wunsch nach Sichtbarkeit jüdischen Lebens in der Stadt eine Rolle. Die alte Bornplatzsynagoge, freigestellt wie sie war – es war ja auch ein Novum, dass eine Synagoge freistehend errichtet werden durfte –, hatte jene zeichenhafte Qualität. Vom Wiederaufbau erhofft man sich heute natürlich eine vergleichbare Wirkung in der Stadt.

Man kann nicht so tun, als ob das neue Gebäude historisch gewachsener Repräsentant der Gemeinde wäre

SK Aber die Frage ist doch, ob so ein Wiederaufbau nicht vielmehr übertünchen würde, was tatsächlich an Leid geschehen ist? Ich meine, die nationalsozialistische Judenvernichtung gehört ja zu den beispiellosen Vorgängen, die es in der Geschichte gegeben hat – und das soll mit einer Fassade versteckt werden? Ich verstehe es nicht. Es kann doch nicht sein, dass man jetzt so tut,

JS Exactly, and the result would actually be a newly constructed building. Supporting this argument is the fact that the idea of reconstituting the facade, but handling the interior in a completely unrelated way, was discussed in both Hamburg and Berlin. In Hamburg, of course, such an approach would be especially challenging, since the Bornplatz Synagogue was a centrally planned building whose interior spatial configuration correlated closely with the exterior design.

SK But the question nonetheless remains: what do today's communities gain by reproducing a style from the highly conflicted period of synagogue building? A style that, in purely chronological terms, has nothing to do with them—it would be different if the majority of the Hamburg community consisted of descendants of German Jews. But that's not the case. Which is why it's doubly questionable to opt for a reconstruction.

JS Mirjam Wenzel, with whom we've discussed this topic intensively, suspects that the community in Hamburg aspires to reconnect with a major tradition of Jewish life in Germany, one seen as grand, something they perceive in the first third of the twentieth century.

SK Yes, but during the period when the synagogues were built, that tradition was more than ambivalent—and to me, an attempt to salvage such a tradition now, at a time when this ambivalence no longer exists, appears senseless.

JS Playing a role here, from my perspective, is above all a desire for greater visibility for Jewish life in the city. The old Bornplatz Synagogue, which was freestanding—and it was a novelty back then for a synagogue to be erected as a freestanding structure—had an emblematic quality. And it is hoped, of course, that a reconstruction will have a comparable impact on the city.

You cannot simply pretend that the new building represents the community in a historically evolved way

SK But the question remains whether a reconstruction of this kind doesn't instead gloss over the suffering that has occurred? I mean, the National Socialist extermination of the Jews is among the unparalleled events of history—and you want to conceal that with a facade? I don't get it. You can't simply pretend it never happened—simply pretend that the new building represents the present-day community in a historically evolved way. Today's community has a different historical background—and the Bornplatz Synagogue building stands for a completely different history. This means that contradictions emerge here that remain incomprehensible to me.

JS It really is astonishing how eagerly and facilely this historical image is nonetheless taken up—as an architect, it surprises me. In Berlin, on Fraenkelufer, things are similar: there is a discussion about completely rebuilding the synagogue, together with its main facade—

2
Alte Synagoge, Dresden, Foto: undatiert
Dresden's old synagogue, photo: undated
—
Gottfried Semper 1840 (zerstört/destroyed 1938)

als wäre nichts geschehen – und als ob dieses neue Gebäude ein historisch gewachsener Repräsentant der heutigen jüdischen Gemeinde wäre. Die aktuelle Gemeinde hat doch eine andere Vorgeschichte – und das Gebäude der Bornplatzsynagoge steht doch wiederum für eine ganz andere Geschichte. Insofern tun sich hier Widersprüche auf, die für mich nicht verständlich sind.

JS Es ist in der Tat erstaunlich, wie gerne und leicht man sich dennoch diesem historischen Bild annähert – das wundert mich als Architekt. In Berlin am Fraenkelufer ist es ja ähnlich: Dort gibt es die Diskussion, dass man die Synagoge wieder vollständig samt der Hauptfassade aufbauen könnte – aktuell existiert ja lediglich der Seitenflügel mit der ehemaligen Jugendsynagoge als Fragment. Zwar verlangt die dortige Gemeinde einen Wiederaufbau nicht explizit, zumal ein solcher auch gar nicht ihrem Selbstverständnis entsprechen würde, was auch ganz offen kommuniziert wird. Andererseits ist man für jede Unterstützung dankbar. Und so würde man auch eine Rekonstruktion der alten Fassade in Kauf nehmen.

    SK Also ich war immer der Meinung, dass eine jüdische Gemeinde in Deutschland nach 1945 die eigene, ganz besondere Geschichte in ihrem Gebäude darstellen oder zumindest symbolisieren sollte.

JS Hier wird es interessant. Zu diesem Gedankengang sagte Philipp Stricharz einmal: Diese Erinnerung zu zeigen, sei keine Aufgabe der jüdischen Gemeinde und ihrer Häuser, sondern eine Aufgabe der nicht-jüdischen deutschen Gesellschaft.

Die Erinnerung zu zeigen, gehört auf beide Seiten

    SK Diese Einstellung ist meiner Meinung nach falsch – die Erinnerung zu zeigen, gehört auf beide Seiten. Sowohl die jüdische Gemeinde als auch die nicht-jüdische Gemeinschaft sind von der Geschichte unmittelbar betroffen, jede auf ihre Art. Insofern sollten beide ein Interesse haben, dieser Dinge auf ihre jeweilige Weise zu gedenken. Man kann sich nicht als jüdische Gemeinde, die in Deutschland lebt, aus der deutschen Geschichte abkoppeln. Direkt oder indirekt ist die Gemeinde immer mit ihr verbunden – ob sie es will oder nicht. Sie kann diese Geschichte nicht einfach ausblenden und sagen: Wir leben hier auf der Insel der Seligen – mit den Verbrechen der Deutschen sollen sich die Deutschen auseinandersetzen. Das geht nicht.

JS Das führt uns wieder zu einer architektonischen Frage, denn: Welcher Art sollte dann ein solches Zeichen der Erinnerung sein? Sie haben hier in Frankfurt am Main das Haus der jüdischen Gemeinde entworfen [→ Abb. 3]. Ein Neubau bedeutenden Maßstabs, über den viel berichtet und geschrieben wurde. Sie selbst haben sich auch prägnant geäußert, in dem Sie dieses Gebäude als Zeichen des Bleiben-Wollens in Erwartung einer Sicherheit bezeichnen. Trotzdem ist dieses Haus um einen Bruch herum gebaut. Für mich ist interessant, dass Sie diesen Bruch seinerzeit als gesellschaftlichen

currently, only the side wing containing the former youth synagogue exists as a fragment. Of course, the community there is not explicitly demanding a reconstruction, especially since that wouldn't correspond at all to their self-understanding, something that is conveyed quite openly. On the other hand, they're grateful for any support received. So a reconstruction of the old facade is regarded as acceptable.

    SK It has always been my view that a Jewish community in Germany after 1945 should represent, or at least symbolize, its own, utterly singular history in a building.

JS This is where it gets interesting. Regarding this line of thought, Philipp Stricharz once said: to display this memory is not a task for the Jewish community or its buildings, but is instead a task for non-Jewish German society.

Both sides are responsible for exhibiting memory

    SK In my view, that attitude is false—both sides are responsible for exhibiting memory. Both the Jewish community and non-Jewish society are directly affected by history, each in its own way. So both should have an interest in commemorating these things, each in its own way. As a Jewish community living in Germany, you cannot decouple yourself from German history. Directly or indirectly, the community is always bound up with it—whether they like it or not. You can't simply suppress this history and say: we live here on the island of the blessed—the Germans have to deal with the crimes of the Germans. That's impossible.

JS Which leads us back to an architectural question: what character should such a symbol of remembrance have? Here, in Frankfurt am Main, you designed a building for the Jewish community [→ Fig. 3]. A new building on a substantial scale, about which much has been said and written. And you have expressed yourself quite incisively, referring to the building as a symbol of the desire to remain, and moreover in the hope of security and safety. All the same, this building is constructed around a discontinuity. For me, it's interesting that back then, you characterized this discontinuity as a societal discontinuity in the present tense—it is not, then, a symbol of the Shoah, but instead an expression of a caesura, one that continues to exist and have an impact on present-day society. Is the staged, graphically depicted discontinuity, then, still an adequate and, in a sense, timeless symbol? Or could this moment of the strange (again) play a role here as a new narrative?

Today as well, the ambivalence of Jewish existence in Germany should be made visible

    SK In "Polycrates' Ring," Schiller says: "A life of pure joy is not bestowed upon mortals." As an architect, that's true for me as well. When fulfilling a task, even when we do it well, we always have to live with the fact that it might not be perfect. With this building, I attempted to symbolize and to display the ambivalence of Jewish

3
Jüdisches Gemeindezentrum, Frankfurt am Main
Jewish Community Center, Frankfurt am Main
—
Salomon Korn & Architektengemeinschaft Gerhard Balser
1986

Bruch im Präsens beschrieben hatten – er ist also nicht Symbol der Shoah, sondern Ausdruck einer Zäsur, die in der gegenwärtigen Gesellschaft fortdauert und fortwirkt. Ist der inszenierte, bildhaft dargestellte Bruch also auch weiterhin dieses adäquate und gewissermaßen zeitlose Zeichen? Oder wäre es vielleicht erneut dieses Moment des Fremdartigen, das als neues Narrativ (wieder) eine Rolle spielen könnte?

Die Ambivalenz der jüdischen Existenz in Deutschland sollte auch heute noch sichtbar gemacht werden

SK Schiller hat in seinem Ring des Polykrates gesagt: «Des Lebens ungemischte Freude ward keinem Irdischen zuteil.» Das gilt auch für uns Architekten. Wir werden immer, wenn wir eine Aufgabe lösen – auch wenn wir sie gut lösen – damit leben müssen, dass es vielleicht nicht perfekt ist. Ich habe mit diesem Gebäude versucht, die Ambivalenz der jüdischen Existenz in Deutschland sowohl aus der Vergangenheit als auch aus der Gegenwart zu symbolisieren und zu zeigen. Hierbei gibt es Dinge, die man sieht und solche, die man nicht sieht. So wurden Namen der 11.000 deportierten und ermordeten jüdischen Frankfurterinnen und Frankfurter in den Grundstein der Synagoge eingelassen. Man sieht sie also nicht – aber dieser Gedanke setzt sich für alle sichtbar in den darüberliegenden gebrochenen Gesetzestafeln fort. Hier muss sich jeder Mensch, der davorsteht, fragen: Was sind das für Brüche? Selbst wenn man sich nicht mit der deutsch-jüdischen Geschichte auseinandergesetzt hat, muss einem diese Frage doch sofort einfallen. Das ist also die Stelle, die irritiert, an der man aufmerksam und neugierig wird und anfangen soll, über diese Dinge nachzudenken. Das ist das, was dieses Gebäude tun soll. Ich habe aber ebenso drei siebenarmige Leuchter über dem Eingang platziert, um zu zeigen: Das Leben geht weiter; es ist nicht nur durch Trauer, sondern auch durch Freude und Zukunftsglauben geprägt! Zuletzt kommt noch als drittes wesentliches Element der Brunnen hinzu. Er ist der Brunnen des Lebens, denn er hat 18 Speier und diese Zahl hat auf Ivrit einen Gleichklang mit dem Wort für Leben. So etwas wissen zwar Nicht-Juden in der Regel nicht, aber Jüdinnen und Juden müssten diesen Zusammenhang bemerken, wenn sie die drei Davidsterne mit den jeweils sechs Speiern sehen. Aber selbst wenn sie nicht auf diese Allegorie kommen, ist der Brunnen doch Symbol an sich, denn das Wasser fließt ja, es ist etwas Lebendiges.

Wenn man nun alle diese Dinge zusammennimmt, kommt jene Ambivalenz zustande, von der ich glaube, dass sie auch heute noch möglichst sichtbar gemacht werden sollte. Denn auch heute ist die jüdische Gemeinschaft in Deutschland immer noch eine gemischte Gemeinschaft. Ich meine, vor dem Krieg gab es in Deutschland etwa eine halbe Million Jüdinnen und Juden – heute sind es gerade einmal 200.000. Die meisten von ihnen sind zugewanderte Jüdinnen und Juden aus der ehemaligen Sowjetunion; einige wenige sind die sogenannten «displaced persons» der ersten Generation. Daher gibt es gewissermaßen kein deutsches Judentum im engeren Sinne mehr. Wir sind vielleicht auf

existence in Germany, in the past as well as the present. In this case, there are things you see, and things that remain unseen. For example, the names of the 11,000 deported and murdered Jews of Frankfurt are embedded in the foundation stone of the synagogue. Which means you don't actually see them—but this idea is extended up above, and visible to all, in the broken Tablets of the Law. Anyone standing in front of them has to ask: "What kind of fractures are these?" Even for someone who has never dealt with German-Jewish history, the question suggests itself immediately. So it's a place that gives rise to irritation, that makes you attentive, curious, prompts you to begin reflecting on these matters. That's the building's intention. I also placed three seven-armed candelabra (menorahs) at the entrance, in order to say: "Life goes on; and life is not just shaped by sorrow, but also by joy and a faith in the future!" Finally, there is a third essential element, the fountain. It is the fountain of life, for it has eighteen spouts, and in Ivrit, modern Hebrew, this number sounds like the word for life. As a rule, that's something non-Jews won't be aware of, but Jews will make the connection when they see the three Stars of David, each with six spouts. But even if they don't notice this allegory, the fountain is a symbol of life, since the flowing water has something lifelike about it.

Now, when you bring all of these things together, you generate an ambivalence, which, I believe, should be made as visible as possible today. For today, as well, the Jewish community in Germany is a mixed community. I mean, before the war, there were half a million Jews in Germany—today there are just 200,000. Most of them immigrated from the former Soviet Union; a few are the so-called "displaced persons" from the first generation. In one sense, there are no longer German Jews, strictly speaking. We are, perhaps, on the path toward a new German Jewry, which may form itself in the course of several generations, but we're still in a kind of transitional period. And this transitional period is gradually coming to an end, because with the fourth or fifth generations, this chapter of German history will no longer be as present in consciousness as it is for us, who lived through the war and the postwar era, and who didn't learn about all of these things from history books, but instead from direct experience.

Do works of architecture wear out when they attempt to visualize memory?

JS To touch now on a different topic: you have made a number of contributions to debates about memorials—texts on very fundamental topics and concerns, but particularly in the context of discussions of a memorial in Berlin for the murdered Jews of Europe [→ Fig. 4]. In them, the idea of the "wearing out" of memorials over time played a major role. I'd like to go more deeply with you into this aspect—to me, it seems significant in particular for Jewish buildings, which always qualify to some extent as architecture of memory. To what extent, in your view, does this aspect play a role here? Do works of architecture, too, "wear out" when they attempt to thematize memory, to visualize memory?

dem Weg zu einem neuen deutschen Judentum, was in einigen Generationen vielleicht zustande kommen mag, aber noch sind wir in einer Art Übergangsperiode. Diese neigt sich allmählich dem Ende zu, weil auch mit der vierten oder fünften Generation dieses Kapitel deutscher Geschichte nicht mehr so sehr im Bewusstsein stehen dürfte wie noch bei uns, die wir ja den Krieg und die Nachkriegszeit erlebt haben und das Ganze also nicht nur aus Geschichtsbüchern, sondern aus unmittelbarem Erleben kennen.

Verschleißen Architekturen, wenn sie versuchen, Erinnerung zu verbildlichen?

JS Um noch ein anderes Thema zu streifen: Sie selbst haben sehr viele Beiträge zu Denkmaldebatten verfasst – sowohl Texte zu ganz grundlegenden Themen und Überlegungen, aber vor allem auch Schriften im Kontext der Diskussionen um das Denkmal für die ermordeten Juden Europas in Berlin [→ Abb. 4]. Dabei ist auch der «Verschleiß» der Denkmale über die Zeit ein Gedanke, der bei Ihnen eine große Rolle spielt. Diesen Aspekt möchte ich gerne mit Ihnen vertiefen – er scheint mir besonders für jüdische Bauwerke, die ein Stück weit immer auch Architekturen der Erinnerung sind, bedeutsam zu sein. Inwieweit, vermuten Sie, spielt dieser Aspekt hier eine Rolle? «Verschleißen» auch Architekturen, wenn sie versuchen, Erinnerung zu thematisieren, Erinnerung zu verbildlichen?

SK Ja, das tun sie. Ich meine, wenn man heute vor einem Reiterstandbild Friedrichs des Großen steht, dann wird man kaum noch eine Verbindung zu diesem haben. Oder nehmen wir zum Beispiel die aktuelle Diskussion um die «Judensäue» an Kirchen: Sollte man sie entfernen oder nicht? Meiner Meinung nach sollte man sie an den Fassaden belassen, aber man muss Menschen aufklären, was es mit ihnen auf sich hat. Das kann entweder mit einer Hinweistafel oder durch entsprechendes Personal geschehen. Es ist also tatsächlich so: Die Dinge selbst sprechen nicht mehr zu uns, sie müssen uns erläutert werden. Entweder über schriftliche Dokumente oder über den Austausch mit Menschen, die uns erzählen, was sie zu bedeuten haben. Insofern veralten Denkmäler sehr schnell, wenn der Betrachter keinen Bezug mehr zum Dargestellten herstellen kann.

JS Für Architekturen gilt das möglicherweise ebenso. Wobei hier interessant ist, dass gerade zeitgenössische Synagogen häufig mit dem Moment des Fremd- und Andersartigen arbeiten, also eine selbstverständliche Einbindung in die umgebende Stadt gar nicht suchen. Manuel Herz' Neue Synagoge in Mainz ist ein sehr prägnantes Beispiel dafür [→ Abb. 5]. Wenn man nun vor diesem Gebäude steht und die intendierte Assoziation zum hebräischen Schriftzug vielleicht nicht unmittelbar versteht, so fragt man sich doch zunächst einmal: Warum ist dieses Haus gerade so, wie es ist?

SK Yes, they do. Today, standing in front of an equestrian statue of Frederick the Great, you have no connection with it. Or let's take the example of current discussions about the "Jewish sows" that still remain on old churches: should they simply be removed, or left in place? In my opinion, they should be left on the church facades, but you need to explain to people what they're all about. This can be done either with an information plaque, or through the appropriate personnel. The fact is, these things no longer speak to us directly, they require explanation. Either through written documents, or through exchanges with people who can explain their significance to us. In this sense, memorials age very rapidly, when visitors no longer have any connection to what is presented.

JS Things may be similar for works of architecture. Of interest here is the fact that contemporary synagogues in particular often work with the foreign, the different, and hence make no attempt to bring about a self-evident integration into the surrounding urban fabric. Manuel Herz's new synagogue in Mainz is a striking example of this [→ Fig. 5]. Standing in front of this building, and perhaps not immediately grasping the intended association with Hebrew writing, you may begin by asking: why is this building the way it is?

It's important to diverge from visual habits and to awaken curiosity

SK That's right, because it cuts right into everyday visual habits. With such buildings, it's important to diverge from visual habits and to awaken curiosity. Today, when you copy a synagogue from the nineteenth century, people stand in front of it, and to begin with, think nothing at all. But standing in front of such a modern synagogue, that is utterly confusing, because the horizontal and the vertical are out of whack, and our curiosity is piqued. The building needs to deviate from the habitual, otherwise it won't achieve its purpose.

JS On this point, when it comes to architecture and its potentialities, I'm somewhat more skeptical. What I mean is that a building stands for a long time in the same place, so people encounter it repeatedly, over time, it becomes a habitual presence. Which is why, it seems to me, the moment of surprise in architecture is not a particularly viable strategy.

4
Denkmal für die ermordeten Juden Europas, Berlin
Memorial to the Murdered Jews of Europe, Berlin
—
Peter Eisenman
2005

Es ist wichtig, dass man von den Sehgewohnheiten abweicht und Neugier erweckt

SK Richtig, denn es schneidet in die alltäglichen Sehgewohnheiten ein. Es ist wichtig, dass man mit solchen Gebäuden von den Sehgewohnheiten abweicht und Neugier erweckt. Wenn man heute eine Synagoge aus dem 19. Jahrhundert kopiert, dann steht man davor und denkt sich zunächst einmal gar nichts. Aber wenn wir vor einer solchen modernen Synagoge stehen, die uns völlig durcheinanderbringt, weil hier Horizontalität und Vertikalität nicht mehr stimmen, dann wird unsere Neugier geweckt. Das Gebäude muss also vom Üblichen abweichen, sonst wird man das, was man bezwecken will, nicht erreichen.

JS Wobei ich in diesem Punkt, was die Architektur und ihre Möglichkeiten betrifft, doch skeptischer bin. Ich meine, Architekturen stehen sehr lange an demselben Ort, die Menschen begegnen dem Haus immer wieder, es tritt also mit der Zeit eine Art Gewohnheit ein. Daher glaube ich, dass das Moment der Überraschung in der Architektur keine besonders tragfähige Strategie ist.

SK Aber, schauen Sie, wir Menschen haben die Rechtwinkligkeit gewissermaßen als allgemeines Erfahrungsgut verinnerlicht: Es gibt die Horizontlinie und wir stehen senkrecht darauf. Wenn jetzt von dieser Orthogonalität augenscheinlich abgewichen wird, verunsichert uns das – das erkennen wir bei Architekturen von Daniel Libeskind ganz besonders. Insofern hat es doch etwas die Neugier Weckendes, wenn man mit den allgemeinen Sehgewohnheiten bricht. Wobei dieses Moment zugegebenermaßen nicht auf Dauer reicht. Ein Beispiel hierfür ist das Denkmal für die ermordeten Juden in Berlin. Denn hier ist der bedeutendste Teil nicht das Stelenfeld an sich, sondern vielmehr das Informationszentrum, welches unter ihm in der Erde steckt. Erst wenn Sie dieses besuchen, erfahren Sie tatsächlich etwas über das nationalsozialistische Menschheitsverbrechen – dieses Gefühl und Bewusstsein um das Beispiellose würde sich Ihnen oben aus dem Stelenfeld allein nicht erschließen. Ohne diese Ergänzung wäre es wirklich nur ein versteinertes Denkmal – erst in Verbindung mit der Gedenkausstellung wird es lebendig, da nun die Aufklärung gewissermaßen unmittelbar unter den Dingen liegt.

JS Aber was würden diese Überlegungen für den Neubau einer Synagoge, zum Beispiel in Hamburg an so einem exponierten Ort, bedeuten?

SK Naja, man könnte zum Beispiel eine kleine Informationsstelle dort einrichten, in der man die Besucherinnen und Besucher über das Judentum, die synagogale Architektur oder die Geschichte der Juden in Deutschland aufklärt – das wäre natürlich ein Idealbild.

JS Ein kleines Museum – wie in München.

SK But, you see, as human beings, we've in a sense internalized orthogonality as a universal experience: there is the horizon line, on which we stand vertically. And we find any apparent deviation from this orthogonality to be unsettling—something that becomes particularly clear with the architecture of Daniel Libeskind. And there's something about rupturing such universal habits of vision that stimulates our sense of curiosity. But, of course, this moment is insufficient in the long run. An example of this is the Memorial to the Murdered Jews of Europe in Berlin. Here, the most important element is not the Field of Stelae as such, and instead the information center, set below ground level. Only when you visit it do you really learn anything about the crimes against humanity committed by the National Socialists—up above, in the Field of Stelae, you don't really get a feel for, an awareness of, the unparalleled nature of these crimes. Without being supplemented by the center, it would be little more than a stony memorial—it only comes alive in connection with the commemorative exhibition, with enlightenment being so to speak located directly beneath the objects themselves.

JS But what do these considerations mean for the construction of the new synagogue in Hamburg, for example, at this exposed location?

SK Well, for example, you could install a small information center, where visitors could learn something about Judaism, about synagogue architecture, or about the history of the Jews in Germany—of course, that would be an ideal solution.

JS A little museum—as in Munich.

The aim should be to create a synagogue for our own time

SK Yes, for example. And beyond that, the aim should be to create a synagogue for our own time. A synagogue that not only says something about the present moment, but also about what happened during the period of persecution of the Jews in Germany. I mean, in Germany, the Jews have suffered through a history that is unprecedented and unique. You can't simply gloss over these past events with a decorative building, producing something that ultimately seems ahistorical. That would be a declaration of bankruptcy on the part of architecture, and bankruptcy when it comes to an awareness of what Jewish history in Germany actually means. Of course, this history is ambivalent. You can't simply reshape this ambivalence by constructing things that were conventional in the nineteenth century—and which were, even then, already pale imitations of the Middle Ages. Today, with such a reconstruction, you'd be constructing a facade of a facade! When an opportunity arises for a new building, it's important to realize that the architecture can't simply look like all other architecture, you can't just pretend that the National Socialist campaign of extermination against the Jews never happened. Which is why I hope that discussion will continue in Hamburg, and that a space for

Es sollte das Ziel sein, eine Synagoge unserer Zeit zu entwerfen

SK Ja, zum Beispiel. Darüber hinaus sollte es aber auch das Ziel sein, eine Synagoge unserer Zeit zu entwerfen. Eine Synagoge, die nicht nur über unsere Gegenwart erzählt, sondern auch etwas darüber aussagt, was in der Zeit der Judenverfolgung in Deutschland passiert ist. Ich meine, Juden haben in Deutschland eine Geschichte erlitten, die beispiellos und einzigartig ist. Man kann daher nicht einfach mit einem dekorativen Gebäude über diese Vergangenheit hinweggehen oder etwas tun, was am Ende ahistorisch wirkt. Das wäre eine Bankrotterklärung der Architektur und des Bewusstseins dessen, was die jüdische Geschichte in Deutschland bedeutet. Sie ist nun einmal ambivalent. Daher sollte man diese Ambivalenz auch nicht überformen, indem man Dinge konstruiert, die im 19. Jahrhundert gängig waren – und die bereits dort schon ein Abklatsch des Mittelalters waren. Das heißt, wir würden mit einer solchen Rekonstruktion heute eine Fassade der Fassade bauen! Wenn man schon die Gelegenheit für einen Neubau hat, dann muss man auch zu dem Schluss kommen, dass die Architektur nicht eine sein kann, die aussieht wie jede andere und so tut, als ob es diesen nationalsozialistischen Vernichtungsfeldzug gegen Jüdinnen und Juden nicht gegeben hat. Daher hoffe ich, dass das in Hamburg noch weiter diskutiert wird und man sich hierbei auch Spielräume offenlässt. Am Ende sollte der Entwurf einen Bezug auf die leidvolle Vergangenheit der Jüdinnen und Juden in Deutschland aufweisen – aber nicht etwas imitieren, was es zwar einmal gab, aber mit der Geschichte der Gemeinde letztlich nichts zu tun hat.

Die Möglichkeit, das zeichenhaft Andersartige zu bauen, gibt es heute nicht mehr

JS Diese Suche nach der adäquaten Gestalt halte ich jenseits der gesellschaftlichen Dimension, die sie ohnehin hat, für eine Frage, die für uns Architekten und Architektinnen eine große Relevanz hat – vor allem auch in der Entwicklung unserer Fachdisziplin, da sie ganz unmittelbar grundlegende Fragen berührt: Wie verhalten wir uns mit unseren neuen Gebäuden eigentlich zu dem, was gewesen ist? Inwieweit kann Architektur Bedeutung transportieren und Zeichen sein? Und: Wie schnell verschleißen solche Zeichen? Letzteres ist eine große Gefahr, die man immer mit bedenken sollte. Ich denke sogar, dass es die Möglichkeit, das zeichenhaft Andersartige zu bauen, heute gar nicht mehr gibt.

SK Ja, das ist fast nicht mehr möglich. Es existieren ja so viele Dinge nebeneinander, die niemand in Gänze überblicken kann. Nicht zuletzt haben wir auch gelernt, die gewohnten Sehweisen abzulegen und Ungewöhnliches zu akzeptieren – wodurch auch dieses dann wieder gewöhnlich wird. Aber es muss ja auch nicht unsere Aufgabe sein, immer wieder etwas Außergewöhnliches zu schaffen. Es reicht schon, wenn wir etwas einigermaßen Gutes zustande bringen: Ein Bauwerk, das sich vertreten lässt und bei dem man das Gefühl hat, dass es immer wieder aufs Neue Interesse wecken kann.

maneuver will be kept open. In the end, the design should make reference to the painful past of the Jews in Germany—but it shouldn't imitate something that existed previously, something that has nothing to do, ultimately, with the history of the community.

There is no longer any possibility today of building the symbolic differently

JS Going beyond the social dimension, which is implicit in it anyway, I regard this search for an adequate shape to be a question of great relevance for us architects— in particular for the development of our discipline, for it touches directly on fundamental issues: what is the impact of our new buildings on what already exists? To what extent can architecture convey meaning and function as a symbol? And: how quickly do such symbols wear out? This last one is an enormous danger, and we always need to bear it in mind. Which is why, I believe, there is no longer any possibility today of building the symbolic differently.

SK True, it has become almost impossible. So many things exist alongside one another that no one has an overview any longer. Not least of all, we have also learned how to shed customary habits of vision, to accept the exceptional—which as a result becomes ordinary in its turn. But it need not always be our task to create something extraordinary. It's enough when we can get something done that is reasonably good: a building that can be defended, that gives you the feeling that it is capable, again and again, of arousing fresh interest.

5
Neue Synagoge, Mainz
The New Synagogue, Mainz
—
Manuel Herz
2010

Mario Marcus & Dekel Peretz im Gespräch mit / in conversation with Andreas Fuchs & Ivan Reimann

Der Plan, das Hauptgebäude der Synagoge am Fraenkelufer in Berlin-Kreuzberg zu rekonstruieren, ist eigentlich älter als die Entscheidung für den Wiederaufbau der Bornplatzsynagoge in Hamburg. Erstaunlicherweise gab es aber hier um die Wiederherstellung der historischen Gestalt der zerstörten Synagoge keine in einer breiteren Öffentlichkeit geführte Auseinandersetzung. In dem vor allem am Hamburger Beispiel geführten Diskurs um die Rekonstruktion zerstörter Synagogen spielt das Berliner Vorhaben kaum eine Rolle. Vielleicht liegt das daran, dass die Rekonstruktion als solche für die Gemeinde in Berlin nicht in der gleichen Weise mit Bedeutung aufgeladen zu sein scheint wie in Hamburg. Anders als dort hat in Berlin die kleine Wochentagssynagoge die Reichspogromnacht überstanden; schon 1945 gab es hier wieder jüdische Gottesdienste. Im Gespräch mit Mario Marcus und Dekel Peretz wird die eigene Perspektive deutlich.

IR Meine erste Frage zielt auf die Bedeutung des Ortes für Sie und die Gemeinde insgesamt ab. Am Fraenkelufer stand eine der größten Synagogen Berlins. Gerade bei so wirkmächtigen Gebäuden ist es oftmals der Fall, dass die Erinnerung an das ehemals Vorhandene die Zeit der Zerstörung überdauert und auch in der Gegenwart immer noch sehr präsent ist. So präsent, dass alle, die sich mit dem Ort beschäftigen, fast unweigerlich das Bild des Vergangenen vor Augen haben und es gewissermaßen als Ideal auch noch die zukünftigen Entwicklungen beeinflusst. Daher interessiert uns, welche Bedeutung die Erinnerung an die zerstörte Synagoge für die Gemeinde hat – und auch vielleicht für Sie persönlich, weil Sie ganz unterschiedliche Biografien und Bezüge zu dem Ort haben. Vielleicht könnten Sie beide dazu etwas sagen?

MM Man sollte in dieser Debatte zunächst beachten, dass es sich bei der Synagoge am Fraenkelufer nicht um eine Hauptsynagoge handelt, die eine zentrale Rolle im Gemeindeleben Berlins nach dem Holocaust innegehabt hätte. Im vereinten Berlin lag der Fokus vor allem auf der großen Neuen Synagoge in der Oranienburger Straße [→ S.156], welche dementsprechend auch

The plan to reconstruct the main synagogue building on Fraenkelufer in Berlin-Kreuzberg actually predates the decision to reconstruct the Bornplatz Synagogue in Hamburg. Until recently, however, and astonishingly, the project received very little support. It played practically no role in discussions about the reconstruction of destroyed synagogues. Perhaps that is due to the fact that the Berlin reconstruction has not been charged with meaning for the community in the same way the Hamburg project has. In Berlin, in contrast to Hamburg, the small weekday synagogue survived the Kristallnacht; Jewish religious services took place here again as early as 1945. In this conversation, Mario Marcus and Dekel Peretz contribute their perspective to this topic of discussion.

IR My first question concerns the importance of the site itself for you and for the community as a whole. Standing on Fraenkelufer was one of Berlin's largest synagogues. Such impressive buildings often survive in memory long after their destruction, and can retain a powerful presence right up to the present. This can be so powerful that everyone who is involved with the location retains an image of it, almost involuntarily, in their mind's eye, allowing it to influence future developments as a kind of ideal. Which is why we're interested in this question: what significance do memories of the destroyed synagogue have for the community—and perhaps for you personally as well, since the two of you have very different biographies in relation to the site? Perhaps each of you could say something about this.

MM In this discussion, it should perhaps be mentioned to begin with that the synagogue on Fraenkelufer is not a main synagogue, which would therefore have played a central role in community life in Berlin after the Holocaust. In a united Berlin, the focus was primarily on the synagogue on Oranienburger Straße [→ p.156], which was therefore restored, in part as a memorial site, with the Centrum Judaicum facing the street, and the articulated void of the rear courtyard. After the war, in contrast, the synagogue on Fraenkelufer was never the main focus—whether politically or in relation to the

als Gedenkort mit dem Centrum Judaicum zur Straßenseite und der dezidierten Leere im Hinterhof wiederhergestellt wurde. Die Synagoge am Fraenkel-ufer lag dagegen nach dem Krieg – sowohl für die Politik als auch für die jüdische Gemeinde selbst – immer etwas abseits vom Fokus. Das heißt aber nicht, dass sie per se unbedeutend gewesen wäre. Für all jene, die dereinst dort gebetet haben, war sie immer wichtig. Nach 1945 hatte allerdings die Mehrzahl der Gemeindemitglieder keinerlei persönliche Verbindung mehr zur Vorkriegssynagoge. Somit waren auch die Überreste des Hauptgebäudes für sie lediglich eine Ruine, die mehr oder weniger gestört hat und dann auch relativ zügig in den 1950er-Jahren abgetragen wurde. Es war also der stehen gebliebene Seitenflügel, welcher für die Gemeinde immer das Zentrum und mehr oder weniger eine Heimat gewesen ist. Auch für die jungen Leute, die jetzt dort wieder etwas aufbauen, ist die alte Synagoge Historie. Ich persönlich bin in diesem Punkt zwiegespalten. Meine Frau ist zum Beispiel noch mit dieser Ruine der alten Synagoge aufgewachsen; von meinen Urgroßeltern weiß ich, dass sie dereinst dieses Gotteshaus besucht haben. Allerdings sind das alles eher Beziehungen auf der Metaebene und keine konkreten Verbindungen – denn ich selbst kenne dieses Haus und auch die Ruine nicht, da bereits meine Großmutter und meine Eltern vor dem Krieg nicht mehr in der Synagoge am Fraenkelufer gebetet hatten. Es gab doch einige Synagogen in Berlin, da hat sich die jüdische Gemeinschaft gewissermaßen verteilt.

Es gibt eine ideelle Beziehung zum Bild der alten Synagoge

DP Meine Beziehung zu diesem Gebäude ist sehr stark, da meine Frau und ich sowie viele andere engagierte Jüdinnen und Juden dort seit zehn Jahren aktiv tätig sind. Damals sollte diese Synagoge eigentlich geschlossen werden – mittlerweile sieht es so aus, dass wir ein großes Gemeindeleben aufgebaut haben und nun mehrere hundert Menschen verschiedenster Herkunft und aller Altersschichten an diesem Ort zusammenkommen. Diese Entwicklung und der damit verbundene Bedarf an neuen Räumlichkeiten waren die Anregung dafür, die bestehende Synagoge nun durch eine Erweiterung zu ergänzen. Wie Mario schon erwähnt hat, kann mit dem ehemaligen Hauptsaal der Synagoge heute kaum jemand verbunden sein, da ihn schlichtweg keiner mehr kennt. Dennoch gibt es eine ideelle Beziehung zu diesem Bild der alten Synagoge, da es doch auch eine Vision ausstrahlt. Man muss sich nur einmal die Entstehungsgeschichte der Synagoge anschauen: Um 1900 hatten sich in Friedrichshain-Kreuzberg viele, vor allem osteuropäische Jüdinnen und Juden angesiedelt, somit gab es einen großen Bedarf an einem neuen Gotteshaus. Bemerkenswert ist, dass die Synagoge am Kottbusser Ufer [→ Abb. 1], wie sie seinerzeit hieß, bereits damals ebenso als Gemeindezentrum und nicht nur als Gebetshaus gedacht wurde. Es gab also neben dem Gebetssaal auch Räumlichkeiten, welche auf die sozialen Bedürfnisse der Jüdinnen und Juden in der Umgebung abgestimmt waren, wie zum Beispiel einen

Jewish community itself. Which by no means suggests that it was unimportant. For everyone who used to pray there, its significance remains. After 1945, however, the majority of the community members no longer had any personal connection to the prewar synagogue. For them, the remains of the main building were simply a ruin that was more or less disturbing, and was then cleared away relatively speedily during the 1950s. It was therefore the surviving side wing that has functioned as a center for the community, serving more or less as a home. For the young people, as well, who are rebuilding something there now, the old synagogue is a piece of history. On this point, personally, I'm ambivalent. My wife, for example, grew up with the ruins of the old synagogue; my great-grandparents have told me they used to attend services there. For me, these are not concrete connections, and instead relationships that exist on the metalevel—I myself never knew the building, nor the ruins, since my grandmother and my parents stopped praying at the synagogue on Fraenkelufer before the war. There were a number of synagogues in Berlin; the Jewish community was somewhat dispersed.

There exists a spiritual relationship to the image of the old synagogue

DP My connection to this building is very strong: my wife and I, along with many other committed Jews, have been active there for ten years now. Back then, the synagogue was to have been closed—meanwhile, it seems as though we've built up a large community life, and now many hundreds of people from the most diverse backgrounds, and of all ages, come together at this location. This development, and the associated need for new spaces, served as a stimulus to supplement the existing synagogue through an extension. As Mario has already mentioned, practically no one still has a connection to the main prayer hall of the synagogue, simply because no one is left who actually knew it. Nonetheless, there exists a spiritual connection to the image of the old synagogue; it still radiates a kind of vision. You only have to consider the history of the synagogue's origins: around 1900, many Jews, mainly from Eastern Europe, settled in Friedrichshain-Kreuzberg, which led to the need for a new place of worship. Remarkably, the synagogue on Kottbusser Ufer [→ Fig. 1], as it was known at the time, was already conceived as a community center as well,

1
Synagoge Kottbusser Ufer (heute Fraenkelufer), Berlin, Foto: um 1917
The synagogue on Kottbusser Ufer (today Fraenkelufer), Berlin, photo: ca. 1917

Trausaal, einen Hort oder einen Ort für Jugendprogramme und Ähnliches. Damit besteht eine große Ähnlichkeit zur heutigen Situation und zum aktuellen Projekt der Erweiterung der Bestandssynagoge. Die jüdische Bevölkerung Berlins ist in den letzten 20, 30 Jahren rasant gewachsen, auch in der näheren Umgebung der Synagoge am Fraenkelufer leben viele Jüdinnen und Juden. Zudem kommen zu unseren Veranstaltungen bereits Besucherinnen und Besucher aus Marzahn, Lichtenberg, Neukölln und auch aus anderen Stadtteilen im Norden und Westen Berlins. Das Fraenkelufer wird wie vor hundert Jahren wieder zu einem zentralen Ort jüdischen Lebens im Südosten Berlins – daher soll das neue Gemeindezentrum auch ein Impulsgeber für den Aufbau einer vielfältigen jüdischen Infrastruktur in der Umgebung sein. Vielleicht noch ein letzter Gedanke zur Bedeutung des Ortes: Wir haben 2016 zur Hundert-Jahr-Feier der Synagoge eine Ausstellung realisiert und uns damals ebenso die Frage gestellt: Wie erzählt man die Geschichte einer Synagoge, die durch den Krieg zum großen Teil zerstört wurde – und dies auch noch an einem Ort, an dem es kaum persönliche Kontinuitäten unter den Gemeindemitgliedern gibt, an dem kaum jemand sagen kann: «Hier haben meine Großeltern schon vor dem Krieg gebetet»? Unsere Antwort ist, dass die historische Kontinuität in der Rolle liegt, welche die Synagoge bei den diversen Migrationswellen nach Berlin spielte. Sie war immer ein Anlaufpunkt: sei es in den 1950er- und 60er-Jahren für die polnischen Jüdinnen und Juden, in den 80er-, 90er-Jahren für Migrantinnen und Migranten aus der ehemaligen Sowjetunion – oder heute für all jene, die aus den USA, aus Israel und anderen Ländern nach Berlin kommen. Das ist gewissermaßen eine funktionale Kontinuität des Ortes, die immer aktuell bleibt.

Ist die monumentale Präsenz der alten Synagoge heute wünschenswert?

IR Es ist interessant, welche Bedeutung die Synagoge doch im gesamtstädtischen Kontext hat! Das war uns, glaube ich, in der Form bislang nicht bewusst. Damit hängt für mich aber auch eine Frage zusammen, die in einer gewissen Weise ebenso mit dem zerstörten Originalbau zu tun hat: Die alte Synagoge war ein sehr monumentales und repräsentatives Gebäude mit einem großen Vorplatz an der Uferseite, es bediente sich einer wirkmächtigen, antikisierenden Architektursprache und loste sich auch sonst aus der umliegenden Bebauung heraus. Daher: Welche Rolle spielt heute für die Gemeinde die Architektur des Hauses? Wäre eine ähnlich starke Präsenz – unabhängig von der Frage, ob die alte Fassade wieder aufgebaut werden soll oder nicht – überhaupt gewünscht? Wie repräsentativ und präsent sollte das neue Gebäudeensemble aus Sicht der zukünftigen Nutzerinnen und Nutzer sein?

MM Zur Präsenz eines Gotteshauses gibt es historisch gesehen in der Synagogenarchitektur im Grunde zwei Wege: einerseits den «alten» Weg, bei dem die Synagogen nicht aus der Umgebungsbebauung herausstechen, sich also niedrig zwischen die Nachbarhäuser

not simply a house of prayer. In addition to the prayer hall, there were spaces designed to accommodate the social requirements of Jews living in the vicinity, for example a wedding hall, a daycare center, a space for youth programs, and so forth. There was therefore a strong resemblance to the contemporary situation, as well as to the current project for an extension of the existing synagogue. Over the past twenty or thirty years, the Jewish population of Berlin has grown rapidly, with many Jews living in the immediate vicinity of the synagogue on Fraenkelufer. Attending our events, moreover, are visitors from Marzahn, Lichtenberg, Neukölln, and other districts in the north and west of Berlin. Fraenkelufer is becoming a central place for Jewish life in southeastern Berlin, just as it was a century ago—so the new community center should be the driving force for the development of a diverse Jewish infrastructure in the vicinity. A final thought, perhaps, on the importance of the site: in 2016, to celebrate the centenary of the synagogue, we organized an exhibition, and we also posed the question: how do you tell the story of a synagogue that was for the most part destroyed during the war? And, moreover, at a location for which the members of the community lack virtually any sense of personal continuity, since virtually no one can say: "It was here that my grandparents prayed before the war"? Our answer was that this historical continuity resides in the role played by the synagogue for the various waves of migration to Berlin. It was always a point of contact, whether during the 1950s and 1960s for Polish Jews, or from migrants from the former Soviet Union during the 1980s and 1990s. Or today for everyone who arrives in Berlin from the United States, from Israel, or from other countries. In a sense, it is this that constitutes the location's functional continuity, one that always remains current.

Is the monumental presence of the old synagogue still desirable today?

IR It's interesting to hear about the importance of the synagogue in the larger urban context. I'd have to say that is something we weren't fully aware of up until now. For me, it also raises a question that is also related in a sense to the destroyed original building: the old synagogue was a monumental and representative building with a large forecourt facing the canal, taking the form of a powerful, antique-style architectural language and contrasting in other ways as well with the surrounding buildings. Hence the question: what role does the building's architecture play for the community today? Would a similarly powerful presence be regarded as desirable today—independently of the question of whether the old facade should be reconstructed or not? From the perspective of future users, how representative and how present should the new architectural ensemble be?

MM Essentially, from a historical perspective, there are two basic paths in synagogue architecture when it comes to the presence of a house of worship: first, there is the "old" path: here, the synagogue avoids being a conspicuous presence within the surroundings; it is as

geduckt haben oder in Hinterhöfen errichtet wurden. Das hatte zum einen die Funktion der Privatheit und des Schutzes der Gemeinde, zum anderen war es auch bestimmten Zwängen, die von außen auferlegt wurden, geschuldet – so durfte eine Synagoge die umliegende Bebauung nicht überragen. Daher wurde zum Beispiel die alte Synagoge in der Heidereutergasse in eine Senke hineingebaut, damit sie die anderen Gebäude, wie die nebenan befindliche Marienkirche, eben nicht überragt und somit auch nicht in dieser Nachbarschaft auffällt. Dann gab es das Zeitalter der großen Emanzipation, als in der zweiten Hälfte des 19. Jahrhunderts das jüdische Selbstbewusstsein in Mitteleuropa erwachte. Hier bekamen auf einmal die Synagogen eine ganz andere Sichtbarkeit – die Neue Synagoge in der Oranienburger Straße [→ S.156] ist wohl einer der wichtigsten Repräsentanten dafür. Sie ist mit ihrer turmartigen Kuppel ein großer, präsenter Bau, der sich aber auch in seiner ganzen Architektursprache mit den maurischen Elementen eindeutig von Kirchen unterschied – hier wollte man also explizit zeigen: Dieser Stil ist nicht christlich, aber genauso repräsentativ. Dieses ganze architektonische Spektrum war auch in der Synagogenbaugeschichte von Berlin zwischen 1860 und 1934 vertreten: Da gab es die Synagoge in der Fasanenstraße [→ Abb.2&3], die ähnlich repräsentativ wie die in der Oranienburger Straße war; man errichtete neoklassizistische Bauten wie zum Beispiel am Fraenkelufer, die mit ihrer Tempelform sehr präsent waren und nicht mehr Kirchen imitierten; es existierte aber immer noch die Bauform von Synagogen, die sich eher im Hintergrund hielten, wie die in der Rykestraße [→ Abb.4], oder auch kleinere Synagogen in Hofsituationen wie in der Pestalozzistraße [→ Abb.5]. Den Abschluss bildete gewissermaßen die klassische Bauhaus-Synagoge in der Prinzregentenstraße [→ Abb.6]. Diese Entwicklungen liefen aber alle parallel nebeneinanderher und es gab viele verschiedene Ansätze, wie präsent oder repräsentativ ein Gotteshaus sein sollte. Was man auch beachten muss: Die Synagoge am Fraenkelufer wurde ja nicht gezielt für eine bestimmte Gemeinde gebaut. Vielmehr hatte die jüdische Gemeinde Groß-Berlin festgestellt, dass an diesem Ort Bedarf an einer orthodoxen Synagoge bestand. In den umliegenden Bezirken lebten viele Jüdinnen und Juden, aber es war eben kein solches Gotteshaus fußläufig erreichbar, was ja am Schabbat wichtig ist. Somit wurde dann den Jüdinnen und Juden, die dort in der Gegend wohnten und sich bislang in Gruppen von 80 oder 100 Leuten in kleineren Shtiblekh getroffen hatten, eine zentrale Synagoge gebaut. Es ist also nicht so, dass dort eine Gemeinde ein solches Gebäude explizit in Auftrag gegeben hätte.

Mit der zweiten und dritten Generation von in Deutschland geborenen Jüdinnen und Juden ist die Frage der Repräsentation jetzt wieder wichtig

IR Das finde ich interessant, aber es war nicht ganz die Intention meiner Frage. Ich wollte eher die Zukunft und den Auftritt der heutigen Gemeinde in der Öffentlichkeit in den Blick nehmen. Also, wenn man heute eine Synagoge für eine konkrete Gemeinde neu baut, wie

low as possible, or is erected in a rear courtyard. First, this approach serves the function of ensuring the privacy and protection of the community; secondly, however, it was also due to the presence of external constraints—a synagogue could not rise higher than the surrounding buildings. The old synagogue on Heidereutergasse, for example, was built in a depression in order to avoid having it rise above adjacent buildings, including the neighboring Marienkirche, thereby avoiding attracting attention in the neighborhood. Then came the great era of emancipation, with Jewish self-confidence coming to life in Central Europe during the second half of the nineteenth century. Now, all of a sudden, synagogues acquired a very different level of visibility—the new synagogue on Oranienburger Straße [→ p.156] is probably the most representative instance of this shift. With its tower-style cupola, it's a grand, emphatically present building, one that is however clearly distinguishable from Christian churches by virtue of its architectural language as a whole, with its Moorish elements—there was a desire to say quite explicitly: this building may not be Christian, but it's equally representative. The entire architectural spectrum was represented in the history of synagogue building in Berlin between 1860 and 1934: there was the synagogue on Fasanenstraße [→ Figs.2&3], which was representative to a degree similar to the one on Oranienburger Straße; there were neo-classical buildings such as the one on Fraenkelufer, which achieved a strong presence through its temple form, and which no longer imitated churches; but also surviving were synagogues that withdrew into the background architecturally, such as the one on Rykestraße [→ Fig.4], as well as smaller synagogues that occupied courtyards, such as the one on Pestalozzistraße [→ Fig.5]. A terminus of sorts was reached with the classically Bauhaus synagogue on Prinzregentenstraße [→ Fig.6]. All of these developments ran parallel to one another, and there were many different approaches to the question of how present or representative a Jewish place of worship should be. What needs to be taken into account is the fact that the synagogue on Fraenkelufer was not built for a specific community. Instead, the Jewish community of metropolitan Berlin had decided that an Orthodox synagogue was needed at that location. Many Jews lived in the neighboring districts where no house of worship was accessible on foot, which is of course of the greatest

2
Gebetsraum Synagoge Fasanenstraße, Berlin,
Foto: 1935
Prayer hall, synagogue on Fasanenstraße, Berlin,
photo: 1935

3
Synagoge Fasanenstraße, Berlin,
Foto: 1930
The synagogue on Fasanenstraße, Berlin,
photo: 1930

—
Ehrenfried Hessel
1912 (zerstört/ destroyed 1938/58)

präsent in Größe und Form sollte sie dann sein? Und ergänzend dazu: Sie, Herr Marcus, hatten ja gerade erwähnt, dass man im späten 19., frühen 20. Jahrhundert einen eigenen architektonischen Stil wählte, um sich von den Kirchen abzuheben – welche Architektursprache wäre dementsprechend heute angemessen?

DP Ich finde, dass dennoch auch bei dieser Frage der Akkulturationsprozess, den Mario soeben erwähnt hat, wichtig ist – also in dem Sinne, dass es sich dabei um eine immerwährende Entwicklung handelt. Man muss gar nicht so weit zurückblicken: Auch die Neubauten der 1970er-, 80er-Jahre hatten ebenso dieses Narrativ des «Versteckens» und wollten nicht unbedingt in der Öffentlichkeit präsent sein. Mit der Tatsache, dass es nun eine zweite oder dritte Generation von in Deutschland geborenen Jüdinnen und Juden gibt und sich auch ein anderes Selbstbewusstsein herausgebildet hat, ist diese Frage der Repräsentation jetzt wieder wichtig geworden. Auch bei unserem Projekt der Synagogenerweiterung spielt sie eine sehr zentrale Rolle. Wie sich allerdings dann die damalige und die heutige Repräsentation und der Umgang mit unserer spezifischen Geschichte konkret in diesem Gebäude zeigen sollen, ist eine noch offene Frage. Wir sprechen bei dem Projekt am Fraenkelufer ja nicht über eine 1:1-Rekonstruktion, daher müssen wir solche Dinge auch wieder neu ausloten. Also: Wie kombinieren wir die Erinnerung an die architektonische Geschichte mit dem Bruch des Holocausts und repräsentieren gleichzeitig die aktuell in Berlin lebenden Jüdinnen und Juden mit ihrem heutigen Lebensgefühl in einem Gebäude? Hierbei muss man auch über die Außenwirkung nachdenken: Wir wissen, dass die meisten Passanten, die an unserem Grundstück vorbeigehen, gar nicht mitbekommen, dass sich da eine Synagoge befindet. Sie merken nur, dass dort Sicherheitsanlagen sind. Wäre es, zugespitzt formuliert, also nicht eigentlich egal, was die Architekten hier planen, da letztlich die Sicherheitsanlagen das Gemeindezentrum repräsentieren werden? Schließlich wären sie das Einzige, was die Öffentlichkeit von diesem Gebäude mitbekommt. So eine Entwicklung wäre aber weder für die Repräsentationsfunktion des Hauses noch für das Lebensgefühl der zukünftigen Nutzerinnen und Nutzer gut. Daher ist das auch ein Element, das wir unbedingt bei der Planung bedenken müssen.

IR Wenn ich hier nachhaken darf: Ist es nicht dennoch so, dass die ganzen Sicherheitsproblematiken immer dazu führen werden, dass sich das Gemeindehaus doch etwas absondern wird und es eine verschlossene Einheit bleibt? In der Diskussion, die wir mit den Studierenden geführt haben, existierte immer das Bedürfnis, das Haus zu öffnen und somit auch einen sozialen Austausch zu ermöglichen. Allerdings gab es bei allen Beteiligten ebenso das Wissen um die Sicherheitsanforderungen und die Notwendigkeit einer Zugangskontrolle. Das ist ein gewisser Widerspruch in sich: einerseits der Wille, sich der Öffentlichkeit zuzuwenden und zu kommunizieren, andererseits die Unabdingbarkeit, sich als Gemeinde zu sichern. Wie stehen Sie dazu?

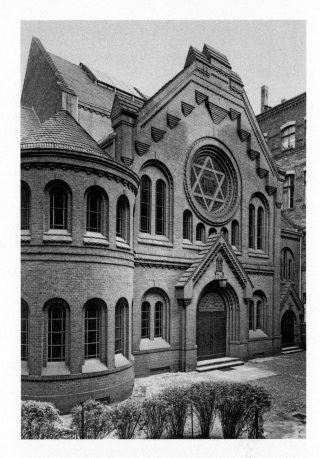

importance on Shabbat. As a result, a central synagogue was built for Jews living in the area, and had up to then come them together in groups of between eighty and a hundred in smaller shtiebels. It's therefore not the case that one particular community commissioned a synagogue building at this location.

With a second and a third generation of German-born Jews, the question of representation has regained its importance

IR I find that interesting, but it wasn't really the intent of my question. What I wanted to address instead was the future and the self-presentation of the contemporary community in the public sphere. Which is to say: when a new synagogue is built today for a specific community, how present should it be with regard to size and shape? And adding to this: you, Herr Marcus, have mentioned that in the late-nineteenth and early-twentieth centuries, an identifiable architectural language was chosen in order to distinguish synagogues from churches—which architectural language would then be appropriate today?

DP I believe the acculturation process just mentioned by Mario is important with regard to this question as well—in the sense that it's a question of a continuous development. You don't have to go back all that far: the new buildings of the 1970s and 1980s illustrate this narrative of "self-concealment," and didn't necessarily want to be publicly present. Now, with a second and a third generation of German-born Jews, who have also given shape to a different self-awareness, the question

4
Gebetsraum Synagoge Rykestraße, Berlin, Foto: 1905
Prayer hall, synagogue on Rykestraße, Berlin, photo: 1905
—
Johann Hoeinger 1904

5
Synagoge Pestalozzistraße, Berlin, Foto: undatiert
The synagogue on Pestalozzistraße, Berlin, photo: undated
—
Ernst Dorn 1912

DP Ich würde es eine Herausforderung nennen. Es sind in jeden Fall entgegengesetzte Ansprüche, aber ich glaube nicht, dass man nun zwingend eine «Burg» bauen muss, um dem Sicherheitsaspekt gerecht zu werden. Es wird eher zum Problem, wenn man diesen Gesichtspunkt nicht von vornherein eingeplant und bedacht hat und die Defizite nachträglich durch Sicherheitsmaßnahmen zu kompensieren versucht. Unser Wunsch ist es, den Stadtraum von sichtbaren Sicherheitsanlagen freizuhalten und sie so stark wie möglich nach innen zu verlagern. Das widerspricht zwar dem aktuellen Planungskonsens, aber ich glaube, diese Diskussion, wie sich solche Anlagen ins Stadtbild einfügen können, ohne bedrohlich zu wirken, wäre auch im Blick auf andere sensible Orte in Berlin wünschenswert.

Das Gemeindezentrum soll weder ein reines Denkmal noch ein hermetischer Neubau sein

MM Der Sicherheitsaspekt ist eine aktuelle Fragestellung, aber man darf nicht vergessen, dass es während der Entwicklung des Synagogenbaus auch schon früher verschiedene Strömungen in Hinblick auf die Sichtbarkeit gegeben hat. Dies hatte auch immer mit dem jeweiligen Selbstverständnis der Gemeinden zu tun. Die großen Synagogen zeigten das Narrativ: «Wir sind hier, mitten in der Stadt und mitten in der Gesellschaft.» Andererseits gab es auch immer wieder Gemeinden, die für sich sagten: «Wir sind zwar Jüdinnen und Juden, wollen das aber nicht weiter thematisieren. Wir gehen lieber in ein Haus hinein, und dann in den Hinterhof zur kleinen Synagoge und sind dann unter uns.» Die Frage ist jetzt natürlich: Wie soll unsere Ausstrahlung in die Öffentlichkeit sein? Beziehungsweise muss man auch fragen: Wie will die Öffentlichkeit uns sehen? Das Interessante ist ja, dass der Wunsch einer Rekonstruktion des historischen Vorbilds vorrangig von der nicht-jüdischen Gesellschaft geäußert wurde. Mit dem neuen Gemeindezentrum soll also auch gezeigt werden, dass es wieder aktives jüdisches Leben an einem historischen Ort gibt. Es soll also weder ein reines Denkmal noch ein hermetischer Neubau sein, vielmehr wünschen wir uns eine Kombination aus beidem. Da das Grundstück in seiner ehemaligen Form noch existiert, haben wir dafür natürlich auch ideale Voraussetzungen.

AF Das ist jetzt eine bemerkenswerte Stellungnahme. Aus Hamburg wissen wir zum Beispiel, dass mit der Rekonstruktion der Bornplatzsynagoge gezielt ein Zeichen gesetzt werden soll, wozu es innerhalb der Gemeinde widersprüchliche Haltungen gibt. Sie haben jetzt gerade gesagt, Herr Marcus, dass im Fall des Fraenkelufers dieser Wunsch nach einer Rekonstruktion maßgeblich von außen herangetragen wurde. Was ich jetzt gelernt habe, ist, dass Sie mit dem Neubau einerseits eine Kontinuität der Geschichte erzählen möchten und andererseits auch eine Sichtbarkeit herstellen wollen, die der prominenten Lage am Landwehrkanal gerecht wird. Daher finde ich es interessant, dass diese Rekonstruktion des Portikus von Alexander Beer seitens der Gemeinde gar nicht als Lösung in den Blick genommen wurde – oder gibt es dazu verschiedene Haltungen?

6
Synagoge Prinzregentenstraße, Berlin, Foto: um 1930
The synagogue on Prinzregentenstraße, Berlin, photo: ca. 1930
—
Alexander Beer 1930 (zerstört/destroyed 1938/58)

of representation has regained its importance. It also plays a central role in our synagogue extension project. Just how the representative character of the building, both then and today, along with the handling of our specific history, should be concretely manifested in this building remains an open question. With the project on Fraenkelufer, after all, we're not talking about a 1:1 reconstruction, so these concerns will need to be reexamined. How do we combine memory and architectural history in this building with the radical break of the Holocaust, and at the same time represent the Jews currently living in Berlin and their attitude toward life? Here, it also becomes necessary to reflect upon its outward impact: we know that passersby will simply be unaware there is a synagogue there. The only thing they notice is the security system. To exaggerate slightly: isn't it actually irrelevant what the architects achieve here, since in the end it's the security system that actually represents the community center? Ultimately, it's the only thing the public is going to notice about the building. It would hardly be positive, either for the representative function of the building, nor for the attitudes of future users. Which means that this element absolutely must be considered when it comes to planning.

IR If I could follow up on that: isn't it the case that the entire security problem inevitably leads toward the community building being somewhat isolated, remaining a self-contained unit? Expressed consistently in our discussions with students was the need to open up the building, to make social exchange possible. Of course, all of the participants were well aware of the security requirements, of the need for controlled access. This involves a contradiction of sorts: on the one hand, the desire to turn toward the wider public, to communicate; on the other, the imperative for the community to protect itself. What is your position on this?

DP I would call it a challenge. These are certainly antithetical demands, but I don't believe you need to build a "fortress" in order to do justice to the security aspect. It becomes a problem rather when this aspect is not given due consideration in the planning measures from the start, necessitating attempts after the fact to compensate for security deficits. Our aim is to keep the urban environment unencumbered by visible security measures, shifting it inward as far as possible. This contradicts the current planning consensus, of course, but I believe a discussion about how such facilities might be integrated into the urban landscape without making a menacing impression would be desirable, with an eye as well toward other problematic locations in Berlin.

The community center is to be neither a pure memorial nor a hermetic new building

MM The security aspect is a current concern, but don't forget that during the development of synagogue building, earlier on as well, there were already various tendencies with regard to visibility. These were always related to the self-understanding of the respective community. The large synagogues displayed the narrative: "We're

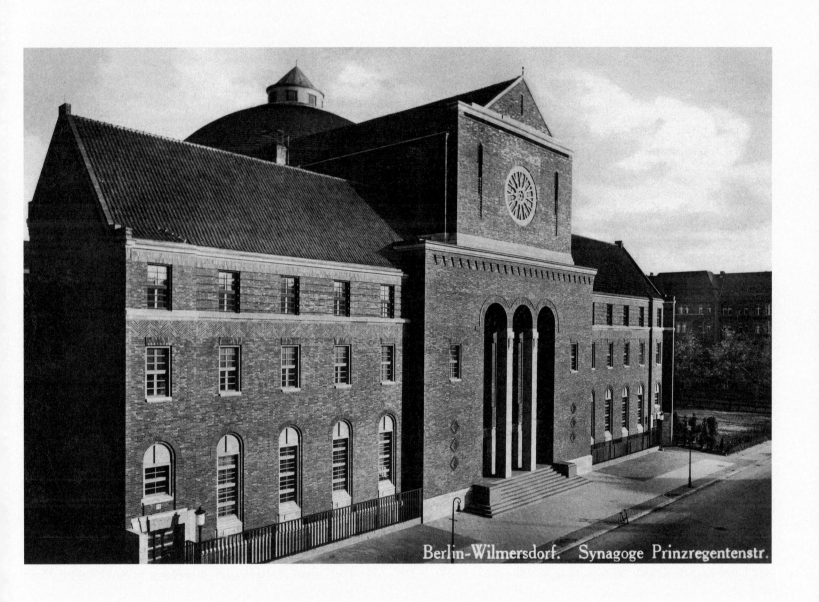

Unser Ziel ist, ein identitätsstiftendes Zeichen zu etablieren, das keine persönliche Verbindung zum Ort voraussetzt

DP Also mit dem Stichwort der Kontinuität müssen wir in diesem Fall aufpassen. Es geht uns nicht darum, das Narrativ «100 Jahre glückliches Leben vor Ort» zu zeigen. Vielmehr wollen wir hier immer auch von dem Bruch erzählen, der ja augenfällig ist, weil eben das Gebäude der alten Synagoge nicht mehr existiert. Unser Ziel ist aber ebenso, ein identitätsstiftendes Zeichen für neue jüdische Zuwanderer nach Berlin zu etablieren, das eben keine persönliche oder familiäre Verbindung zu diesem Ort voraussetzt. Trotz allem wollen wir uns an dem historischen Gebäude und seiner Architektur orientieren. Bei einer Rekonstruktion gäbe es allerdings gewisse Widersprüche zu den aktuellen Nutzungswünschen, ich denke hier vor allem an die Themen Sicherheit und Offenheit, an technische Schwierigkeiten aufgrund einiger Änderungen in den angrenzenden Häusern, aber auch an die Frage nach der Funktionalität des Gebäudes. Schließlich wurde die Synagoge damals als Saal für 1600 Personen und damit für ganz andere Zwecke geplant. Daher sind wir offen, wie genau hier eine gute Lösung gelingen kann. Ich meine, die Fassade ist natürlich das bekannteste Gesicht des Gebäudes. Sie ist gewissermaßen das historische Gedächtnis, an dem sich die Erinnerung reproduziert. Die Frage ist dann, wie sie genau aussehen soll und wie dabei die Erinnerung an die Vergangenheit eine Rolle spielen kann? Das sind wichtige Aspekte, die in die Diskussion um den Wiederaufbau einfließen müssen. Schließlich ist es auch unser Wunsch, dass die Vergangenheit an diesem Ort mitgedacht und in diesem Wiederaufbau präsent wird.

IR Aber das ist schon eine interessante Frage. In dem grandiosen Entwurf von Alexander Beer mit seiner starken Präsenz war alles integriert – er war eine Einheit von Zweck, Ausdruck und Raum. Wenn man nun bei einem Neubau die Erinnerung auf ein sichtbares Zeichen reduziert, dann trennt sich doch die Bedeutung der Fassade von dem, was dahinter passiert. Hier muss ich unweigerlich an Robert Venturis «dekorierten Schuppen» denken. Unsere Aufgabe als Architekten und Architektinnen ist es doch vielmehr, diese beiden Aspekte zusammenzubringen. Dabei stellt sich auch unweigerlich die Frage nach der Bedeutsamkeit, also ob es richtig wäre, die Geschichte auf ein Symbol oder einen Verweis zu reduzieren.

DP Sie wird aber doch nicht auf ein Symbol reduziert! Im Endeffekt ist ja die Synagoge an sich schon gebauter Ausdruck der Dinge, die in ihr geschehen. Sie zeigt, dass jüdisches Leben einen Ort hat – das ist der Kern der Sache.

IR Das stimmt und das sehen wir alle genauso – aber trotzdem stellt sich die Frage, wie man das nun auch architektonisch adäquat zum Ausdruck bringt.

here, in the middle of the city, in the midst of society." On the other hand, there were always communities that took the position: "Of course we're Jews, but we don't want to thematize that fact further. We prefer just entering the building, and then the little synagogue in the rear courtyard, remaining amongst ourselves." The question now, of course, is: what kind of public aura do we want to have? And, conversely: how does the public perceive us? Interestingly, the desire to reconstruct a historic model is being expressed primarily by non-Jewish society. The new community center is also designed to show that active Jewish life is present here again at this historic site. It should therefore be neither a pure memorial nor a hermetic new building; instead, we want a combination of the two. Since the property still exists in its earlier form, the ideal preconditions are of course present here.

AF That's a remarkable statement. From Hamburg, for example, we know that the reconstruction of the Bornplatz Synagogue is intended to send a deliberate signal, and that there are conflicting attitudes about this within the community. You have just said, Herr Marcus, that in the case of Fraenkelufer, this desire for a reconstruction came to a large extent from outside. I've now learned that, with the new building, you strive first to narrate a continuous history, and secondly to generate a form of visibility that does justice to the prominent location on Landwehrkanal. Which is why I find it interesting that the reconstruction of Alexander Beer's portico was not viewed as a viable solution at all by the community—or are there differing views about this?

Our aim is to establish a symbol that promotes a sense of identity but assumes no personal connection with this location

DP Well, in this instance, we need to be careful with the catchword continuity. We're not trying to give form to the narrative "one hundred years of joyous life on this site." Instead, we always want to say something about the radical break as well, which is of course strikingly conspicuous, since the old synagogue building no longer exists. But our aim is also to establish a symbol for the sake of recent Jewish immigrants to Berlin, one that promotes a sense of identity but assumes no personal or family connection with this location. Despite everything, we seek to orient ourselves toward the historic building and its architecture. With a reconstruction, however, there are certain conflicts with current utilization needs—I'm thinking in particular of the topics of security and openness, of technical difficulties arising from alterations to the adjacent buildings, but also to the question of the building's functionality. Back then, finally, the synagogue was planned as a hall for 1,600 people, and hence for a very different purpose. So we're open to proposals for good solutions that promise success. I mean, the facade is of course the building's most familiar aspect. In a sense, it's the focus of the reproduction of historical memory. The question then becomes: how, exactly, should it appear, and how can memories of the past play a role here? These are

Wenn man den Originalentwurf wiederherstellen würde, würde der Bruch verschwinden

MM Wenn wir die Bauaufgabe einmal ganz pragmatisch betrachten, gibt es aktuell für die Gemeinde die Notwendigkeit, sich räumlich zu vergrößern. Was wir hierfür allerdings nicht brauchen, wäre ein repräsentativer, großer Synagogensaal; vielmehr benötigen wir Funktionsbauten und einige multifunktionale Räumlichkeiten, die idealerweise für einen direkten räumlichen Zusammenhang mit der existierenden Synagoge kombiniert werden sollten. Natürlich haben wir auch einen gewissen ästhetischen Anspruch – egal, was dort gebaut wird, es soll sich harmonisch in die Umgebung einpassen. Aber hier schließt sich gewissermaßen auch die Frage nach der Erinnerung an die Geschichte mit all ihrer Widersprüchlichkeit an. Also: Wie können wir all diese Sachen so verbinden, dass wir ein funktionierendes Gebäude haben, dass das Moment des Erinnerns sichtbar wird und dass wir gleichzeitig in dem Erinnern darstellen, welchen Bruch es einmal gab? Das ist ganz wichtig. Um noch einmal auf die Rekonstruktion zurückzukommen: Wenn man den Originalentwurf von Alexander Beer wiederherstellen würde, würde meines Erachtens der Bruch verschwinden. Dann heißt es irgendwann: Am Fraenkelufer gibt es ein wunderbares großes Gebäude, was sich hübsch in die Umgebung einfügt – das ist eine Synagoge und war schon immer eine Synagoge. Das wäre nicht die Wirkung, die ich mir vorstelle. Wir brauchen zwar ein Gebäude, was sichtbar und repräsentativ ist, aber man muss dem Entwurf immer auch gleichzeitig den Bruch in der Geschichte anmerken und sich als Betrachter oder Betrachterin fragen, ob hier nicht etwas fehlt.

DP Ich möchte hier nur noch hinzufügen, dass sich ja auch das Selbstverständnis von «Wie praktiziere ich Jüdisch-Sein?» gewandelt hat, so dass vor allem die sozialen und kulturellen Bedürfnisse mehr Raum einfordern. Aber um noch einmal auf die Frage nach dem architektonischen Ausdruck zurückzukommen: Am Fraenkelufer ist es auch im Gegensatz zu Hamburg so, dass wir uns nicht damit auseinandersetzen müssen, wie man sich als neues Gebäude zu einem Nazibunker postiert, sondern wir müssen darüber nachdenken, wie sich ein Erweiterungsbau zu dem bestehenden Seitenflügel [→ Abb. 7] verhalten sollte. Was der Neubau in jedem Fall leisten muss, ist, mit den erhalten gebliebenen Bestandteilen des Originalgebäudes zu kommunizieren.

IR Ja, das sehen wir genauso. Das ist sehr wichtig.

AF Was mich noch interessieren würde: Wir haben mit dem synagogalen Raum, den Kultur- und Gemeinderäumen und dem Kinderhaus drei neue funktionale Pfeiler des Gemeindehauses definiert: Stehen diese Teile für Sie gleichwertig zueinander oder gäbe es einen Bereich, der Ihrer Meinung nach dort bedeutender wäre als die anderen? Der Entwurf von Daria Federova formt aus diesen Programmteilen zum Beispiel eine Art Konglomerat, das sich aus verschiedenen kleinen Gebäuden mit jeweils einer eigenen architektonischen Identität

important aspects, and must flow into discussions about reconstruction. Finally, we hope to see the site's historical past given due consideration, to see it present in the reconstruction.

IR That's an interesting question. In Alexander Beer's magnificent design, with its powerful presence, everything was integrated—it was a unity of function, expression, and space. If its memory is reduced now, in a new building, to a visible symbol, then the significance of the facade becomes separated from what occurs behind it. I can't avoid being reminded of Robert Venturi's "decorated shed." But our task as architects is instead to bring these two aspects together. Unavoidably, this raises the question of meaningfulness, whether it's correct to reduce history to a symbol or reference.

DP But it isn't being reduced to a symbol! Ultimately, the synagogue is in essence the built expression of the things that transpire within it. It shows that Jewish life has a place—that's the heart of the matter.

IR That's true, and all of us see it that way—nevertheless, there's the question of how this can be expressed adequately in architectural terms.

If the original design was recreated, the radical break would disappear

MM Considering the construction task from a purely pragmatic standpoint, we have the present need on the part of the community to expand spatially. What we don't need, however, is a large, representative synagogue hall; required instead are functional buildings and a number of multifunctional spaces that can, ideally, be combined directly in spatial terms with the existing synagogue. Of course, there are also certain aesthetic demands—regardless of what is built there, it should be adapted harmoniously to the surroundings. And this is also linked, in a sense, to the question of historical memory, with all its contradictions. The question therefore is: how do we combine all of these things in such a way that the result is a functional building, that the aspect of memory becomes visible, and that, in remembering, we also represent the radical break that has occurred? That's very important. To return again to the idea of a reconstruction: in my view, if Alexander Beer's original design was recreated, the radical break would disappear. At some point, you would hear people say: "There is a large, marvelous building on Fraenkelufer which fits beautifully into the surroundings—it's a synagogue, and always was a synagogue." That would be the effect as I would imagine it. Of course, we need a building that is visible and representative, but, at the same time, the design must always express an awareness of the radical break in history, so that visitors will ask themselves whether something is missing here.

DP I'd just like to add that our self-conception regarding the question "how do I practice my Jewishness?" has changed, that social and cultural needs in particular demand greater scope. But to return again to the

und Adressbildung zusammensetzt [→ S. 68–71]. Hier gäbe es somit keinen dominierenden Solitärbau mehr, wie er zum Beispiel für den Entwurf Alexander Beers prägend war.

DP Ich denke, dass sich die Hierarchie der Funktionen für jede Nutzerin und jeden Nutzer unterschiedlich darstellt. Es gibt daher keinen Ort, von dem wir als Bauherren sagen würden, dass auf ihm unser Augenmerk liegen würde und er wichtiger als alles andere wäre. Was mir aber bei vielen Entwürfen fehlt, ist eine Grünfläche als öffentlicher und gemeinsam genutzter Raum – vor allem an einem Ort wie Kreuzberg wäre das natürlich repräsentativ und besonders auch im Hinblick auf den angedachten Kindergarten wünschenswert. Das wäre meiner Meinung nach also ein Element, was zu einer zeitgenössischen Repräsentation gehört und auch unseren heutigen Ansprüchen sowie dem Geschmack der Gemeinde entsprechen würde.

Wäre es überhaupt richtig, das Gemeindezentrum durch eine Synagoge zu repräsentieren?

IR Das stimmt. Ich glaube, wenn man das ganze Grundstück für den Neubau nutzen dürfte, ergäbe sich so eine Situation von ganz allein: Am Kanalufer hätte man den repräsentativen öffentlichen Platz, dann käme das Gemeindehaus, an das sich der Garten und der Kindergarten anschließen würden. – Nun hätte ich aber noch eine letzte Frage, die auch mit der Thematik der Nutzung und der damit verbundenen Außenwirkung zusammenhängt: Wir haben unser Projekt ja «Synagogen-Projekt» genannt und auch hier die ganze Zeit von Synagogen gesprochen. Aber Sie, Herr Peretz, betonten gerade, dass die synagogale Nutzung nur eine neben vielen anderen ist und dass es dabei auch keine feste Hierarchie der Funktionen gibt. Wenn es so ist, wäre es dann überhaupt richtig, das geplante Gemeinde- und Kulturzentrum architektonisch durch eine Synagoge zu repräsentieren? In den meisten Entwürfen der Studierenden wurde die Synagoge wirkmächtig nach vorne gestellt, während die anderen Nutzungen im Hintergrund angeordnet sind. Daher: Ist eine solche Geste dann inhaltlich-programmatisch gesehen überhaupt der richtige Ausdruck? Oder wäre es nicht konsequenter, die Synagoge als einen Raum unter vielen zu behandeln? Wir haben uns sogar gefragt, ob sie nicht irgendwo im Haus integriert sein könnte und gar nicht als eigenständiger Raum in Erscheinung treten sollte.

MM Ich weiß jetzt nicht ganz genau, wie Sie und die Studierenden an diese Aufgabe herangegangen sind – aber wenn ich die Entwürfe betrachte, sehe ich doch die Forderung: Man plant einen Synagogenraum sowie einen Mehrzweckraum und verteilt dann alle anderen Nutzungen drumherum. Ehrlich gesagt ist das für uns kein Raumprogramm, das wir als Gemeinde so aufstellen würden. 90 Prozent unserer Gottesdienste halten wir in der bestehenden Synagoge ab – und einen schönen, großen Synagogenraum bereitzuhalten, um ihn nur ein- oder zweimal im Jahr zu nutzen, ist nicht das, was

question of architectural expression: on Fraenkelufer, we don't have the problem of deciding how to position the new synagogue in relation to the Nazi bunker, as in Hamburg; here, the issue is how the extension building should relate to the existing side wing [→ Fig. 7]. What is required of the new building is that it communicates effectively with the surviving components of the original building.

IR Yes, we feel the same way. That's very important.

AF Something else that interests me: with the synagogal space, the cultural and community spaces, and the children's house, we have defined the three functional pillars of the community center: do these elements stand alongside one another on equal terms, or are some areas, in your view, more important than others? Daria Federova's design, for example, forms a kind of conglomerate from these programmatic elements, composed of various small buildings, each with an independent architectural identity and recognition value [→ pp. 68–71]. Here, there is no longer any dominant solitaire building of the kind so characteristic of Alexander Beer's design.

DP I think the hierarchy of functions is different for each individual user. As the builders, there is therefore no single area that requires special attention, that's more important than all the others. What's missing for me in many of the designs is a green space that would function as a public, commonly used area—in a district like Kreuzberg, in particular, it would of course be representative, and would be especially desirable with regard to the envisaged kindergarten. In my view, such an element would be consistent with contemporary needs for representation, and would also be consistent with the current demands and tastes of the community.

Is it even correct for the planned community center to be represented by a synagogue?

IR That's true. I believe that if the entire premises were used for the new building, a certain situation would arise automatically: facing the canal would be a public, representative plaza, then the community building, with the adjoining garden and kindergarten—but I still have one final question that relates to utilization, and to

7
Seitenflügel der Synagoge am Fraenkelufer, Foto: 1987
Side wing, synagogue on Fraenkelufer, photo: 1987

wir brauchen. Lieber sollte man den Gebetsraum als Mehrzweckraum gestalten, so dass er für beides nutzbar ist, wie man es zum Beispiel in den 1950er-Jahren bei der Synagoge in der Fasanenstraße gehandhabt hat. In diesem großen Raum können die verschiedensten Veranstaltungen stattfinden: Hochzeiten, Tanzveranstaltungen, Versammlungen, Jugendtreffs. Hinter der Bühne befindet sich der Tora-Schrank – und in dem Moment, in dem sich die Tora-Rollen in ihm befinden, wird dieser Raum eben auch zur Synagoge.

IR Diese Frage nach der Multifunktionalität haben wir auch im Vorfeld sehr intensiv diskutiert. Unsere Schlussfolgerung war, dass es eben genau der Gebetsraum ist, welcher als spezifischer Raum ein Gemeindehaus von anderen Gebäuden unterscheidet. Wenn wir diesen dann multifunktional gestalten würden, würde dem Gebäude etwas Identitätsstiftendes fehlen. Mag sein, dass das der Blick der Menschen ist, die jenseits der Gemeinde stehen. Wir haben auch schon gemerkt, dass es Gemeinden gibt, die eben diesen Anspruch an einen feierlichen Gebetsraum haben und andere haben ihn nicht.

DP Ich bin da optimistischer als Mario, in dem Sinne, dass auch ein zweiter Gebetsraum in der Zukunft wichtig sein und öfter verwendet werden könnte. Schließlich ist unsere Hoffnung, dass noch weitere Jüdinnen und Juden nach Berlin kommen werden und sich auch in diesem Stadtteil niederlassen.

MM Wobei ich im Hinblick auf solche Überlegungen aber noch einmal betonen möchte: Den synagogalen Raum, der sich in dem Fragment der alten Synagoge befindet, würden wir auch in Zukunft nicht aufgeben oder umnutzen wollen – er ist und bleibt unser Gebetsraum. Alles, was neu gebaut wird, muss dann auch neu gedacht werden. Das halte ich für einen wichtigen Aspekt.

the related issue of the building's outward impact: we called our project "The Synagogue Project," and have been speaking the whole time about synagogues. But you, Herr Peretz, have just been emphasizing that the synagogal utilization is only one among many others, and that no fixed hierarchy of functions exists here. If that's the case, then is it even correct for the planned community and cultural center to be represented architecturally by a synagogue? In most of the student designs, the synagogue is positioned in front for maximum impact, while the other utilizations are configured in the background. Can such a gesture really be the appropriate expression from the perspective of content and program? Wouldn't it be more logical to handle the synagogue as one space among others? We even asked ourselves whether it couldn't be integrated into the building somehow, whether it needs to take the form of a freestanding structure at all.

MM I don't know exactly how you and the students approached this task—when I study the designs, I perceive the task as: plan a synagogue space as well as a multi-use space, and distribute all the other utilizations around them. To be honest, that's not a spatial program we would have come up with as a community. I mean, 90 percent of our religious services are held in the existing synagogue—and to keep a large, beautiful, synagogue space available in order to use it just once or twice a year is not what we need. It would be better to design the prayer hall as a multifunctional space, so that it's usable for both, which is how things were managed, for example, in the 1950s in the synagogue on Fasanenstraße. The most diverse events could take place in this large space: weddings, dance performances, gatherings, youth clubs. Found behind the stage is a Torah cabinet—and the moment when the Torah scrolls are stored in it, the space becomes a synagogue. That would be my comment.

IR The issue of multifunctionality is something we discussed intensively beforehand. We concluded that it's precisely the specific space of the prayer hall that distinguishes a community center from other buildings. If it were designed in a multifunctional way, the building would be missing part of what shapes its identity. It may be that this perspective is held by people outside of the community. We also became aware that some communities are quite definite about the need for a formal prayer hall, while others feel differently.

DP I'm more optimistic than Mario, in the sense that, at some point in the future, a second prayer hall may become important, may be used more frequently. Finally, we're hoping more Jews will come to Berlin, and will settle in our district.

MM Although with regard to such considerations, I'd like to emphasize again: we wouldn't want to give up or convert the synagogal space that is found in the fragment of the old synagogue—it is and remains a space of prayer. Everything that is newly built must also be newly conceived. I regard that as an important aspect.

Synagoge Fraenkelufer Synagogue

1
Blick vom Landwehrkanal, Foto: um 1917
View from the Landwehrkanal, photo: ca. 1917

Synagoge Fraenkelufer
    Fraenkelufer Synagogue

    Fraenkelufer 10–16, Berlin
    Alexander Beer
    1916 (zerstört/destroyed 1938/59)

Die Synagoge am Fraenkelufer war die letzte große Synagoge Berlins und zählte bei ihrer Entstehung 1916 zu den größten Synagogen der Stadt.[1] Neben dem Hauptgebetssaal umfasste das Raumprogramm eine Wochentagssynagoge, einen Saal für den Jugendgottesdienst, einen Trausaal, Versammlungs- und Wohnräume sowie einen Kindergarten.[2]

Um 1900 wurde die prosperierende Stadt Berlin um mehrere Außenbezirke erweitert. Zur schnell wachsenden Bevölkerung zählten auch viele Juden und Jüdinnen, die unter anderem aufgrund von Pogromen in Osteuropa und Russland nach Westeuropa flohen. Den sich vergrößernden jüdischen Gemeinden standen für Zusammenkünfte zunächst nur weiter entfernte Synagogen im Stadtzentrum oder kleinere Privatsynagogen und Festsäle zur Verfügung. Zudem war die Gesamtzahl der Synagogen in Berlin bei weitem nicht ausreichend. Auch im Bezirk Kreuzberg begannen daher Planungen für den Neubau einer Synagoge am Fraenkelufer.[3] Im Jahr 1911 erwarb die jüdische Gemeinde den Bauplatz am Landwehrkanal. Nach kriegsbedingter dreijähriger Bauzeit konnte die Synagoge am 17. September 1916 eingeweiht werden.[4]

Die Synagoge am Fraenkelufer bestand aus dem über einen dreieckigen Vorplatz erschlossenen und dem Landwehrkanal zugewandten Hauptgebäude und mehreren Nebengebäuden. Von Alexander Beer als dreischiffige Anlage konzipiert, folgte das Hauptgebäude dem Typus der frühchristlichen Pfeilerbasilika mit einem viersäuligen dorischen Portikus an der Eingangsfassade und einer rückseitigen Exedra, ergänzt durch den im spitzwinkligen Teil des Grundstücks zum Landwehrkanal hin gelegenen, heute noch erhaltenen, ursprünglich als Jugendsynagoge genutzten Seitenflügel mit einer Fassadengliederung aus dorischen Halbsäulen.[5] Diese Hinwendung der jüdischen Gemeinde zu einem damals in der Architektur aufkommenden Neoklassizismus, der «dazu

The synagogue on Fraenkelufer was Berlin's last large synagogue, and was among the largest in the city when it was completed in 1916.[1] In addition to the main prayer hall, the ground plan encompassed a weekday synagogue, a hall for youth religious services, a wedding hall, rooms for gatherings, residential spaces, as well as a kindergarten.[2]

Around 1900, a prospering Berlin began expanding into a number of outlying districts. The rapidly growing population included many Jews, some of whom had fled to Western Europe to escape pogroms in Eastern Europe and Russia. Initially, only three relatively distant synagogues located in the city center, and smaller private synagogues and festival halls, were available to the growing Jewish community for gatherings. It was apparent that the number of synagogues in Berlin was far from adequate. Plans for the construction of a new synagogue (on Fraenkelufer) were therefore initiated in the Kreuzberg district as well.[3] In 1911, the Jewish community acquired the building site on Landwehrkanal. Following an extended three-year period of construction, a consequence of wartime conditions, the synagogue was dedicated on September 17, 1916.[4]

The synagogue on Fraenkelufer consisted of a main building and a number of ancillary structures that were accessed via a triangular forecourt and oriented toward the Landwehrkanal. Conceived by Alexander Beer as a three-aisled structure, the main building conformed to the type of the Early Christian pillared basilica with a Dorian portico having four columns on the entrance facade and a rear exedra; this was supplemented by a surviving lateral wing set in the acute-angled section of the parcel facing Landwehrkanal, its facade articulated by Dorian half-columns, which was originally used as a youth synagogue.[5] This recourse on the part of the Jewish community to a then nascent architectural neo-classicism, which "tended to—or was made to—serve as a new, unifying style for all architectural genres,"[6] distinguished the synagogue strikingly from its predecessors, which had relied upon orientalizing architectural forms, and can be interpreted as an expression of the prevalent Jewish patriotism of that time.[7]

The main prayer hall had space for more than 2,000 congregants, with roughly equal seating for men and women.[8] The continuous, three-sided gallery for women, standard for Orthodox synagogues, was accessed via a spacious vestibule typical of synagogue architecture.[9] The main nave, 17 meters wide, 24 meters in depth, and 21 meters in height, and spanned by a wooden coffered ceiling,[10] was oriented—in conformity with basilica typology—axially toward the Torah shrine with its domed baldachin in the northeast, and the bimah

2
Luftbild: 1933
Aerial view: 1933

tendierte bzw. dazu gebracht wurde, als neuer einheitlicher Stil für alle Baugattungen zu dienen»⁶, unterschied die Synagoge in erstaunlicher Weise von ihren an orientalischen Bauformen angelehnten Vorgängern und kann als Ausdruck des jüdischen Patriotismus dieser Jahre gelesen werden.⁷

Der Hauptgebetssaal bot Platz für über 2000 Menschen, mit etwa gleich vielen Sitzplätzen für Männer und Frauen.⁸ Die dreiseitig umlaufenden Frauenemporen der orthodoxen Synagoge wurden über die großzügigen, für den Synagogenbau typischen Vorhallen erschlossen.⁹ Das 17 Meter breite, 24 Meter tiefe und 21 Meter hohe, von einer Holz-Kassettendecke überspannte Hauptschiff¹⁰ war, dem Typus der Basilika folgend, axial auf den Toraschrein mit überkuppeltem Baldachin im Nordosten und auf die unmittelbar davor befindliche Bima hin orientiert. Obergaden entlang der Seitenfassaden belichteten den Raum und verstärkten dessen längs gerichteten Charakter.

In den Jahren der zunehmenden systematischen Ausgrenzung der jüdischen Bevölkerung ab 1933 wurde auch die Synagoge am Fraenkelufer immer häufiger zur Zielscheibe antisemitischer Übergriffe.¹¹ In dieser Zeit nahm der Gebäudekomplex verschiedene soziale Einrichtungen wie das Jüdische Wohlfahrts- und Jugendamt, die Jüdische Winterhilfe und später auch eine Wohlfahrtsküche auf. In der Reichspogromnacht am 9. November 1938 wurde die Synagoge in Brand gesetzt, aber nicht zerstört – vermutlich auch, weil eine Ausbreitung der Flammen auf die direkt angrenzende städtische Schule verhindert werden sollte.¹² Die Nutzung des Hauptgebetssaals war infolgedessen nicht mehr möglich, jedoch konnte die Gemeinde bis 1942 noch Gottesdienste in der Jugendsynagoge im Seitenflügel des Gebäudes durchführen.¹³ 1942 besetzte die Gestapo die verbliebenen Baulichkeiten, die kurze Zeit später bei einem Bombenangriff erneut schwer beschädigt wurden.¹⁴ Die verbliebenen Überreste des Hauptgebaudes wurden schließlich 1958/59 abgerissen.¹⁵

Besondere Bedeutung kommt dem heute noch erhaltenen Gebäudeteil der ehemaligen Jugendsynagoge zu, da dieser Gebetsraum als einer von wenigen der Zerstörung entging. Die Synagoge am Fraenkelufer war damit eine von nur sieben Berliner Synagogen, die nach den Novemberpogromen 1938 zumindest teilweise, auch von angrenzenden Gemeinden, genutzt werden konnten. Als erste Synagoge in Berlin wurde die Jugendsynagoge zum jüdischen Neujahrsfest Rosh ha-Schana im September 1945 wiederhergerichtet.¹⁶ Seit ihrer Wiedereinweihung 1959 wird sie durchgängig für Gebete und Gemeindeleben einer in den letzten Jahren immer weiter anwachsenden Gemeinde genutzt.

situated immediately in front of it. The space was illuminated by a clerestory running along the side facades, reinforcing the longitudinal character of the space.

To an ever-greater degree during the years of the increasing and systematic exclusion of the Jews that followed 1933, the synagogue on Fraenkelufer became a target of anti-Semitic attacks.¹¹ During this period, the building complex accommodated various social facilities, such as the Jewish welfare and youth office, Jewish winter aid, and later a charity kitchen as well. During the Reich's Pogrom Night (Kristallnacht) of November 9, 1938, the synagogue was set on fire, but not destroyed—presumably partly because of the need to prevent the flames from spreading to the municipal school directly adjacent.¹² Subsequently, the main prayer hall could no longer be used, but the congregation continued to celebrate religious services in the youth synagogue in the side wing of the building until 1942.¹³ In that year, the remaining buildings were occupied by the Gestapo, and were again heavily damaged shortly thereafter during an air raid.¹⁴ Finally, the remnants of the main building were demolished in 1958/59.¹⁵

Particular importance is attributed to the still-surviving sections of the former youth synagogue, since this prayer room is one of the few to escape destruction. The synagogue on Fraenkelufer was therefore one of only seven Berlin synagogues that were at least partially usable after the pogrom night of 1938, and were consequently opened to adjoining communities as well. In September of 1945, the youth synagogue was the first synagogue in Berlin to be restored for the occasion of the Jewish New Year's festival of Rosh Hashanah.¹⁶ Since its rededication in 1959, it has remained in continuous use for prayer and social activities by a community that has seen significant growth in recent years.

3
Blick vom Fraenkelufer, Foto: um 1916
View from Fraenkelufer, photo: ca. 1916

4
Blick vom Planufer, Zeichnung: um 1970
View from Planufer, drawing: ca. 1970

1 Vgl. Harold Hammer-Schenk: *Synagogen in Deutschland. Geschichte einer Baugattung im 19. und 20. Jahrhundert (1780–1933)*, Teil 1, Hamburg 1981 (Hamburger Beiträge zur Geschichte der deutschen Juden, Band VIII), S. 459.
2 Vgl. Daniela Gauding und Christine Zahn: *Die Synagoge Fraenkelufer (Kottbusser Ufer) 1916 – 1959 – 2009*, in: *Jüdische Miniaturen. Spektrum jüdischen Lebens*, hg. von Hermann Simon, Berlin 2009, S. 16.
3 Vgl. ebd., S. 13 ff.
4 Vgl. ebd., S. 22.
5 Vgl. Harold Hammer-Schenk: *Synagogen in Deutschland*, S. 459.
6 Ebd., S. 462.
7 Vgl. ebd., S. 461.
8 Vgl. Daniela Gauding und Christine Zahn: *Die Synagoge Fraenkelufer*, S. 16.
9 Vgl. Harold Hammer-Schenk: *Synagogen in Deutschland*, S. 459.
10 Vgl. Daniela Gauding und Christine Zahn: *Die Synagoge Fraenkelufer*, S. 19.
11 Vgl. ebd., S. 34 ff.
12 Vgl. ebd., S. 38.
13 Vgl. ebd.
14 Vgl. ebd., S. 42 f.
15 Vgl. ebd., S. 47.
16 Vgl. ebd., S. 43.

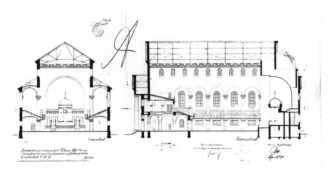
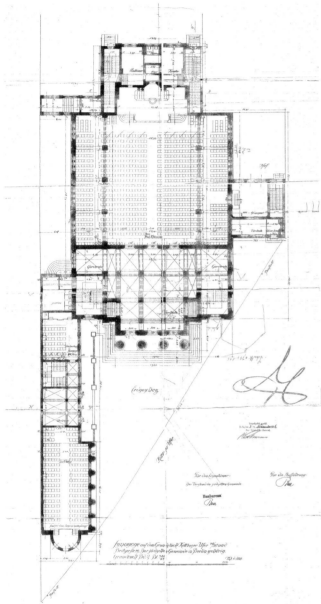
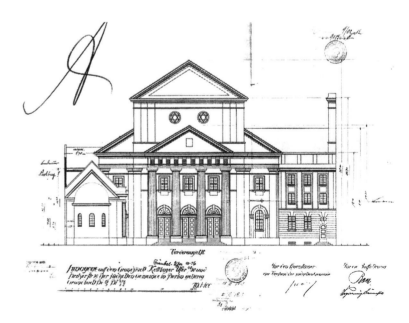

5
Schnitte durch den Gebetsraum
Sections through the prayer room

6
Erdgeschoss
Ground floor

7
Ansicht Fraenkelufer
elevation

8
Unvollendetes Gemälde von Curt Leschnitzer: um 1920
Unfinished painting by Curt Leschnitzer: ca. 1920

Marie Isabel Cara Menninger

Technische Universität Dresden
Prof. Ivan Reimann, Prof. Thomas Müller

Ein zentraler Gemeindegarten zeichnet den Umriss des historischen Gebetsraumes nach und übersetzt den zerstörten Innenraum in einen Außenraum. Zahlreiche Rundbögen und die Andeutung einer Apsis verweisen auf die ursprüngliche Größe sowie Raumwirkung und geben der Erinnerung einen Ort. Um den introvertierten Garten gruppiert sich ein Gefüge von spezifisch gestalteten Baukörpern, denen je ein Gemeindebereich zugeordnet ist. Zusammen mit dem Kinderhaus entwickelt das Ensemble eine komplexe Struktur aus differenzierten Außenräumen, die mit dem Lese-, Nutz- und Gemeindegarten sowie dem städtischen Platz ein reiches Angebot an Freiräumen bietet. Zum Fraenkelufer präsentiert sich das Haus mit großformatigen Rundbogenfenstern, die einerseits einen Dialog mit dem erhaltenen Gebäudeflügel eingehen und andererseits die öffentliche und sakrale Bedeutung des Neubaus betonen. Gelockert wird der historische Bezug durch blau gefliste Fensterrahmungen auf rotem Natursteinhintergrund. Die Gestaltung erinnert an expressionistische Architekturen und testet den angemessenen Grad an architektonischer Erinnerung und Erneuerung.

A central community garden traces out the contours of the historical prayer room, translating the now-destroyed interior space into an outdoor area. Numerous round arches and a suggestion of an apse allude to the room's original size and spatial impact, providing a space for memory. Grouped around the introverted garden is a constellation of individually designed volumes, each assigned a specific community area. Together with the childcare center, the ensemble develops a complex structure of differentiated exterior spaces, offering a wealth of open areas for reading, the kitchen, community gardens, and an urban plaza. Toward Fraenkelufer, the building—with its large round-arched windows—engages in a dialogue with the preserved wing, at the same time emphasizing the new building's public and sacred significance. Historical references are loosened by the use of blue-tiled window frames against a background of red natural stone. The design is reminiscent of expressionistic architecture, and seeks to test the appropriate degree of architectural memory and architectural renewal.

1
Lageplan
Site plan

2
Blick vom Fraenkelufer
View from Fraenkelufer

—
1:2500

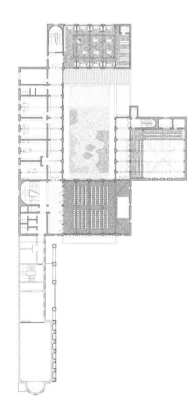

3
Gebäudekomplex
mit Vorplatz
Building complex
with forecourt

4
Erdgeschoss
Ground floor

5
1. Obergeschoss
First floor

—
1:1000

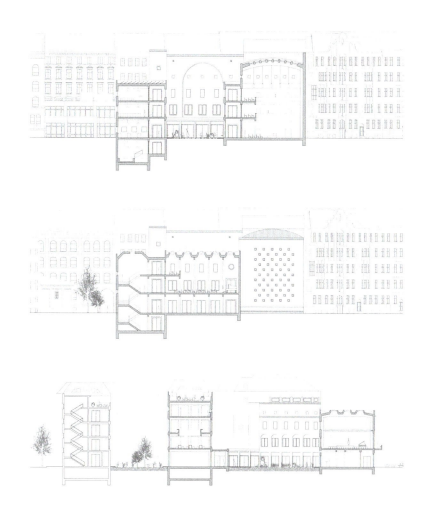

6
Querschnitt
mit Gebetsraum
Cross section
with prayer room

7
Querschnitt
durch Festsaal
Cross section
through
banquet hall

8
Längsschnitt
Longitudinal
section

9
Gebetsraum
Prayer room

—
1:1000

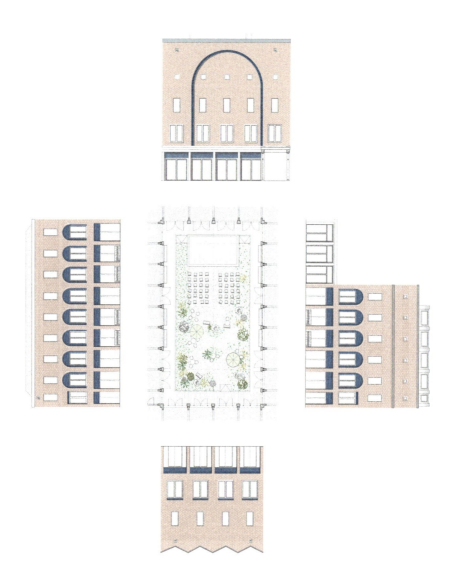

10
Abwicklung Hof
Elevations, courtyard

1:500

11
Innenhof
Inner courtyard

Heinrike Aue & Kira Wrigge

HafenCity Universität Hamburg
Prof. Gesine Weinmiller

Als kräftiger Solitär präsentiert sich der Synagogenneubau am Fraenkelufer. Diese städtebauliche Dominante markiert selbstbewusst den Ort und die Präsenz jüdischen Lebens in Berlin. Durch den sich öffnenden Eingangsbereich werden Besuchende und Interessierte aller Religionen und Kulturen in das Gebäude eingeladen und können sich nach dem Passieren der Sicherheitsschleuse frei im Gemeindezentrum bewegen. Dicke Mauern vermitteln ein Gefühl von Schutz. Das gesamte Bauwerk ist in Materialität und Form monolithisch gedacht, um eine Harmonie zwischen sakralen sowie profanen Nutzungen zu erzeugen. Die Ausformulierung der Räume folgt dem Konzept des Aushöhlens eines massiven Blockes. Von der Mikwe bis zum Synagogenraum fügen sich die unterschiedlichen Räume zu einem Ganzen. Im Kontrast zu seinem bewegten Innenleben präsentiert sich der Baukörper zur Stadt als ruhiger Baustein, der erst in der Nutzung seine Reichhaltigkeit offenbart.

The synagogue building on Fraenkelufer takes the form of a powerful solitaire. A dominant element within the urban environment, it assertively announces the location and presence of Jewish life in Berlin. Through the welcoming entrance area, visitors and interested individuals from all religions and cultures are invited into the building, and can move freely within the community center after passing through the security checkpoint. Thick walls convey a sense of protectiveness. In materiality and form, the entire building is conceived as a monolith, and is designed to generate harmony between sacred and secular uses. The articulation of the spaces is based on the concept of the hollowing out of a solid block. From the mikveh to the synagogue space, the diverse areas cohere to form a larger whole. In contrast with its animated inner life, the building presents itself to the city as a serene block whose richness is revealed only through use.

1
Lageplan
Site plan

2
Gebetsraum
Prayer room

—
1:2500

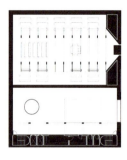
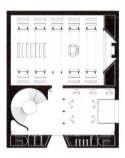

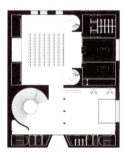
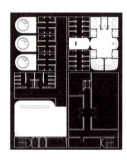

3
5. Obergeschoss
Fifth floor

4
3. Obergeschoss
Third floor

5
2. Obergeschoss
Second floor

6
1. Obergeschoss
First floor

7
Untergeschoss
Basement level

8
Erdgeschoss
Ground floor

9
Café

—
1:1000

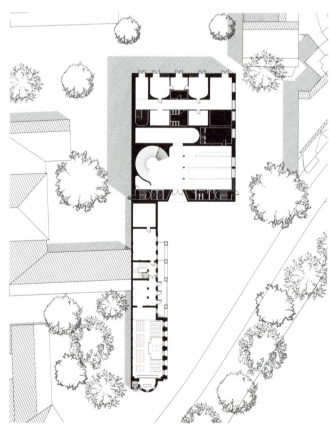

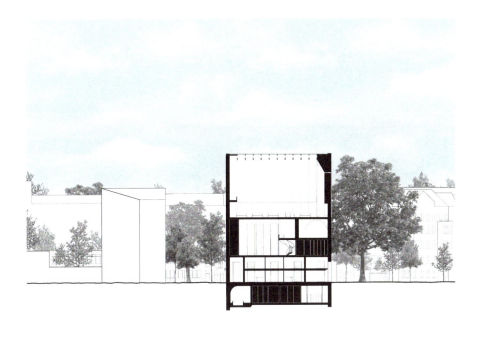

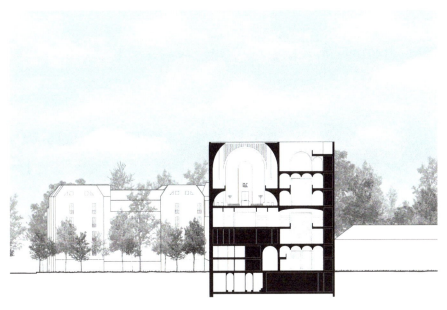

10
Querschnitt
Cross section

11
Längsschnitt
Longitudinal section

12
Seitenansicht
Fraenkelufer
side elevation

—
1:1000

Marthe Betsch & Leonie Ederer

Bauhaus-Universität Weimar
Prof. Jörg Springer

Die Heiligen Schriften des Judentums stehen im Mittelpunkt des Gebäudeentwurfs – gelesen wie gesprochen. Das vom Fraenkelufer erschlossene und äußerlich zurückhaltend gestaltete Hauptgebäude verwahrt eine freistehende mehrgeschossige Struktur, in deren Zentrum der Gebetssaal von einem vielschichtigen hölzernen Stabwerk umschlossen wird. In diesem umseitig angeordneten Raumgeflecht liegt eine Bibliothek mit Studienplätzen. Der großmaßstäbliche Gebetssaal als Ort des gemeinschaftlichen und geräuschvollen Austauschs wird auf diese Weise von Räumen des individuellen Studiums und Lernens umschlossen. Im Sinne der Vermittlung und Weitergabe der Heiligen Schriften des Tanach gehen gelesenes und gesprochenes Wort eine räumliche Symbiose ein, in der nur beide Teile gleichsam existieren können.

The sacred texts of Judaism—both written and spoken—are central to the conception. With its outwardly restrained design, the main building—which is accessed from Fraenkelufer—contains a freestanding, multistory structure at whose center the prayer hall is enclosed by a multilayered wooden framework. Set within this circumjacent spatial mesh is a library with study places. In this way, the large-scale prayer hall—a place of collective, energetic exchange—is encircled by spaces devoted to individual study and learning. In the spirit of the transmission and dissemination of the sacred texts of the Tanakh, the written and spoken word enter into a spatial symbiosis where the two aspects necessitate one another's existence.

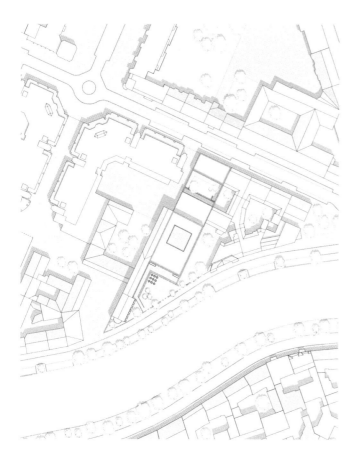

1
Lageplan
Site plan

2
Gebetsraum
Prayer room

—
1:2500

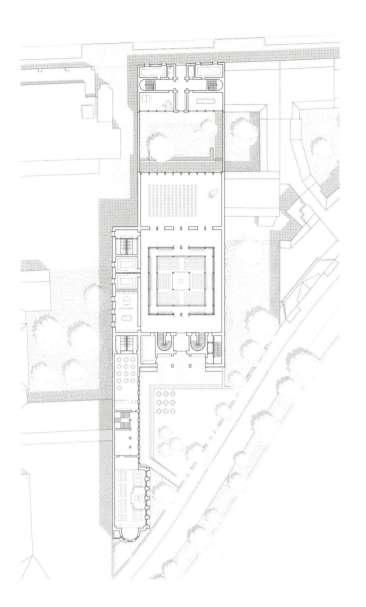

3
Erdgeschoss
Ground floor

4
Schwellenraum
Threshold space

—
1:1000

5
Bibliothek
Library

6
Querschnitt
Cross section

7
Längsschnitt
Longitudinal section

—
1:1000

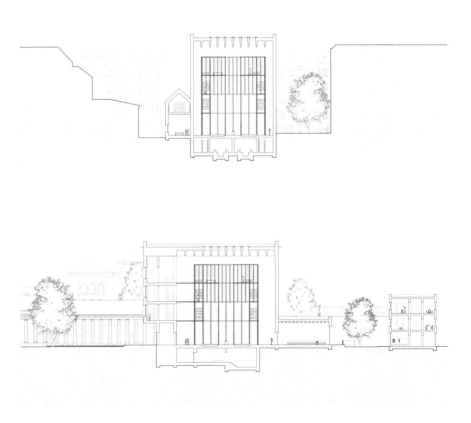

Marie Carraux

Technische Universität Dresden
Prof. Ivan Reimann, Prof. Thomas Müller

Ein großes kompaktes Haus nimmt alle öffentlichen Nutzungsbereiche der Gemeinde auf und orientiert sich mit einer selbstbewussten architektonischen Geste zum Fraenkelufer. Die lebendige Formensprache des Hauptgebäudes mit seinen Loggien, Balkonen und Dachterrassen sowie die verspielte Materialität zeugen von einem neuen Selbstbewusstsein jüdischen Lebens, zugleich treten sie in Interaktion mit der Nachbarschaft. Im Inneren des Gebäudes öffnet sich eine reiche Welt von unterschiedlich thematisierten Räumen. Die übereinandergeschichteten Bereiche wie die Mikwen, der Festsaal, die Synagoge und die Bibliothek erhalten ihren eigenen Charakter mit spezifischer Atmosphäre. Zwischen dem Gemeindezentrum am Fraenkelufer und dem Kinderhaus an der Kohlfurter Straße spannt sich ein großzügiger grüner Außenraum auf, der zum Spielen, Zusammenkommen und Erinnern einlädt.

A large, compact building, oriented toward Fraenkelufer with an assertive architectural gesture, accommodates all areas devoted to public community use. The animated formal idiom of the main structure, with its loggias, balconies, and roof terraces, along with the playful use of materiality, testify to a new self-confidence in Jewish life, at the same time interacting with neighboring buildings. Opening up within is an opulent world whose individual rooms are devoted to diverse themes. Each of the stacked zones, including the mikveh, banquet hall, synagogue space, and library, is given a singular character and a distinctive atmosphere. Set between the community center on Fraenkelufer and the daycare center on Kohlfurter Straße is a spacious landscaped outdoor area that invites community members to play, come together, and remember.

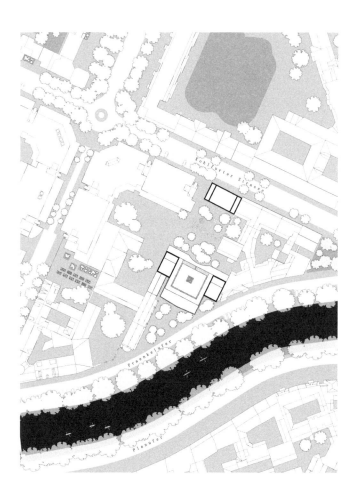

1
Lageplan
Site plan

2
Blick vom
Fraenkelufer
View from
Fraenkelufer

—
1:2500

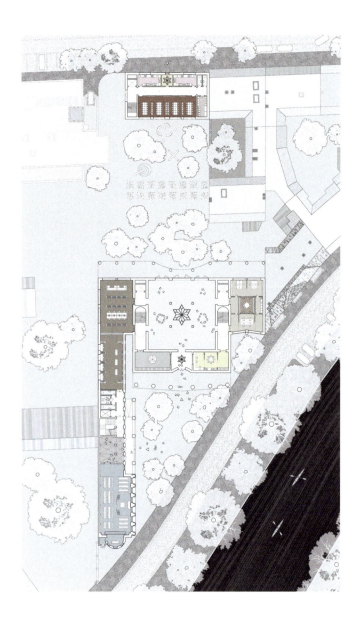
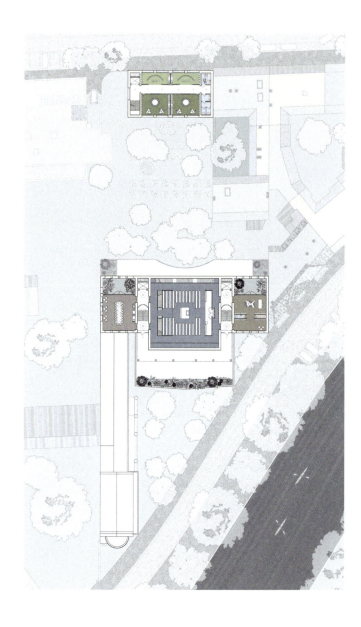
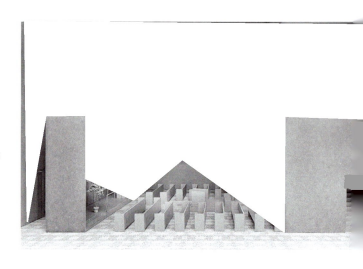

3
Erdgeschoss
Ground floor

4
4. Obergeschoss
Fourth floor

5
Gebetsraum
Prayer room

—
1:1000

6
Stadtloggia
City loggia

7
Ansicht
Kohlfurter Straße
elevation

8
Querschnitt
Cross section

9
Längsschnitt
Longitudinal
section

—
1:1000

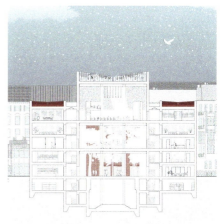

Daria Federova

Technische Universität Dresden
Prof. Ivan Reimann, Prof. Thomas Müller

Das eigenständige Erscheinungsbild des neuen Gemeindehauses wird durch eine Komposition von spezifisch gestalteten Baukörpern gebildet. Anstelle des historischen Solitärs werden baukastenartig die unterschiedlichen Raumbereiche zusammengefügt. Die Aufgliederung des Hauses in einzelne Volumina erzeugt eine spannungsreiche Silhouette zum Fraenkelufer, die durch die Gestaltung von expliziten Dachformen den Gebetsraum und den Festsaal als wichtige Elemente ablesbar macht. Eine großzügige Treppenhalle im Inneren des Gebäudes wird zum verbindenden Element des Ensembles aus verschiedenartig gestalteten Räumen. Die Außenhülle aus gefärbten Ziegelsteinen fügt die Baukörperfiguration zu einem einheitlichen Ganzen zusammen und zeigt im Detail ein vollflächiges Ornament an jüdischen Motiven, das die neue jüdische Präsenz im Stadtraum betont.

The idiosyncratic appearance of the new community center emerges from a composition based on individually designed volumes. In place of the historical solitaire, the various spatial areas are assembled through a modular system. The segmentation of the building into individual volumes generates a captivating silhouette toward Fraenkelufer, while the clear-cut contrast between roof designs renders the prayer room and the banquet hall clearly identifiable. The spacious stair hall in the building's interior functions as a connective element for the larger ensemble, whose diverse spaces are given variegated designs. The exterior shell, consisting of colored brickwork, merges the larger configuration into a unified entity, the entire surface covered with detailed ornamentation based on Jewish motifs, emphasizing a renewed Jewish presence in this urban setting.

1
Lageplan
Site plan

2
Gebetsraum
Prayer room

—
1:2500

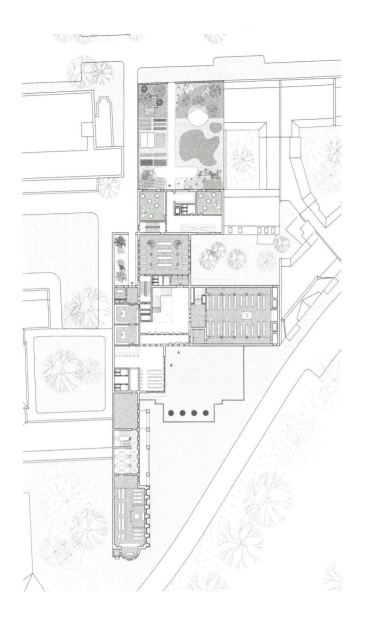

3
Erdgeschoss
Ground floor

4
Querschnitt
Cross section

5
Längsschnitt
Longitudinal section

6
Ansicht
Fraenkelufer
elevation

—
1:1000

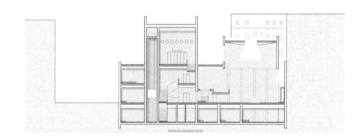

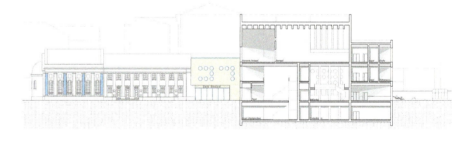

7
Blick vom
Fraenkelufer
View from
Fraenkelufer

8
Festsaal
Banquet hall

Marie Göben & Emilia Kuhlendahl

HafenCity Universität Hamburg
Prof. Gesine Weinmiller

Über dem großen, lang gestreckten Innenhof thront die Synagoge als zentraler Baustein und bietet den Besuchenden gleichermaßen einen geschützten Ort des Rückzugs und des Zusammenkommens. Das Haus ist über zwei differenzierte Adressen zu erreichen, einen profanen Zugang im Norden sowie eine repräsentative Adresse zum Fraenkelufer. Die räumliche Komposition und Anmutung bleiben bei aller Klarheit immer zweideutig: sowohl massiv als auch filigran, sowohl steinern als auch grün, sowohl erhaben als auch heiter, sowohl repräsentativ als auch zurückhaltend. Nach außen hin übermittelt das Haus die Bedeutung des Ortes auf subtile Art und Weise: Wie ein Schatten liegt die Zerstörung der Synagoge über dem Areal am Fraenkelufer. Eine Gravur als eine Art Inschrift zeichnet die zerstörte Synagoge auf der Textur der Fassade nach.

The synagogue sits enthroned as the central element above an extensive, elongated interior courtyard, and offers visitors a sheltered space of retreat as well as a place for coming together. The building is accessible via two differentiated street addresses, a secular entrance to the north, and a prestigious street address facing Fraenkelufer. Despite all its clarity, the spatial composition and the impression it makes on visitors remain consistently ambiguous: both massive and filigree, stony as well as verdant, sublime as well as light-hearted, impressive yet restrained. Toward the outside, the building conveys the importance of this location with subtlety: the destruction of the synagogue hangs above the zone around Fraenkelufer like a dark shadow. Engraved lines that resemble a kind of inscription trace out the contours of the destroyed synagogue on the texture of the facade.

1
Lageplan
Site plan

2
Blick vom
Fraenkelufer
View from
Fraenkelufer

—
1:2500

3
Innenhof mit
Tagessynagoge
Inner courtyard
with day synagogue

4
Erdgeschoss
Ground floor

5
1. Obergeschoss
First floor

—
1:1000

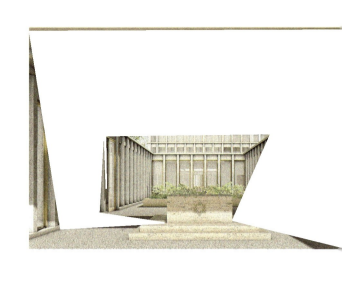

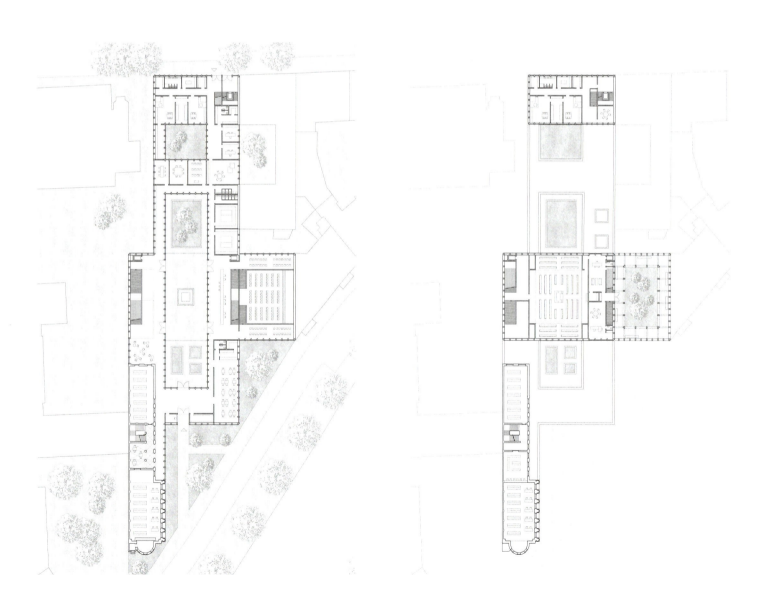

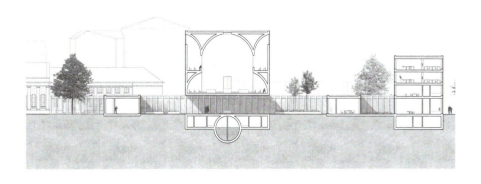

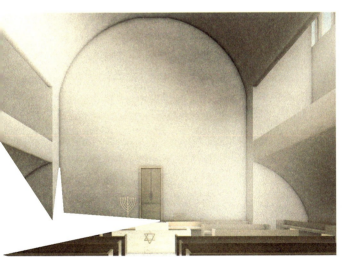

6
Längsschnitt
Longitudinal section

7
Gebetsraum
Prayer room

8
Festsaal
Banquet hall

—
1:1000

Janis Kukral

Bauhaus-Universität Weimar
Prof. Jörg Springer

Ohne zu rekonstruieren oder abstrahierend zu zitieren, erinnert der Neubau in Kubatur und Architektur mit einigen subtilen Anspielungen an die zerstörte Synagoge am Fraenkelufer. Vielmehr werden, wie lose aus dem Gedächtnis nachgezeichnet, Elemente wie die Schaufassade oder der Portikus mit ihren tektonischen Gliederungen in kraftvolle heutige Formen übertragen. Im Inneren bildet ein zentrales, von Lufträumen über alle Geschosse verbundenes Foyer das Herzstück des Baus, an das alle Gebäudeflügel mit den jeweiligen Funktionsbereichen angegliedert sind – so auch der Gebetssaal im ersten Obergeschoss. Dieser erhält eine innere mehrschichtige Fassade, die, ebenso wie die darüber spannende durchbrochene Kuppel, mit Holzpaneelen ausgekleidet ist und dem Raum so, trotz seiner Größe und räumlichen Tiefe, Geborgenheit verleiht.

Through a number of subtle allusions, and without engaging in reconstruction or abstract citation, the cubature and architecture of the new building recall the destroyed synagogue on Fraenkelufer. Instead, however, and as though sketched loosely from memory, elements such as the main facade and the portico, with their tectonic subdivisions, are taken up again in powerful new forms. Within, a central foyer continues through all levels via airspaces, forming the building's core, to which all of the building's wings, with their respective functional areas, are connected—including the prayer hall on the first upper level. The hall has a multilayered facade which is clad—like the pierced dome that rises above it—with wooden paneling, giving the room a sense of protectiveness despite its dimensions and spatial depth.

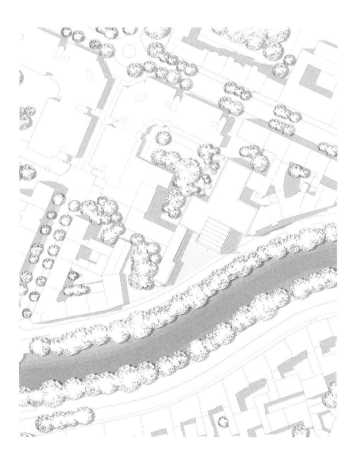

1
Lageplan
Site plan

2
Blick vom
Fraenkelufer
View from
Fraenkelufer

—
1:2500

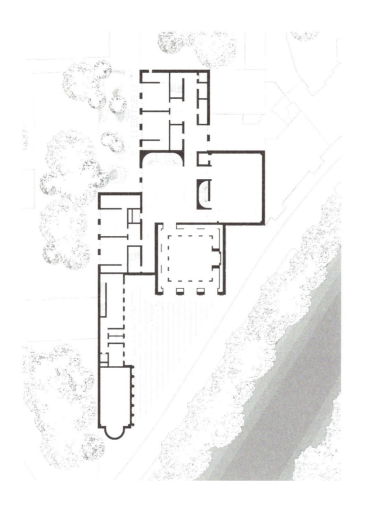

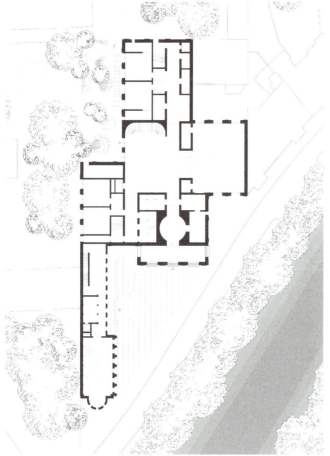

3
Foyer

4
1. Obergeschoss
First floor

5
Erdgeschoss
Ground floor

—
1:1000

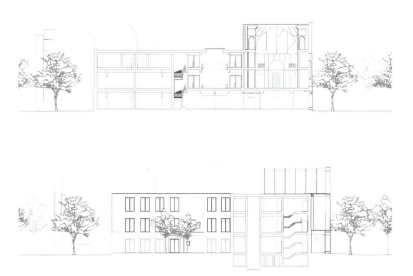

6
Längsschnitt
mit Gebetsraum
Longitudinal
section with
prayer room

7
Längsschnitt
mit Garten
Longitudinal
section
with garden

8
Seitenansicht
Fraenkelufer
Side view
Fraenkelufer

—
1:1000

9
Fassadendetail
Facade detail
—
1:250

10
Gebetsraum
Prayer room

Robert Wehner

Technische Universität Dresden
Prof. Ivan Reimann, Prof. Thomas Müller

Die programmatische Kernidee des neuen jüdischen Kulturzentrums bildet ein zentraler «Klosterhof». Der mit einem Wandelgang umfasste Lichthof gibt dem facettenreichen Gemeindeleben eine neue Mitte, um die alle Raumbereiche gleichwertig angeordnet sind. Durch eine subtile Differenzierung der Gebäudekubatur und der Fassadengestaltung bleiben der Festsaal und der Gebetsraum jedoch ablesbar. Das zum Fraenkelufer orientierte Baukörperkonglomerat formuliert einen Vorplatz, an dem Haupteingang und Café situiert sind. Die Bildwirkung der Fassade schwingt zwischen dem Wunsch nach einer neuen repräsentativen Sichtbarkeit und einer beinahe wehrhaften Zurückhaltung im Stadtraum. Der Charakter der Innen- und Außenräume lässt sich durch die ausgewogene Proportionierung der sparsam eingesetzten architektonischen Elemente und die feinen Farbnuancen mit einer eleganten Bescheidenheit beschreiben.

The core programmatic idea of the new Jewish culture center is its central "monastery courtyard." The atrium, which is enclosed by a covered walkway, provides a new center for the multifaceted life of the community, around which all of the other spatial areas are configured on equal terms. Through the subtle differentiation of the building's cubature and facade design, the banquet hall and the prayer room nonetheless maintain their distinctive identities. The conglomerate of structures oriented toward Fraenkelufer creates a forecourt where the main entrance and café are situated. The visual effect of the facade oscillates between the desire for a new and prestigious visibility and an almost defensive restraint within the urban environment. Through balanced proportions, a sparing use of architectural elements, and subtle chromatic nuances, both the interior and exterior spaces are characterized by an elegant modesty.

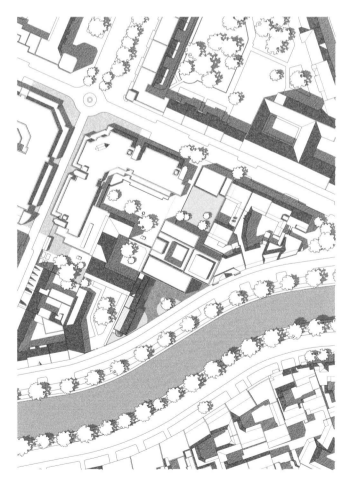

1
Lageplan
Site plan

2
Blick vom
Fraenkelufer
View from
Fraenkelufer

—
1:2500

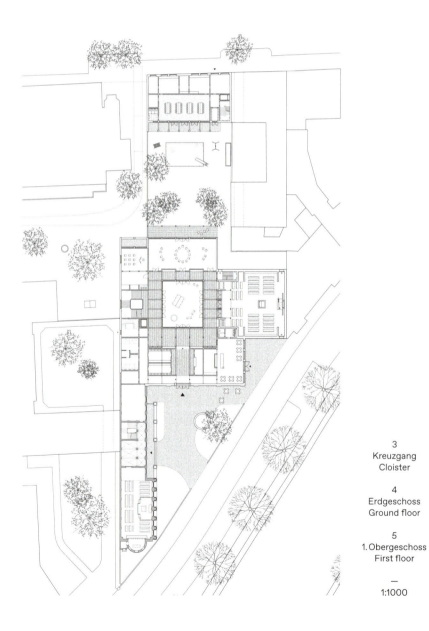

3
Kreuzgang
Cloister

4
Erdgeschoss
Ground floor

5
1. Obergeschoss
First floor

—
1:1000

84

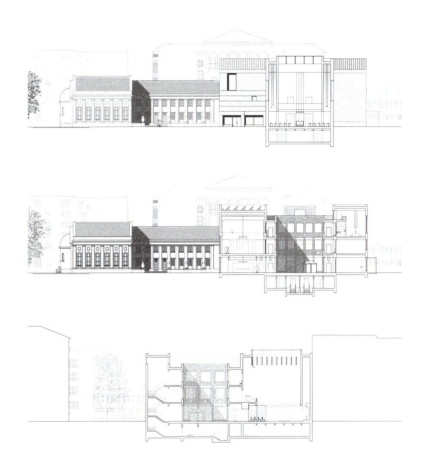

6
Längsschnitt durch Gebetsraum
Longitudinal section through prayer room

7
Längsschnitt durch Hof
Longitudinal section through courtyard

8
Querschnitt durch Gebetsraum
Section through prayer room

9
Gebetsraum
Prayer room

—
1:1000

Edward van Voolen im Gespräch mit
in conversation with
Ivan Reimann & Gesine Weinmiller

Edward van Voolen setzt sich seit vielen Jahren mit «Jüdische[r] Identität in der zeitgenössischen Architektur» (so der Titel eines von ihm 2004 mitherausgegebenen Buches) auseinander. Nicht nur als Jurymitglied in mehreren wichtigen Architekturwettbewerben ist ihm der Diskurs mit uns Architekten vertraut. In seinen Vorträgen zur Vorbereitung des Synagogen-Projekts hat er mit seinem profunden Wissen den Studierenden sowohl einen historischen Überblick des Synagogenbaus durch die Jahrhunderte als auch die baulichen Gesetzmäßigkeiten zum Bau einer Synagoge vermittelt. Während des Entwurfsprozesses war er der Ansprechpartner für Fragen der Studierenden in historischer, theologischer und baulicher Hinsicht.

GW In den Entwurfskursen, in Dresden, Weimar, Darmstadt und Hamburg, haben sich Studierende mit verschiedensten religiösen Hintergründen und Erfahrungen auf das Abenteuer eingelassen, eine Synagoge zu entwerfen. Dabei war sehr interessant, dass die wenigsten je in einer Synagoge waren, geschweige denn an einem Gottesdienst teilgenommen haben. Zu Planen ohne eigene Anschauung ist natürlich ureigenes Architektengeschäft – man muss ja auch nicht im Kloster gelebt haben, um ein Kloster zu bauen. Daher sind wir es gewöhnt, mit unbekannten Typologien umzugehen. Du, Edward, hast uns alle mit Deinen einleitenden Vorträgen sehr informativ in die Welt des Synagogenbaus eingeführt, daher nun die Frage: Haben die Studierenden Deine Anregungen aufgenommen? Wie fandest Du die Entwürfe? Haben sie Dich angesprochen oder wurde aus Deiner Sicht an den Bedürfnissen der Gemeinde vorbeigeplant?

Eine Synagoge ist ein Bet ha-Knesset – ein Haus der Versammlung, ein Bet ha-Midrasch – ein Haus des Lernens, ein Bet ha-Tefillah – ein Haus des Gebetes

EvV Mir hat es zunächst einmal sehr gut gefallen, dass sich die Studierenden so stark auf die Aufgabenstellung eingelassen haben und versucht haben, zu ergründen, was das Wesen einer Synagoge ist. Schließlich ist eine Synagoge etwas anderes als eine Kirche –

For many years now, Edward van Voolen has been preoccupied with "Jewish Identity in Contemporary Architecture" (to cite the title of a book he coedited in 2004). He is familiar with the architectural discourse, not only through his participation in juries for a number of major architectural competitions. In his lectures in preparation for the Synagogue Project, he drew on his profound knowledge to provide the students with a historical overview of synagogue construction through the centuries as well as teaching them the structural laws for building a synagogue. During the design process, he acted as the contact person for students' questions on any matters historical, theological, or structural.

GW In the design courses in Dresden, Weimar, Darmstadt, and Hamburg, students with the most diverse religious backgrounds and experiences embarked on the adventure of designing a synagogue. Interestingly, very few of them had ever been in a synagogue, let alone participated in a religious service there. To engage in planning in the absence of a personal perspective is, of course, a quintessential architectural activity—you don't need to actually live in a monastery in order to build one. We are accustomed to dealing with unfamiliar typologies. In your introductory lectures, Edward, you gave all of us a highly informative entry point into the world of synagogue building, so the question now is: did the students adopt your suggestions? What did you think of the designs? Did they speak to you, or did they instead, from your perspective, disregard the needs of the community?

A synagogue is a Bet ha-Knesset—a house for gathering, a Bet ha-Midrash—a house of learning, and a Bet ha-Tefillah—a house of prayer

EvV To begin with, I was delighted to see that the students were so committed to the task and attempted to determine the essential traits of a synagogue. In the end, a synagogue is very different from a church—it's not simply a place where you practice your faith, but above all a building where people come together, a

sie ist nicht nur ein Ort, an dem man seinen Glauben ausübt, sondern vor allem ein Haus, in dem Menschen zusammenkommen, ein Haus der Gemeinschaft. Daneben ist sie ebenso ein Zentrum, wo man sein Leben lang – von Kindesbeinen an bis ins hohe Alter – lernt und das Judentum studiert; und natürlich ist sie auch ein Gebetshaus.

In ihr kommen alle Funktionen zusammen. Eine solche Nutzungsvielfalt kann man schon im 17. Jahrhundert zum Beispiel bei der Portugiesischen Synagoge in Amsterdam [→ Abb. 1] sehen. Dort gibt es neben dem großen Raum für Gottesdienste auch viele kleinere Räumlichkeiten für alle funktionalen Erfordernisse, welche das Gemeindeleben mit sich bringt. Es gibt Räume, in denen die Erwachsenen lernen und studieren, eine Schule für die Kinder, einen Trausaal für Hochzeiten, eine Wohnung für den Rabbiner, rituelle Bäder und einen Raum, in dem man die Toten für die Beerdigung vorbereitet. In der Synagoge findet das ganze Gemeindeleben statt – und dieser Grundgedanke zum Charakter des Hauses zieht sich durch alle Zeiten. Gute moderne Beispiele sind die Synagogen Erich Mendelsohns [→ Abb. 2 & 3], die er Mitte des 20. Jahrhunderts in den USA gebaut hat.

IR Wenn wir schon einmal bei der Architekturgeschichte sind: In der Vergangenheit war es ja so, dass sich die jüdischen Gemeinden aus den unterschiedlichsten Gründen die etablierten Architektursprachen Europas «ausgeliehen» haben. Sei es im Mittelalter, weil ihnen dort schlichtweg der Beruf des Baumeisters verwehrt wurde und sie sich mit nicht-jüdischen Architekten behelfen mussten, oder aber später im 19. Jahrhundert, als sie solche Baustile bewusst als Ausdruck der Assimilation wählten. Gibt es daher aus Deiner Sicht überhaupt so etwas wie eine jüdische Architektursprache oder nicht?

Es gibt nicht die eine dezidiert jüdische Architektursprache

EvV Es gibt keine jüdische Architektursprache – weder im Mittelalter noch im 19. Jahrhundert, und es gab sie auch nicht in der Moderne. Es gibt nicht die eine dezidiert jüdische Architektursprache – es gibt nur Gebäude, die für eine bestimmte Funktion, nämlich die der Nutzung als Synagoge, Gemeindezentrum und Lehrhaus geeignet sind und eine dementsprechende Ausstrahlung haben. Das ist eigentlich das Einzige, was man dazu sagen kann. Lediglich bei der Inneneinrichtung eines synagogalen Raums gibt es bestimmte liturgische Bedingungen, die erfüllt werden sollten – aber auch sie sind nicht an eine bestimmte Stilistik oder Formensprache gebunden. Es gibt also die unterschiedlichsten Gestaltungsmöglichkeiten. Was man aber in der Debatte um viele Synagogen des 19. und frühen 20. Jahrhunderts sieht, ist, dass im 19. Jahrhundert bestimmte Architekturstile zu bestimmten ideologischen Zwecken verwendet wurden. So hat man wie bei der Bornplatzsynagoge ganz bewusst einen typisch «deutschen» Baustil gewählt, um zu symbolisieren: «Wir Jüdinnen und Juden sind Teil der deutschen Gesellschaft.»

home for the community. But it's also a center for learning, for the study of Judaism—throughout your lifetime, from early childhood all the way to advanced old age; and it's also, of course, a house of prayer.

A synagogue is a Bet ha-Knesset—a house for gathering, a Bet ha-Midrash—a house of learning, and a Bet ha-Tefillah—a house of prayer. All of these functions come together in it. This diversity of purposes can be observed as early as the seventeenth century in the Portuguese synagogues of Amsterdam [→ Fig. 1]. Found there alongside a large space for religious services were a number of smaller spaces designed to fulfill all of the functional needs associated with community life. There are spaces where adults learn and study, a school for children, a hall for weddings, an apartment for the rabbis, ritual baths, and a room where the dead are prepared for burial. Community life as a whole takes place in the synagogue—and this core idea concerning the character of the building has remained a constant throughout history. Good modern examples are the synagogues built by Erich Mendelsohn [→ Figs. 2 & 3] in the United States in the mid-twentieth century.

IR Since we're already getting into architectural history: in the past, for the most diverse reasons, Jewish communities "borrowed" from the established architectural idioms found in Europe. Whether in the Middle Ages, when they were simply forbidden from practicing the occupation of master builder and had to rely on non-Jewish architects, or later, in the nineteenth century, when they consciously chose certain building styles as expressions of assimilation. From your point of view, does anything resembling a specifically Jewish architectural language exist at all?

There isn't one decidedly Jewish architectural language

EvV There is no Jewish architectural language—neither in the Middle Ages, nor in the nineteenth century, nor even in modernism. There isn't one decidedly Jewish architectural language—there are simply buildings that are suitable for a specific function, namely to use as a synagogue, a community center, or a place of teaching, and which have a corresponding aura. That's really all that can be said about it. It's only with the interior design of a synagogue space that specific liturgical requirements need to be fulfilled—but even these are not bound up with any specific stylistic or formal language. The most diverse design possibilities are therefore possible. What you often encounter in debates about synagogues from the nineteenth and early twentieth centuries is that, in the nineteenth century, specific architectural styles were used for certain architectural purposes. As in the case of the Bornplatz Synagogue, when a typically "German" building style was chosen in order to signal that, "We Jews are a part of German society." At the same time, there are synagogues that make use of the Moorish idiom [→ Fig. 5]. That architectural style was used to refer to the fact that in medieval Spain, Jews, Muslims, and Christians were able to coexist in a way that was impossible in Germany, and which,

1
Portugiesische Synagoge, Amsterdam, Stich: 1723
Portuguese synagogue, Amsterdam, engraving: 1723
—
Elias Bouwman
1675

Zur gleichen Zeit gibt es Synagogen, die sich der maurischen Formensprache bedient haben [→ Abb. 5]. Mit diesem Architekturstil wollte man darauf hinweisen, dass im mittelalterlichen Spanien Juden, Muslime und Christen auf eine Art zusammenleben konnten, die in Deutschland unmöglich war, und die es, wenn man die Situation der Muslime heute bedenkt, noch immer nicht gibt. Ja, eine Synagoge funktioniert also durchaus auch als Zeichen nach außen – und war und ist noch immer ein Hoffnungszeichen dafür, dass ein friedliches Zusammenleben verschiedener Konfessionen möglich sein muss. Warum es in bestimmten Kreisen noch immer für nötig gehalten wird, auf eine völlig antiquierte Architektursprache und damit auf einen älteren Diskurs zurückzugreifen, kann ich nur nachvollziehen, weil man sich damit vielleicht etwas aneignet, das zuerst absichtlich von den Nazis vernichtet und danach von Parkgaragen oder Warenhäusern überbaut, unsichtbar gemacht wurde, um alle Erinnerungsspuren auszulöschen. Ich verstehe diese Haltung, aber ich teile sie nicht. Neue Synagogen sollten meiner Meinung nach in einer modernen Architektursprache auf die heutigen Herausforderungen reagieren, die gesellschaftlichen und ökologischen. Da hat sich seit Anfang des 20. Jahrhunderts eine große Vielfalt entwickelt, die sich auch bis heute mit vielen spannenden Entwürfen ständig weiterentwickelt.

GW Im Fall der Bornplatzsynagoge haben die Nationalsozialisten ja an genau der Stelle, wo sich vormals das Hauptportal der Synagoge befand, einen Bunker errichtet. Ziel war es, diesen Städtebau zu zementieren, um zu verhindern, dass die Bornplatzsynagoge jemals wiederaufgebaut wird. Dieser Bunker steht auch heute noch dort, er ist mittlerweile zu einem Universitätsgebäude umgebaut worden – und er zerschneidet weiterhin den Stadtraum und behindert die städtebauliche Entwicklung an diesem Ort. Es gab allerdings ein paar Entwürfe, die sich ihn als eine Art Sockel zunutze gemacht haben und die Synagoge auf dem Dach des Bunkers platziert haben. Wäre das für Dich vorstellbar und eine denkbare Art, mit diesem Desaster des Bunkers umzugehen?

Sollten wir im 21. Jahrhundert nicht so frei sein, dass wir unsere Identität selbst definieren können?

EvV Hier stellt sich für mich die Frage: Müssen wir unbedingt auf die Nazis reagieren? Ist es nötig, dass wir uns noch einmal mit ihnen auseinandersetzen? Oder sollten wir im 21. Jahrhundert nicht so frei sein, dass wir unsere Identität selbst definieren können? Allerdings sehe ich es auch so, dass man einen Umgang mit dem Bunker finden muss. Ich bin auch davon überzeugt, dass hier eine akzeptable Lösung gefunden werden kann – doch ob diese unbedingt darin bestehen muss, dass man ihn in Zukunft als Synagoge umnutzt, da habe ich meine großen Zweifel. Ich meine: Kann man sich denn überhaupt in dieser neuen Synagoge wohlfühlen, wenn man weiß, dass der Kern des Gebäudes ein Nazibunker war? Ich jedenfalls nicht. Ich muss nicht beweisen, dass ich mir einen Nazibunker aneignen

when you think of Muslims specifically, doesn't exist today either. So, a synagogue functions very much as a symbol toward the outside world—it was and remains a symbol of hope that the peaceful coexistence of the various confessions might still be possible. I understand the view, which prevails in certain circles, that it's necessary to resort to an utterly antiquated architectural language, and hence to an earlier discourse, which signals a desire to appropriate something that was deliberately destroyed by the Nazis, and then built over with parking garages or department stores, rendered invisible, in order to erase all traces of its memory. I understand this attitude, but I don't share it. In my view, new synagogues should respond to contemporary challenges, whether social or ecological, through a modern architectural language. Beginning in the early twentieth century, an enormous variety of approaches has developed, and this continues up to the present with many exciting designs.

GW In the case of the Bornplatz Synagogue, the National Socialists erected a bunker at precisely the location where the main portal of the synagogue had been before. The aim was to cement an urban layout that would make it difficult for the synagogue to be rebuilt at some point in the future. The bunker still stands there today and has meanwhile been converted into a university building—it continues to cut up the urban space, impeding urban planning measures at this location. A couple of designs went as far as using the bunker as a kind of pedestal, positioning the synagogue on the roof. In your view, would that be a conceivable or plausible approach to dealing with the disaster of the bunker?

Shouldn't we be free, in the twenty-first century, to define our own identity?

EvV This, for me, begs the question: do we absolutely have to respond to the Nazis? Is it really necessary for us to once again seek to come to terms with them? Shouldn't we be free, in the twenty-first century, to define our own identity? I also believe, however, that we need to find a modus vivendi for dealing with the bunker. I'm also convinced that an acceptable solution can be found—but I do have grave doubts about whether this must necessarily involve its future use as

2
Synagoge Cleveland, Ohio, Luftbild: undatiert
Synagogue, Cleveland, Ohio, aerial view: undated

3
Synagoge Cleveland, Ohio, Grundrisszeichnung: undatiert
Synagogue, Cleveland, Ohio, layout drawing: undated

—
Erich Mendelsohn
1950/53

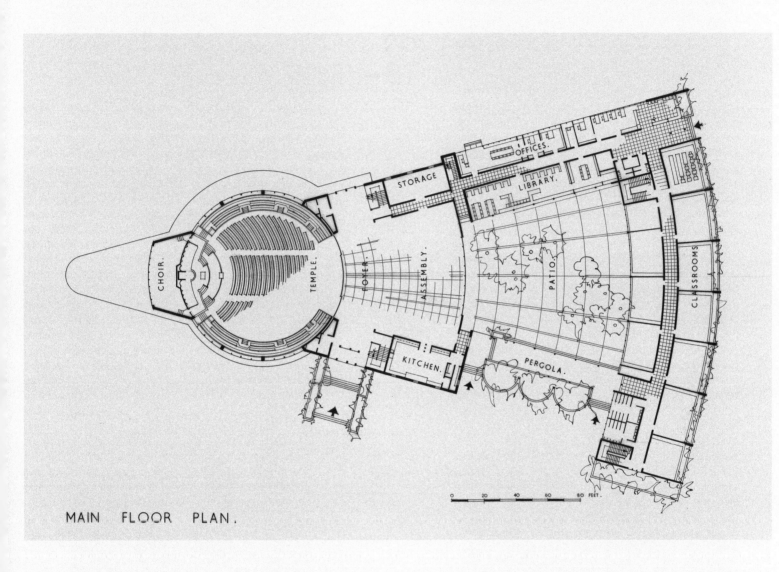

MAIN FLOOR PLAN.

kann. Wozu? Rache? Seit wann ist das Teil einer jüdischen Identität, meiner Identität? In Spanien wurden nach der Reconquista Synagogen und Moscheen in Kirchen verwandelt, jegliche jüdische Spuren gelöscht, als Zeichen des Triumphes des Christentums [→ Abb. 4]. Wäre es also auch für uns heute wichtig, so etwas Ähnliches zu tun? Ich persönlich fände diese Herangehensweise sehr problematisch, damals und jetzt. Keine Frage, Deutschland setzt sich mit seiner belastenden Architektur von Nazis und von Stalinisten auseinander: mit Nazibunkern, mit Nazibauten, mit dem Palast der Republik – aber das ist nicht meine Geschichte.

IR Aber ist ein Synagogenbau an den Standorten der in den Novemberpogromen oder im Krieg zerstörten Synagogen in Deutschland nicht zwangsläufig immer mit einer Auseinandersetzung mit der Geschichte und der Nazizeit verbunden – ob man will oder nicht? Ich meine, allein durch die Tatsache, dass diese Synagogen eben nicht mehr existent sind, kann man dieser Auseinandersetzung nicht entkommen.

EvV Natürlich kann man ihr, kann ich ihr, nicht entkommen, wobei man auch dieser Auseinandersetzung mit der Geschichte eines jeweiligen Ortes, mit dem, was an diesem Ort geschehen ist, nicht entkommen kann. Das ist kein spezifisch deutsches Problem, muss man leider feststellen. Und natürlich, wenn es möglich ist, an den alten Standorten eine neue Synagoge zu bauen, wie zum Beispiel in Dresden, dann ist das wünschenswert – aber meistens gibt es diese Option nicht mehr, einfach weil die Juden ermordet sind – das ist doch klar, wenn man sich in Europa auskennt. In solchen Fällen sollte man sich mit der spezifischen Situation am Ort auseinandersetzen, mit den erhaltenen Spuren, den Resten, leeren Synagogen, jüdischen Schulen, Altersheimen, unbenutzten Friedhöfen sowie Umschlagplätzen und anderen Spuren der Vernichtung und nach einer zweckgemäßen neuen Funktion suchen, welche die Geschichte des Ortes markiert oder auf eine andere Art aufnimmt. Davon gibt es in Deutschland überall gute und würdige Beispiele. Alles besser als ein Wiederaufbau einer Synagoge ohne Juden. Manchmal ist ein Ort so belastet, dass man überlegen sollte, ob man gerade dort nicht bauen sollte, sondern den Neubau einer Synagoge oder eines Gemeindezentrums lieber an einem anderen Standort errichten sollte. Wir müssen Geschichten nicht immer miteinander vermischen. Die Neue Synagoge in Dresden ist ein gelungenes Beispiel: Auf dem Innenhof wurde der Grundriss der alten Synagoge sichtbar gemacht und erinnert so zurückhaltend, aber eindringlich an die Zerstörung durch die Nazi-Deutschen. Die Neue Synagoge selbst bietet einen sicheren und geschützten Raum für das Gebet, ein an Tabernakel und Tempel erinnerndes Zuhause für die Gemeinschaft – und genau gegenüber steht im Gegensatz zu der introvertierten Synagoge das offene, mit seiner verglasten Fassade einladende Gemeindezentrum. In diesem Setting fühle ich mich wohl.

4
Synagoge El Tránsito, Toledo, nach der Umwidmung zum katholischen Gotteshaus, Stich: 1843
The El Tránsito Synagogue, Toledo, after rededication as a Catholic church, engraving: 1843

a synagogue. Could anyone really feel comfortable in a synagogue knowing that the core of the building was once a Nazi bunker? I certainly couldn't. I feel no need to demonstrate that I can appropriate a Nazi bunker. For what purpose? Revenge? Since when is that a part of Jewish identity, of my identity? In Spain, after the Reconquista, synagogues and mosques were converted into churches, and all traces of Jewish life were erased in order to signify the triumph of Christianity [→ Fig. 4]. Is it necessary now for us to do something similar? Personally, I find such a strategy to be problematic, both then and now. Unquestionably, Germany is seeking to come to terms with its burdensome Nazi and Stalinist architecture: with the Nazi bunkers and buildings, with the Palace of the Republic—but that's not my history.

IR But aren't synagogue projects at locations in Germany where synagogues were destroyed during the Kristallnacht or the war inescapably entangled in a confrontation with history and with the Nazi era—whether willingly or unwillingly? What I mean to say is that such a confrontation becomes unavoidable solely through the circumstance that these synagogues no longer exist.

EvV Of course you can't avoid it, I can't avoid it, nor can a confrontation with the history of a specific location, with events that occurred at that location, ever be avoided. And that, I have to point out, isn't a specifically German problem, unfortunately. And of course, wherever it's possible to build a new synagogue in the location of an old one, for example in Dresden, then that's desirable; but for the most part, that option is no longer available, simply because the Jews were murdered—that's obvious to anyone who knows their way around Europe. In such instances, it becomes necessary to come to terms with the specific situation on the site, with the surviving traces, the vestiges, empty synagogues, Jewish schools, retirement homes, disused cemeteries, as well as the transit points for the deportation of the Jews, along with any other traces of the Holocaust, and to search for a new and meaningful function, one that marks the history of the site or honors it in a different way. You can find good and dignified examples of this all over the place in Germany. And all are better than rebuilding a synagogue without Jews. In some instances, a site is so overburdened that it's worth considering whether building there should be avoided altogether, whether a new synagogue or community center should be instead erected at a different location. It isn't always necessary to mix and mingle different historical narratives. The new synagogue in Dresden is a successful example: the layout of the old synagogue is rendered visible in the interior courtyard, recalling its destruction by the Nazis in a restrained yet emphatic way. The new synagogue itself offers a safe and protected space for prayer, a home for the community that is reminiscent of a tabernacle or temple—and standing directly opposite, contrasting with the introverted synagogue, is the open, inviting community center with its glazed facade. I feel comfortable in this setting.

Sollte der Neubau einer Synagoge auf den Anspruch verzichten, ein kraftvolles Zeichen in der Stadt zu sein?

GW Das Beispiel der Neuen Synagoge in Dresden ist hier ein guter Stichwortgeber, weil dieser Neubau fast schon beispielhaft vom gewandelten Selbstverständnis der jüdischen Gemeinden spricht. Wenn wir uns die Nachkriegsgeschichte anschauen, ist es so, dass die Neubauten der meisten deutschen Synagogen nach der Shoah in der Stadt geradezu unsichtbar waren. Dies liegt vor allem daran, dass sie die historisch bedeutenden Orte der ehemaligen Synagogen nicht wieder in Anspruch nehmen konnten und daher an anderen Orten, abseits des Fokus, errichtet werden mussten. Eine wichtige Rolle spielt auch, dass man bei diesen neu gebauten Synagogen ganz explizit auf das nach außen hin Zeichenhafte verzichtete – diese Häuser waren introvertiert bis unscheinbar. Heute ist es dagegen so, dass beim Neubau von Synagogen die Aspekte der Sichtbarkeit und der kraftvollen Präsenz in der Stadt wieder stärker thematisiert werden – siehst Du darin einen positiven Ausdruck der Teilhabe? Oder um die Frage einmal umzukehren: Sollte der Neubau einer Synagoge auch weiterhin auf den Anspruch verzichten, ein sichtbares, kraftvolles Zeichen in der Stadt zu sein?

EvV Letzteres war absolut richtig für die Nachkriegszeit, in den Jahrzehnten, in denen viele deutsche Politiker, Richter, Professoren, Lehrer, Entscheidungsträger, Stadtplaner und Architekten unbestraft weiter schalten und walten konnten wie zuvor. Haben die Städte die von ihnen initiierte Vernichtung der Synagogen kompensiert, haben sie angeboten, die zerstörten Synagogen zu restaurieren, wiederaufzubauen? Hat Deutschland je die vielen tausenden Displaced Persons, diejenigen also, die wegen der sowjetischen Besatzung Zentral- und Osteuropas nicht mehr nach Hause zurückkehren konnten oder wollten (weil alles sowieso vernichtet war und niemand dort überlebt hatte) und die jahrelang in deutschen Lagern gezwungen waren zu arbeiten und jetzt hier wohnen, hat Deutschland ihnen je die deutsche Staatsbürgerschaft angeboten? Ja, die Gebäude sind bescheiden, und ja, so ist ihre Ausstrahlung, und ja, so sind die Straßen, wo sie gebaut wurden. Die deutlichen Zeichen kamen erst eine Generation später, bei der sogenannten Vergangenheitsbewältigung der Deutschen, bei dem Eichmannprozess 1961, nach der Studentenrevolte 1968/69, als die deutsche Nachkriegsgeneration anfing, ihre Eltern über ihre Vergangenheit zu befragen. Und ja, als auch die jüdische Nachkriegsgeneration anfing, mit größerem Selbstbewusstsein zu agieren. Erst seit den 1990er-Jahren verliehen Bauten für Synagogen dem veränderten jüdischen Selbstbewusstsein Ausdruck, jedenfalls in jenen Ländern, wo die noch immer belastete und belastende Vergangenheit persönlich und gesellschaftlich öffentlich angesprochen werden kann. Bei vielen älteren «erhabenen» Synagogen in Europa erzeugt die Vergangenheit in mir Beklemmung, die unvermeidliche Leere. Obwohl man sich bei jedem Synagogenbesuch in Europa und seit kurzem manchmal auch in den USA von bewaffneten Polizisten befragen und kontrollieren

Should a new synagogue building renounce attempts to constitute a powerful symbol within the city?

GW The new synagogue in Dresden is a nice reference here, since this new building testifies in an almost exemplary way to the changed understanding that Jewish communities have of themselves. Turning now toward postwar history, we see that most of the German synagogues that were newly constructed in cities after the Shoah were virtually invisible. This was due primarily to the circumstance that they were unable to lay claim to the historically significant locations of the former synagogues and instead had to be built at different locations, and hardly ever on prominent sites. Important as well was the explicit renunciation of any attempt at outward symbolic presence—the buildings were introverted to the point of inconspicuousness. Foregrounded more strongly again today when a new synagogue is planned is the aspect of visibility, of a powerful presence within the city—do you regard this as a positive expression of participation? Or, turning the question around: should new synagogues continue to renounce any attempt to constitute a visible, powerful symbol within the city?

EvV The latter option was absolutely right for the postwar era, during the decades when many German politicians, judges, professors, teachers, decision-makers, urban planners, and architects associated with the Nazis continued leading active professional lives just as before, escaping all punishment. Did the cities offer compensation for the destruction of the synagogues they initiated? Did they offer to restore, to rebuild the destroyed synagogues? Did Germany offer citizenship rights to the many thousands of displaced persons, people who were unable or unwilling to return home as a result of the Soviet occupation of Central and Eastern Europe (especially since everyone there had been killed, no one had survived), and who were compelled to work for years in German camps, and who now lived here in Germany? Yes, the buildings are modest and so is their aura, and so indeed are the streets where they were built. The clear signals of reconciliation came only a generation later, during the so-called German "Vergangenheitsbewältigung," the process of coming to terms with the past, with the Eichmann trial of 1961 and the student revolts of 1968/69, when the German postwar generation began asking their parents about the past. And, indeed, when the Jewish postwar generation began to act with greater self-confidence. Only from the 1990s did synagogue buildings begin to reflect this renewed Jewish self-confidence, at least in those countries where this still highly fraught history can be spoken about openly, whether in interpersonal or societal terms. For me, with many of the older, "noble" synagogues in Europe, the past engenders a sense of unease, an inescapable emptiness. Although at times, when visiting a synagogue in Europe, and more recently in the United States as well, you have to submit to questioning and inspection by armed police officers (despite knowing it's for my own protection, I still experience a psychological threshold that is to be overcome), I feel

lassen muss – wobei ich mich zwar beschützt weiß, aber eine psychologische Schwelle überwinden muss –, fühle ich mich in vielen modernen Synagogen wohl, geborgen, zuhause – ja klar, auch dank einer Architektur, die mich inspiriert.

Brauchen wir Räume, die synagogal und repräsentativ sind? Oder brauchen wir nicht vielmehr Räume, die für das alltägliche Gemeindeleben geeignet sind?

IR Um noch einmal zu den Entwürfen für das Grundstück in Berlin zu schauen: Bei den Arbeiten, die sich mit der ehemaligen Synagoge am Fraenkelufer befasst haben, gab es im Wesentlichen zwei Lösungsansätze: Der eine ist, ein völlig neu strukturiertes Ensemble aus Gebäuden zu etablieren. Oftmals gibt es hierbei einen Innenhof, um den sich die verschiedenen Nutzungen gruppieren. Die Arbeit von Robert Wehner verfolgt diesen Entwurfsansatz [→ S. 82–85]. Bei dieser Herangehensweise entsteht somit eine komplexe Raumstruktur aus verschiedenen, einzelnen Baukörpern. Dadurch erscheint das neue Gemeindezentrum aufgrund seiner Kleinteiligkeit viel weniger dominant und stadtraumprägend, als es beim früheren Bau von Beer der Fall war. Die andere Möglichkeit war, die frühere Präsenz der Synagoge am Fraenkelufer wiederherzustellen, ohne allerdings das ehemalige Gebäude zu rekonstruieren. Diesen Gedanken hat zum Beispiel Marie Carraux mit ihrem Entwurf umgesetzt und die verschiedenen Nutzungen in einem Gebäude zusammengefasst, so dass sich die Synagoge zum Ufer hin als ein großes, monumental wirkendes Gebäude präsentiert [→ S. 64–67]. Das wären zwei grundsätzlich mögliche Ansätze zu einem Entwurfsprojekt an diesem Standort: also einmal eine komplexe Raumstruktur von Gebäuden zu erzeugen, die das ganze Grundstück bespielen und sich aufgrund der notwendigerweise kleineren Volumetrie zwangsläufig zurücknehmen – oder andererseits ein Gebäude zu errichten, das versucht, die frühere Präsenz im Stadtraum wiederherzustellen. Meine Frage wäre: Was ist Deine Haltung zu diesen beiden Entwürfen?

EvV Hier stellt sich mir immer die Frage: Wenn ein Gebäude so viel Repräsentanz verkörpert, stimmt das denn überhaupt noch mit dem Selbstverständnis der heutigen Gemeinden überein? Ich meine, brauchen wir Räume, die synagogal und repräsentativ sind – oder brauchen wir nicht vielmehr Räume, die für das alltägliche Gemeindeleben geeignet sind? Daher finde ich es immer problematisch, wenn Räumlichkeiten in ihrer Funktion so festgelegt sind, dass sie nur zu einem bestimmten Zweck genutzt werden können. Multifunktionalität ist heute wichtig – man sollte zum Beispiel den Synagogenraum innerhalb von einer Stunde so umbauen können, dass er auch als Konzertsaal oder Vortragsraum verwendet werden kann. Das wäre sinnvoll, da er schließlich nicht die ganze Zeit als Gebetsraum genutzt wird und somit nur leerstehen würde.

comfortable in many modern synagogues, sheltered, at home—partly, of course, thanks to an architecture that inspires me.

Do we need spaces that are synagogal and representative? Don't we instead need spaces that are adapted to everyday community life?

IR Taking a look again at the designs for the site in Berlin: essentially, the projects that address the former synagogue on Fraenkelufer are based on two possible solutions, the first being to establish a completely new configuration of an ensemble of buildings. In many instances, there is an interior courtyard around which various utilizations are grouped. The project by Robert Wehner follows this approach [→ pp. 82–85]. This strategy results in a complex spatial structure composed of various individual volumes. And consequently, the new community center, with its small-scale structure, is far less dominant and shapes the urban space far less than Beer's earlier building did. The other possibility was to recreate the presence of the former synagogue on Fraenkelufer without reconstructing the original building itself, however. This concept was implemented in the project by Marie Carraux, for example, which brings together the various utilizations in a single building, so that the synagogue, which faces the canal, takes the form of a large building that exudes monumentality [→ pp. 64–67]. Essentially, these were the two possible strategies for a design project at this location: to generate a complex spatial structure with multiple buildings that occupy the entire site, and which are unavoidably more subdued by virtue of their necessarily smaller volumes—or to erect a building that attempts to embody the earlier presence of the synagogue within the urban environment. My question is: what is your attitude toward these two approaches?

EvV For me, the question always arises: when a building embodies such representative qualities, is this still consistent with the self-understanding of the contemporary community? What I mean by that is: do we need spaces that are synagogal and representative? Don't we instead need spaces that are adapted to everyday community life? Which is why I always find it problematic when spaces are so fixed in relation to function that they are usable only for a certain purpose. Today, multifunctionality is important—it should be possible, for example, to convert the space of a synagogue within an hour or so for use as a concert or lecture hall. This seems sensible—in the end, the space shouldn't be usable only for prayer purposes so that it ends up sitting there empty the rest of the time.

Isn't a sacred space one that differs from all others?

IR The question of multifunctionality was discussed intensively in all of the design courses—all of the participants shared the view that the prayer hall needs to be the most architecturally specific space, which is to say that it loses incisiveness and power when converted into a multifunctional space. All of the students,

Ist nicht der Sakralraum der Ort, der sich von allen anderen unterscheidet?

IR Diese Frage der Multifunktionalität wurde in allen Entwurfskursen sehr stark diskutiert – die Meinung aller Beteiligten war, dass der Gebetsraum eigentlich der architektonisch spezifischste Raum sein muss, also dass der Raum an Prägnanz und Stärke verliert, wenn man ihn zum Multifunktionsraum macht. Ausnahmslos alle Studierenden haben sich dazu entschieden, explizit einen Gebetsraum zu entwerfen. Meinst Du, dass dies nicht notwendig wäre?

EvV Doch, das ist natürlich notwendig. Es ist notwendig, dass es einen funktionsfähigen, symbolträchtigen Synagogengebetsraum gibt, der eine bestimmte spirituelle Atmosphäre ausstrahlt, aber seine Stimmung je nach Feierlichkeit – ob Fest, Fastentag oder Gedenktag – verändern können muss. Ein hoher Raum über zwei Stockwerke mit einer Empore oben ist vielleicht eindrucksvoll – aber eben auch sehr formell.

GW Aber ist nicht der Sakralraum der Ort, der sich von allen anderen unterscheidet, indem er genau dieses Moment des Erhabenen und Transzendentalen anbietet? Ich glaube schon, genau dieser Unterschied zu allen anderen Räumlichkeiten ist essenziell – und ich sehe den Gebetsraum auch gewissermaßen als identitätsstiftendes Herzstück der Synagoge. Würde hier nicht eine Multifunktionalität immer zu einer großen architektonischen Uneindeutigkeit führen und dem Raum einiges von seinem spezifischen Charakter nehmen?

Man baut eine Synagoge nicht für die Repräsentanz, sondern für eine Gemeinschaft, die nach Identität und Anknüpfungspunkten aus der Tradition sucht

EvV Mit den Begriffen «erhaben» und «transzendental» habe ich ein Problem – sie gehören nicht zum Vokabular, das ich bei einem Auftrag für den Bau einer Synagoge verwenden würde. Aber ja, ich finde natürlich auch, dass es eine Herausforderung ist, einem synagogalen Raum eine besondere Ausstrahlung zu geben; darüber geht ja die Debatte, darum sollte es Auftraggebern und Architekten gehen. Nochmal einen Schritt zurück: Eine heutige jüdische Gemeinde hat viele praktische Bedürfnisse, aber man muss immer auch die sakrale Funktion in den Blick nehmen. Eine Synagoge ist sicher kein reiner Treffpunkt – sie sollte sowohl Spiritualität als auch gleichzeitig Wärme, Geborgenheit ausstrahlen, also eben auch niedrigschwellig sein. Das Sakrale sollte heute nicht wie eine moderne Kathedrale aussehen. Hier gibt es auch subtilere Wege, den Ansprüchen gerecht zu werden. Das ist die Herausforderung. Man baut eine Synagoge nicht für die Repräsentanz, nicht für die Honoratioren einer jeweiligen Stadt, sondern für eine Gemeinschaft, die nach Identität und Anknüpfungspunkten aus der Tradition sucht, um sich weiterzuentwickeln.

IR Ich verstehe Deinen Wunsch nach einer den Menschen zugewandten, selbstverständlichen Architektur without exception, chose to design a prayer room with an explicit identity. Is it your view that this was unnecessary?

EvV It's certainly necessary. You need to have a functional and symbolically effective synagogal prayer space that radiates a certain spiritual atmosphere, but whose mood can shift depending on the ceremonial occasion—whether it's a celebration, a day of fasting, or a day of remembrance. A tall room that extends across two stories with a gallery above can be quite impressive, but also rather formal.

GW But isn't a sacred space one that differs from all the others precisely by virtue of providing a sense of the sublime, the transcendental? I believe that precisely this distinction from all other spaces is essential—and I regard the prayer hall as the centerpiece of the synagogue, the one that, in a sense, gives it an identity. In such a space, wouldn't multifunctionality always lead to a significant degree of architectural ambiguity, robbing the space to some extent of its specific character?

You build a synagogue not solely for representative purposes, but also for a community that is seeking a sense of identity, points of reference in tradition

EvV I have a problem with the terms "sublime" and "transcendental"—they don't belong to the vocabulary I would associate with a commission for a synagogue. But yes, of course, I believe it's a challenge to give a synagogal space a special aura; that's the focus of the debate, and clients and architects need to engage with it. But taking another step back: while a contemporary Jewish community has many practical needs, the sacral function always needs to be considered as well. Certainly, a synagogue is more than just a gathering place—it should radiate spirituality, but at the same time warmth and protectiveness, and should therefore also be low-threshold. Today, a sacred space shouldn't resemble a modern cathedral. There are more subtle ways of doing justice to these demands. That's the challenge. You build a synagogue not solely for representative purposes, for the dignitaries of the respective town, but also for a community that is searching for a sense of identity, points of reference in tradition, in order to develop further.

IR I understand your desire for a self-evident architecture that is oriented toward people, but it's also true that the sublime is in a sense unavoidably opposed to the low-threshold—should the demand that higher things be endowed with expression through architecture be basically abandoned? The point here is: a religious service may be possible in any perfectly ordinary setting, but in the absence of a search for the sublime, the construction of a place of worship would simply be nonsensical.

EvV As I mentioned earlier, the word "sublime" doesn't suit me. I prefer the word "spirituality." It's like this: every human being is created in God's image. When I look

5
Alte Synagoge am Michelsberg, Wiesbaden, Postkarte: undatiert
Old synagogue on Michelsberg, Wiesbaden, postcard: undated
—
Philipp Hoffmann 1869

und es stimmt auch, dass das Erhabene dem Niedrigschwelligen gewissermaßen unvermeidlich entgegensteht – aber sollte man deshalb den Anspruch, das Höhere auch mit den Mitteln der Architektur zum Ausdruck zu bringen, ganz grundsätzlich aufgeben? Ich meine, der Punkt ist doch: Es mag ja sein, dass ein Gottesdienst an jedem noch so gewöhnlichen Ort möglich ist, aber der Bau eines Gotteshauses würde, ohne das Erhabene zu suchen, doch schlicht unsinnig sein.

EvV Wie ich schon gesagt habe, passt mir das Wort «erhaben» nicht. Ich bevorzuge das Wort «Spiritualität». Und zwar so: Jeder Mensch ist geschaffen in Gottes Ebenbild. Wenn ich einem Menschen in die Augen schaue, mit ihm spreche und spiele, studiere und diskutiere oder zusammen bete, ist Gottes Anwesenheit da. Für mich sollte ein synagogaler, religiöser Raum diese Idee verkörpern – und nichts anderes. Das Zeitalter des Erhabenen, der Kathedralen, der Beeindruckung ist vorbei. Wir bewegen uns auf das Post-Anthropozän zu. Meiner persönlichen Meinung nach ist jetzt Bescheidenheit und Zurückhaltung angesagt, auch in der Architektur – in einer Schöpfung, einer Welt, die wir an den Rand des Untergangs gebracht haben.

IR Ist es vielleicht auch so, dass die studentischen Entwürfe, welche ohne Dialog mit der jeweiligen Gemeinde entstanden sind, doch sehr stark von einer mitteleuropäischen, nicht-jüdischen Sichtweise auf sakrale Räume geprägt sind?

EvV Ich fürchte das ein bisschen. Eine Synagoge sollte immer symbolträchtig sein und eine gewisse Spiritualität ausstrahlen – wenn diese allerdings zu überwältigend und prächtig wird, haben die Menschen Hemmungen, diesen Raum zu nutzen. Eine Synagoge, groß oder klein, muss sich also auch immer heimisch anfühlen.

IR Wenn man in der Geschichte zurückblickt, haben die jüdischen Gemeinden des späten 19. und frühen 20. Jahrhunderts doch Synagogen gebaut, bei denen der sakrale Aspekt ganz explizit betont wurde und die auch in ihrer äußeren Erscheinung sehr stark an Kirchen erinnerten. Sie haben sich somit der Sakralität bedient, die Du gerade kritisiert hast.

Wir sollten uns ganz andere Fragen stellen: Was braucht eine jüdische Gemeinde heute?

EvV Genau – und dessen bin ich mir auch bewusst. Das hat aber mit einem Damals zu tun, mit einer jüdischen Welt, einer jüdischen Kultur und einer jüdischen Gemeinschaft, die alle zerstört sind. Um diese Synagogenbauten zu verstehen, muss man den damaligen Diskurs studieren, den jeweiligen historischen Hintergrund kennen. Festzuhalten ist, dass vor dem Zweiten Weltkrieg, vor der Shoah einerseits die städtischen jüdischen Gemeinden sehr viel größer waren, als es heute der Fall ist; dass es dazu eine große Vielfalt von größeren und kleineren Synagogen gab, aus denen man wählen konnte; und dass es diese Vielfalt auch in kleineren Städten und Dörfern auf dem Land gab. Dann kommt

another human being in the eye, when I speak and play with him, study, discuss, or pray with him, then God is present. For me, a synagogal, a religious space should embody this idea—and no other. The age of the sublime, of the cathedrals, of imposing architecture, is now behind us. We are facing the Post-Anthropocene epoch. Personally, I feel that modesty and restraint are called for, in architecture as well—in a Creation, a world, we have brought to the brink of destruction.

IR Might it perhaps be the case that the student designs, which were produced without engaging in dialogue with the community, are very strongly shaped by a Central European, non-Jewish perspective of sacred spaces?

EvV I'm a little afraid that might be the case. A synagogue should always be symbolically effective, should radiate a certain spirituality—but when it becomes too overpowering and splendid, people feel inhibited about using the space. A synagogue, whether large or small, should always feel somewhat homelike.

IR Looking back on history, the Jewish community of the late nineteenth and early twentieth centuries nonetheless built synagogues that very explicitly emphasized the sacral aspect and whose outward appearances were strongly reminiscent of churches. Which means that they took advantage of precisely the sacrality you are criticizing now.

We need to ask ourselves very different questions: what does a Jewish community need today?

EvV Exactly—and I'm well aware of that. But all of that is connected to a past, to a Jewish world, a Jewish culture, and a Jewish community that has been destroyed. To understand these synagogue buildings, you need to study the discussions that took place at that time, to familiarize yourself with the respective historical background. First, it should be pointed out that prior to World War II, before the Shoah, the urban Jewish communities were much, much larger than is the case today; there existed a great diversity of larger and smaller synagogues from which to choose; and this diversity existed even in smaller towns and villages. A second aspect is that in their struggle for equality, rabbis and Jewish scholars throughout Europe were forced to confront not just the state, but also the dominant state religion of Christianity (whether Protestant or Catholic). This kind of hostile debate (which wasn't where it ended, unfortunately), initiated by the state and by representatives of the Christian faith, forced the Jews into a difficult position. The Jews for whom non-Jewish architects built synagogues strove to demonstrate that their buildings were at eye level with Catholic and Protestant churches, both architecturally and in many other respects. They lost this battle. Today, in the twenty-first century, we find ourselves in a different phase of history, and accordingly should be asking ourselves very different questions. Specifically: what does a Jewish community need today? What does the younger generation need in

als zweiter Aspekt hinzu, dass sich die Rabbiner und jüdischen Gelehrten überall in Europa in ihrem Kampf um Gleichberechtigung nicht nur mit dem Staat selbst, sondern auch mit der dominanten christlichen Staatsreligion (evangelisch oder katholisch) auseinandersetzen mussten. Diese Art einer von staatlicher und christlicher Seite initiierten feindseligen Debatte (und dabei ist es leider nicht geblieben) hat Juden in eine schwierige Position gezwungen. Die Jüdinnen und Juden, für die jüdische und nicht-jüdische Architekten Synagogen gebaut haben, wollten beweisen, dass sie auf gleicher Ebene wie die katholischen und protestantischen Kirchen standen, architektonisch und in vielerlei anderer Hinsicht. Diesen Kampf haben sie verloren. Heute im 21. Jahrhundert befinden wir uns in einer anderen Phase der Geschichte und wir sollten uns sinngemäß auch ganz andere Fragen stellen. Nämlich: Was braucht eine jüdische Gemeinde heute? Was braucht die jüngere Generation, um sich dort willkommen zu fühlen, und was benötigt die ältere Generation, damit sie sich dort heimisch fühlt – jüdische Immigranten aus der ehemaligen Sowjetunion, die seit 1923 von ihrer jüdischen Kultur, ihren jüdischen Sprachen (Hebräisch und Jiddisch) und ihrer jüdischen Religion beraubt wurden? Diese radikal andere Lebensrealität sollte man in den Blick nehmen – und auch, dass nicht mal Gläubige regelmäßig eine Synagoge besuchen, wenn man heute ein jüdisches Gemeindezentrum, eine Synagoge baut.

IR Eine Schlussfolgerung wäre doch, dass das komplexe Raumprogramm, was Grundlage der Entwürfe war, mit vielen Räumen von Unterrichtsräumen über Veranstaltungsräume und die Bibliothek bis hin zu den sakralen Räumen wie dem Gebetsraum – welcher dann eigentlich nurmehr ein Raum unter vielen ist – doch das richtige Nutzungskonzept für ein Gemeindehaus unserer Zeit ist. Die Synagoge wird zu einem Ort, an dem das Religiöse nicht mehr singulär im Vordergrund steht, und damit zu einem Treffpunkt für die Mitglieder der jüdischen Gemeinde und ihre Gäste.

EvV Ja, ich denke, dass das so ist. Wir brauchen Ausstellungsräume, Räume, in denen man Vorträge oder Konzerte geben oder Filme zeigen kann – wobei ein Teil dieser Veranstaltungen öffentlich sein sollte, um Austausch und Gespräch zu fördern, damit Nicht-Juden die jüdische Kultur aus einer Innenperspektive kennenlernen. Spannend wäre zum Beispiel hören zu lassen, wie nahe Klezmer und Jazz beieinander liegen. Nicht zuletzt sollte es bei solchen Veranstaltungen dann auch möglich sein, die Synagoge zu besuchen und religiösen Aspekte kennenzulernen. Ich selbst finde es jedes Mal, wenn ich eine Synagoge irgendwo auf der Welt besuche, spannend, wie die jeweiligen Gemeinden ihr Haus nutzen, auf welche Funktionen sie ihren Schwerpunkt legen oder welche Räume aus den unterschiedlichsten Gründen ungenutzt bleiben. Dieser Blickwinkel ist, so meine ich, auch für Architektinnen und Architekten essenziell. Nicht zuletzt deswegen war es mir eine große Freude, an diesem fantastischen Projekt ein wenig als Impulsgeber mitarbeiten zu können.

order to feel welcome, and what does the older generation need so that they feel at home? Jewish immigrants from the former Soviet Union, who were robbed, beginning in 1923, of their Jewish culture, their Jewish languages (Hebrew and Yiddish), and their Jewish religion. It's important to take account of this radically different lived reality when planning a Jewish community center or synagogue, along with the fact that, these days, not even believers visit a synagogue regularly.

IR One possible conclusion, then, would be that the complex spatial program that formed the basis for the designs, with numerous spaces ranging from instruction rooms to event spaces and a library, including sacred spaces such as the prayer hall—which would be only one space among many in that scenario—is the right utilization concept for a community center of our time after all. The synagogue would become a place where religious affairs alone are no longer front and center and would instead be a meeting place for the members of the Jewish community and their guests.

EvV Yes, I believe that's right. We need exhibition spaces, spaces for lectures, or concerts, or film screenings—some events should also be public to promote exchange and dialogue, allowing non-Jews to familiarize themselves with Jewish culture from an insider perspective. It can be exciting to realize, for example, how close klezmer and jazz are to one another. Through such events, it should also be possible to visit the synagogue and become familiar with certain religious aspects. For me, it's always exciting to visit a synagogue somewhere around the world, to see how the respective community uses its building, which functions are emphasized and which spaces remain unused, for the most diverse reasons. Such a perspective, I believe, is also essential for architects. Which is also why it was such a pleasure for me to contribute, even in a small way, some impulses to this amazing project.

Roger Diener
im Gespräch mit
in conversation with
Jörg Springer

Roger Diener war für den Umbau der Synagoge in Basel verantwortlich und er hat für den Neubau der Synagoge in Aachen einen wunderbar leisen und gerade deswegen kraftvollen Entwurf vorgelegt – der leider nicht realisiert wurde. Seine Themen sind die Rolle des einzelnen Hauses in der Stadt und das Verhältnis von Stadtraum und Gebäude. *Das Haus und die Stadt* ist der Titel eines programmatischen Buchs, das er schon 1995 gemeinsam mit Martin Steinmann publiziert hat. Seine fortdauernde Suche nach dem Allgemeingültigen auch in den scheinbar besonderen, exponierten Aufgaben offenbart eine bescheidene, um Genauigkeit bedachte Haltung.

JS In diesem Gespräch möchte ich mit Dir nicht einfach nur diskutieren, ob die Rekonstruktion von Synagogen grundsätzlich denkbar wäre oder nicht. In unserem Synagogen-Projekt hat uns vielmehr die Frage interessiert, welche Beweggründe eigentlich hinter dem Wunsch nach Rekonstruktion stehen – und ob es uns als Architekten nicht gelingen könnte, diese Anliegen auch mit anderen Mitteln als denen des Rekonstruierens zu beantworten. Unsere Gespräche und auch der aktuelle Diskurs haben gezeigt, dass der Wunsch, jüdisches Leben in der Stadt wieder sichtbar zu machen, eines der wichtigsten Motive der Wiederaufbauambitionen ist. Dies gilt vor allem für Hamburg. Die Besonderheit der Bornplatzsynagoge liegt ja darin, dass sie das erste im Stadtraum freistehende jüdische Gotteshaus war. Eine solche Freistellung von Synagogen war bis dahin auch in anderen deutschen Städten nicht möglich. Selbst die große Synagoge in der Oranienburger Straße in Berlin steht ja noch in der Straßenflucht. Insofern war die Bornplatzsynagoge, als sie 1906 gebaut wurde, auch ein einzigartiges Symbol für eine selbstverständliche Präsenz des Judentums in der Stadt – ein Umstand, der auch heute noch für den Wunsch nach Rekonstruktion eine große Rolle spielt.
Du selbst hast ja vor ziemlich genau 30 Jahren einmal eine Synagoge in einer deutschen Stadt entworfen: die Synagoge in Aachen. Ein Projekt, das damals auch in einem der ersten Bücher[1] über Deine Arbeit veröffentlicht wurde. Hier hattest Du die Synagoge ganz anders

Roger Diener was responsible for the conversion of the synagogue in Basel, and produced a marvelously muted—and for that very reason powerful—design for a new synagogue in Aachen, which ultimately remains unrealized, regrettably. His themes are the role of the individual building within the city and the relationship between the urban environment and the building. *Das Haus und die Stadt* (The House and the City) is the title of a programmatic book published back in 1995 by Diener jointly with Martin Steinmann. His continuing search for the universal, even within seemingly exceptional, exposed assignments, reveals a modest attitude and a great concern for accuracy.

JS In this conversation, I want to go beyond the question of whether synagogue reconstructions are, essentially, conceivable or not. In our Synagogue Project, we were far more interested in the question of what motivations are found behind the desire for a reconstruction—and whether we might not be capable, as architects, of responding to these intentions with resources other than reconstruction. Our discussions, along with current debates, have shown that the desire to make Jewish life visible again in the city is one of the most important motives underlying such aspirations for reconstruction. This is true in particular for Hamburg. What made the Bornplatz Synagogue special was that it was the first freestanding Jewish house of God in an urban setting. Up to that point, this type of standalone synagogue was simply impossible, in other German cities as well. Even the large synagogue on Oranienburger Straße in Berlin sits within the larger urban block. When it was built in 1906, the Bornplatz Synagogue was in this respect a singular symbol for the taken-for-granted presence of Judaism in the city—a circumstance that plays a major role today in the desire for a reconstruction.
Exactly thirty years ago, you yourself designed a synagogue for a German city, namely Aachen. A project that was also published in one of the first books[1] about your work. Here, you conceived the synagogue very differently, and—in explicit opposition to the intentions of the competition announcement—positioned it in a way that it would have avoided dominating Synagogue Square—

gedacht und sie – durchaus gegen die Intention der Auslobung – in einer Weise positioniert, dass sie den Synagogenplatz, wie er dann ja wieder genannt wurde, eben nicht dominiert hätte [→ Abb. 1]. Sie sollte in Deinem Entwurf etwas vom Platz abgerückt stehen, sichtbar, aber eher in einer beiläufigen Form anwesend. Statt eines zum Platz hin orientierten Portals hattest Du einen seitlichen Zugang vorgesehen. Auch die Ausrichtung der Baukörper war nicht auf den Platz bezogen, sie folgte stattdessen der orthogonalen Ordnung einer unbedeutenden Seitenstraße. Die Synagoge, eigentlich ja das namensgebende Bauwerk am Platz, hätte sich sehr zurückgenommen [→ Abb. 2]. Was mich an dieser frühen Arbeit von Dir, vor allem vor dem Hintergrund dessen, was derzeit in Hamburg diskutiert wird, interessiert: Wie denkst Du eigentlich heute über die Rolle einer Synagoge in der Stadt? Welche Position und Rolle kann sie heute in einer Stadt, oder genauer: in einer deutschen Stadt, einnehmen? Siehst du das noch genauso wie vor 30 Jahren in Aachen oder möglicherweise inzwischen anders?

In Aachen sollte die Verletzlichkeit der Synagoge auch Ausdruck des Status der jüdischen Gemeinden in Deutschland sein

RD In Aachen haben wir diesem Projekt abverlangt, dass es zugleich zu einem Erinnerungswerk für die Geschichte der Juden im 20. Jahrhundert und für das Verhängnis des Nationalsozialismus wird. Das wird zum einen in der städtebaulichen Position des Hauses deutlich, indem wir die Synagoge bewusst nicht mehr als Teil dieses zu rekonstruierenden Platzes entworfen haben, sondern das Haus, wie Du sagst, etwas von ihm abgerückt haben. Das Zweite, das die Erinnerungskraft sicherstellen sollte, ist der Holzbau [→ Abb. 3], sodass das Haus immer auch in einer gewissen Weise fragil und empfindlich wirken würde. Die Verletzlichkeit könnte auch Ausdruck des Status der jüdischen Gemeinden in Deutschland sein – ein Aspekt, der ja eigentlich bis heute unverändert anhält. Es gab damals in Aachen nicht die ausführliche Diskussion, die gegenwärtig in Hamburg stattfindet. Das Beispiel Hamburg zeigt uns, dass es ebenso eine Fraktion von Bürgerinnen und Bürgern gibt, die mit diesem Vorhaben gewissermaßen nur das Beste für die jüdische Gemeinde will. Sie teilen also nicht im Geringsten die Bedenken, dass man das Geschehene durch die Rekonstruktion vergessen lassen möchte – sondern meinen, dass ein prominenter Wiederaufbau angemessen wäre und auch das sei, was der jüdischen Gemeinde zustünde. Soweit ich das verfolgt habe, wird dieses Vorhaben auch mit dem Argument begründet, dass man ansonsten eben doch der Intention der Nazi-Schergen entspräche, die eine Synagoge an diesem Ort für alle Zeit verhindern wollten. Das ist natürlich eine zunächst entwaffnende Position. Aber ich denke dennoch, dass ein bruchloser Wiederaufbau tatsächlich der Erinnerung zu einer zusätzlichen Hürde zu werden drohte. Daher würde ich auch den Entwurf für die Aachener Synagoge heute nicht anders ausführen.

as it was now once again called [→ Fig. 1]. In your design, it was shifted somewhat away from the square, still visible, but present in a rather incidental kind of way. In place of a portal oriented toward the square, you envisioned a side entrance. Nor was the building oriented toward the square; instead, it followed the orthogonal configuration of an unimportant side street. The synagogue, the building for which the square was known, would have been quite withdrawn in character [→ Fig. 2]. What I find interesting about this early project, especially in the light of current discussions in Hamburg, is: what are your current thoughts about the role of a synagogue in the city? What kind of position or role might it assume today in a city, or more precisely, in a German city? Do you see things exactly the way you did thirty years ago in Aachen, or perhaps in the meanwhile somewhat differently?

In Aachen, this vulnerability could also express the status of the Jewish communities in Germany

RD In Aachen, we demanded of this project that it simultaneously became a work of memory for the history of Jews in the twentieth century and also for the disastrous effects of National Socialism. That is made evident first in the urbanistic position of the building; we deliberately avoided conceiving the synagogue as an integral part of the square that was to be reconstructed, and instead, as you've said, shifted the building away somewhat. The second element that was designed to safeguard the power of memory is the building's timber structure [→ Fig. 3], intended to lend a certain impression of fragility and delicacy. This vulnerability could also express the status of the Jewish communities in Germany, an aspect which in fact remains unchanged up to the present. In Aachen, there wasn't the kind of in-depth discussion currently taking place in Hamburg. What the Hamburg example shows to us is that there exists a faction of the citizenry that, through this undertaking, only wants the best for the Jewish community. They by no means share the concern that a reconstruction would allow past events to be forgotten—instead, they regard a prominent reconstruction as a fitting solution, something that is owed to the Jewish community. To the extent that I have followed the discussion, the endeavor is also justified by the argument that, otherwise, you'd be satisfying the intentions of the Nazi henchmen, who sought to prevent the presence of a synagogue at this location for all time. To begin with, of course, this is a disarming position. All the same, I believe that a seamless reconstruction could have actually become an additional hindrance to memory. For this reason, I wouldn't carry out the design for the synagogue in Aachen any differently today.

JS I'd like to remain for a bit with the role of the synagogue in the city—and perhaps avoid focusing primarily on the design of the building, instead turning toward the question of whether the desire for a powerful presence is genuinely correct or adequate. In Hamburg, meanwhile, the urbanistic position of the Bornplatz Synagogue has been severely disadvantaged by newer

1
Entwurf
Neue Synagoge,
Aachen,
Erdgeschoss mit
Umgebung
Design of the
new synagogue
in Aachen,
ground floor with
surroundings
—
Diener & Diener
Architekten
1991

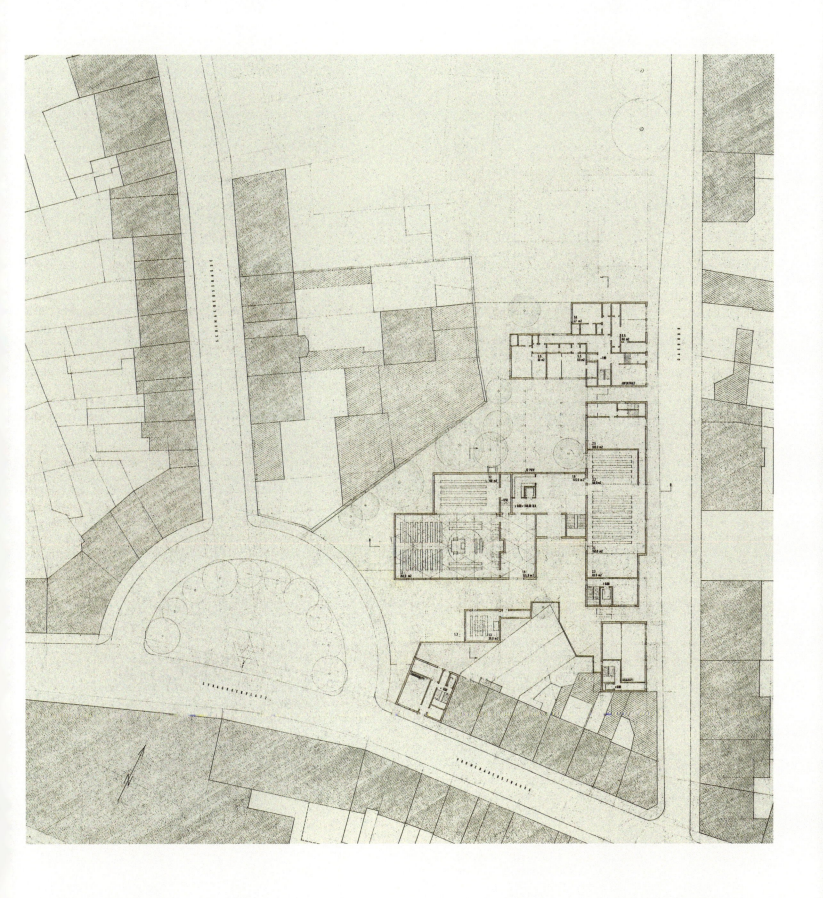

2
Entwurf
Neue Synagoge,
Aachen,
Blick vom Platz
Design of the
new synagogue
in Aachen,
view from the
square
—
Diener & Diener
Architekten
1991

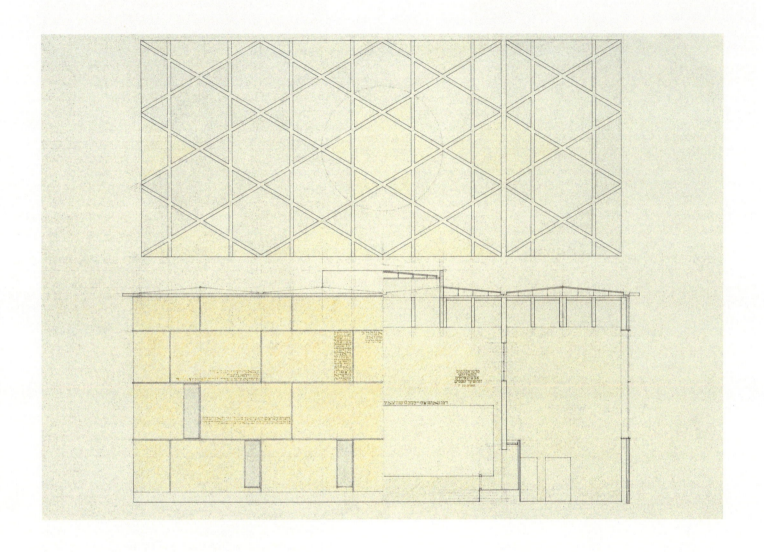

3
Entwurf
Neue Synagoge,
Aachen,
Detailschnitt mit
Ansicht
Design of the
new synagogue
in Aachen,
detail section
with view
—
Diener & Diener
Architekten
1991

JS Ich würde gerne noch ein wenig bei der Rolle der Synagoge in der Stadt bleiben – und dabei vielleicht gar nicht als Erstes auf die Gestalt des Hauses fokussieren, sondern uns zunächst der Frage zuwenden, ob der Wunsch nach einer kraftvollen Präsenz eigentlich richtig und adäquat ist. In Hamburg ist ja die stadträumliche Position der Bornplatzsynagoge inzwischen durch neuere Bestandsgebäude stark beeinträchtigt. Nach 1938 wurde mit Absicht ein Bunker genau an die Stelle gesetzt, an der sich das Hauptportal befunden hatte. Der steht frisch renoviert heute noch dort – im Grunde kann man also die Synagoge nur rekonstruieren, wenn man zugleich den Bunker abbricht. Und dann sind da auch noch die später hinzugefügten Gebäude der Universität, so dass auch die stadträumliche Situation der Bornplatzsynagoge im Grunde zerstört ist. Aber dennoch: jenseits dieser städtebaulichen Einschränkungen war für uns bemerkenswert, dass es – anders als bei den zuvor errichteten jüdischen Neubauten in Deutschland – in Hamburg zum ersten Mal explizit darum geht, die Synagoge wieder im Stadtbild zeichenhaft wirksam werden zu lassen. Das ist, denke ich, das entscheidende Anliegen, das beschäftigt uns – vor allem, weil es sich so sehr von der Haltung unterscheidet, die den meisten Synagogenbauten der Nachkriegszeit und die auch Deinem Aachener Projekt zugrunde liegt.

Wenn man heute in Deutschland Synagogen wiederaufbaut, dann sollten sie eine Präsenz im Stadtraum haben

RD Die Frage nach der Präsenz in der Stadt ist eine evident wichtige Überlegung. Ich weiß aber nicht, inwieweit sie sich unbedingt mit der Frage decken muss, ob ein Gebäude als Teil einer Blockbebauung ausgebildet oder freigestellt wird. Gerade in der Oranienburger Straße, wo die Synagoge Teil einer Blockrandbebauung ist, verleiht ihr ja die Kuppel trotzdem eine große Präsenz im Stadtraum. Zumal es auch diese lange Tradition gibt, sakrale Gebäude in den städtischen Block zu integrieren – hier erinnere ich mich an eine Stelle in Camillo Sittes Städtebaudiskurs, an der er ausführt, dass ein sehr hoher Prozentsatz der Kirchen in Rom eingebaut waren und sind.[2] Daran liegt es also nicht. Ich würde eher sagen, wenn man heute in Deutschland Synagogen wiederaufbaut, dann dürfen und sollten sie eine

buildings. After 1938, a bunker was deliberately constructed on the site where the main portal had been located. It still stands there, now freshly renovated—basically, the synagogue can only be reconstructed provided the bunker is demolished. And then there are the university buildings that were added later—essentially, the urbanistic situation of the Bornplatz Synagogue has been destroyed. Even so, it seemed remarkable to us that beyond these urbanistic limitations, in Hamburg—and in contrast to new Jewish buildings erected previously in Germany—it was explicitly and for the first time a question of allowing the synagogue to become a meaningful symbolic presence within the city once again. And that is, I believe, the decisive issue that preoccupies us—in particular because this attitude is so different from the one that underlies most postwar synagogue buildings, including your own Aachen project.

When synagogues are rebuilt in Germany today, they should be powerfully present within the urban environment

RD The question of the building's presence within the city is clearly an important consideration. But it's not clear to me how far it needs to be necessarily congruent with the question of whether the building is designed as part of the block or freestanding. On Oranienburger Straße, in particular, where the synagogue is part of the perimeter block development, its cupola nevertheless ensures a powerful presence within the urban environment. Especially since there exists this long tradition of integrating sacred buildings into the urban block—I'm thinking now of a passage in Camillo Sitte's discussion of urban development, in which he states that a high percentage of the churches in Rome were and are integrated into the block.[2] So that's not the issue. I would instead say that when synagogues are rebuilt in Germany today, they can and must be powerfully present within the urban environment, and that corresponds qualitatively to the complex aspiration for prominence. Something of the kind should be a requirement.

JS In that case, you might perhaps be slightly critical of your Aachen project.

RD Yes and no. With the Aachen project, urban planning and architecture cannot be looked at separately. I am certain that the painted wooden structure of the synagogue—somewhat averted and set behind a wall—would have stood out against the other buildings. By focusing on the form, we engaged with the meaning. I believe that in this relatively small city, and even at this not especially prominent location, the project's architectural language would have been possible and appropriate. In connection with the larger projects we are discussing here, our Aachen solution would of course not be an option. With the competition for a new building for a Jewish center in Munich, I was very involved in the jury [→ Fig. 4]. I felt that it would have been simply incomprehensible, had they tried to embed the new synagogue on Jakobsplatz in a way that was as unobtrusive as

4
Jüdisches Gemeindezentrum am Jakobsplatz, München
Jewish Community Center on Jakobsplatz, Munich
—
Andrea Wandel, Dr. Rena Wandel-Hoefer, Andreas Hoefer, Wolfgang Lorch, Niklolaus Hirsch
2006

Präsenz im Stadtraum haben, die auch qualitativ dem komplexen Anspruch nach Prominenz entspricht. So etwas wäre einzufordern.

JS In dem Fall würdest Du Deinen Aachener Entwurf ja selbst ein wenig kritisieren.

RD Ja und nein. Im Aachener Projekt sind Städtebau und Architektur nicht voneinander zu trennen. Ich bin sicher, dass sich der bemalte Holzbaukörper der Synagoge, etwas abgekehrt und hinter einer Mauer stehend, von den anderen Gebäuden abgehoben hätte. Indem wir uns mit der Form beschäftigt haben, haben wir uns mit der Bedeutung beschäftigt. Ich glaube, dass die Architektursprache des Projekts in dieser mittelgroßen Stadt und selbst an diesem nicht allzu prominenten Ort möglich und angemessen war. Im Zusammenhang mit den größeren Projekten, die in unserem Gespräch zur Diskussion stehen, wäre unsere Aachener Lösung natürlich keine Option. Anlässlich des Wettbewerbs für den Neubau des Jüdischen Zentrums in München [→ Abb. 4] habe ich mich sehr in der Jury engagiert. Dort empfand ich Unverständnis, wenn man hier den Versuch unternommen hätte, die neue Synagoge am Jakobsplatz möglichst nicht sperrig, sondern nahtlos in das Stadtbild einzubetten. Besonders angesichts dessen, was im Nationalsozialismus von der Stadt München ausgegangen ist.

JS Salomon Korn hat interessanterweise ebenso gefordert, dass neue Synagogen auf eine gewisse Art und Weise sperrig zu sein haben. Er hat sich – ganz ähnlich wie Du jetzt auch argumentierst – ebenfalls gegen eine allzu harmonische Einfügung in die Stadt ausgesprochen [→ S. 19–29].

RD In dieser Sache bin ich tatsächlich verunsichert. Einerseits denke ich, dass das Haus einer Synagoge auch in der Lage sein müsste, zu vermitteln, was geschehen ist. Andererseits traue ich das der Architektur nicht unbedingt zu. Denn auch die Beispiele anderer Erinnerungsarchitekturen, wie das durchaus gefeierte Jüdische Museum in Berlin [→ Abb. 5], haben mir eigentlich gezeigt, dass man die Geschichte der Juden im Nationalsozialismus nicht in ein funktionales Programm von Stadt integrieren kann. Es ist einfach nicht möglich. In dem Sinne würde ich also die Meinung teilen, dass eine Synagogenarchitektur sperrig sein muss. Das allein wäre aber nicht genug. Es geht noch vielmehr um die Information, also um die Aussage, welche hinter dieser architektonischen Haltung steht. Ansonsten droht so eine Entscheidung für eine derartige Architektursprache doch auch immer zu einem Freibrief zu werden, sich dann unbotmäßig über den Bestand eines Ortes oder einer Stadt hinwegzusetzen. Es ist eine Frage von Fall zu Fall.

JS Das sehe ich ähnlich. Vor allem beim Jüdischen Museum in Berlin teile ich Deine Kritik. Das Gebäude unternimmt ja den Versuch, die Shoah abzubilden – das halte ich grundsätzlich für sehr fragwürdig und ich glaube auch nicht, dass die Architektur hierfür

possible, integrating it seamlessly into the townscape. Especially in the light of everything that had emanated from the city of Munich during National Socialism.

JS Interestingly, Salomon Korn also called for having new synagogues that should be in a certain sense bulky. Anyway, in a way that is very similar to what you're arguing now, he also expressed opposition to an excessively harmonious insertion into the city [→ pp. 19–29].

RD Concerning this question, I'm actually somewhat unsettled. On the one hand, I believe that a synagogue building must be in a position to convey what has occurred. On the other, I don't necessarily trust architecture to achieve this. Even enthusiastically celebrated examples of memorial architecture, such as the Jewish Museum in Berlin [→ Fig. 5], have brought home to me that the history of Jews under National Socialism cannot be integrated into a functional program of the city. It's simply not possible. So in this sense, I share the view that a work of synagogue architecture should be highly bulky. On its own, that's not enough. It's instead a question of the information, of the statement, that is found behind the architectural attitude. Otherwise, the choice of such an architectural language always threatens to become a kind of carte blanche to simply ignore the existing architectural environment of a location or city. It's a case-by-case issue.

JS I have a similar perspective. In particular regarding the Jewish Museum in Berlin, I share your reservations. The building attempts to represent the Shoah—which I regard, essentially, as highly questionable; nor do I believe that architecture is a suitable medium for achieving that in the first place. In a conversation, Philipp Stricharz, the head of the Jewish community in Hamburg, posed the question of whether a synagogue should necessarily refer symbolically to the Shoah at all. He replied in the negative. For him, it was instead a question of preventing the Nazis from winning by rebuilding the synagogue at its original location. For him, basically, it's no different from reconstructing destroyed churches immediately after the war. If you want to erect a memorial for the Holocaust, that's certainly legitimate—but not here, "not on our land."

5
Jüdisches Museum, Berlin
Jewish Museum, Berlin
—
Daniel Libeskind
2001

überhaupt ein geeignetes Mittel wäre. In einem Gespräch hatte Philipp Stricharz, der Vorsitzende der Jüdischen Gemeinde in Hamburg, die Frage gestellt, ob eine Synagoge denn überhaupt zeichenhaften Bezug auf die Shoah nehmen müsse.[3] Er hat das für sich verneint. Es gehe vielmehr darum, durch den Wiederaufbau der Synagoge am ursprünglichen Ort die Nazis nicht gewinnen zu lassen. Im Grunde sei es dasselbe wie beim Wiederaufbau zerstörter Kirchen unmittelbar nach dem Krieg. Wenn man denn ein Mahnmal für den Holocaust errichten wolle, dann sei das sicher richtig – aber eben nicht an diesem Ort, «nicht auf unserem Grund und Boden».

Andererseits gibt es Stimmen aus der Gemeinde, die argumentieren, dass die Shoah als Teil der jüdischen Geschichte im Grunde immer präsent sei und somit auch immer mitgedacht werden müsse. Auch das ist nicht von der Hand zu weisen. Allein der Vorwurf, dass eine Rekonstruktion oder ein Neubau Erinnerung auslöschen könnte, trifft aber am Gegenstand einer Synagoge nicht – einer jüdischen Gemeinde diese Absicht zu unterstellen, wäre schlichtweg absurd.

Ich persönlich denke, dass in einer Synagoge in Deutschland die besondere Geschichte doch präsent sein sollte. Die Frage ist: In welcher Art und Weise kann das geschehen?

RD An einem anderen Ort konnten wir unser Projekt auf die Nachbarschaft eines Denkmals stützen. Das ermöglichte, dem Auftrag des Hauses als Ort der Forschungs- und Vermittlungsarbeit ganz konsequent und bedingungslos Vorrang zu geben und ihm auch eine gewisse Monumentalität zu widmen. Ich spreche vom Mémorial de la Shoah in Drancy [→ Abb. 6] bei Paris. In Drancy wurden die französischen Juden von 1941 bis 1944 in der Cité de la Muette, einer zwischen 1932 und 1934 realisierten u-förmigen Wohnsiedlung, interniert und von hier aus in die Konzentrationslager deportiert. In der gegenüberliegenden Straße liegt das Shoah Mémorial. Die Besucher blicken auf ein Denkmal mit einem Eisenbahnwaggon, das vor der Siedlung, die heute bewohnt ist, errichtet wurde und – unbeschadet von seinem künstlerischen Rang – Auskunft über die Geschichte gibt. Ich weiß jetzt allerdings nicht, ob so eine Konstellation auch im Zusammenhang mit einem Synagogenbau denkbar wäre.

JS Gut, in den Entwürfen für den Neubau des Jüdischen Gemeindezentrums in München waren zum Beispiel Ausstellungsflächen vorzusehen – aber so etwas scheint mir kein notwendiger Teil des Raumprogramms einer Synagoge zu sein.

RD Nein, ich fände das auch innerhalb einer Synagoge nicht angemessen. Aber ich weiß nicht, wie es Dir geht, man hat doch irgendwie ein ungutes Gefühl, wenn man an die Rekonstruktion dieser prächtigen Synagoge in Hamburg denkt.

JS Unbedingt. Man rekonstruiert, das kommt noch dazu, auch ein Bild, das sich in seinen ursprünglichen Ansprüchen und Absichten heute eigentlich als nicht

On the other hand, there are forces within the community which essentially argue that, as a part of Jewish history, the Shoah must always be present, must always be given due consideration. A position that can hardly be dismissed out of hand. When we are speaking about a synagogue, the reproach that a reconstruction or a new building is capable of extinguishing memory is, frankly, irrelevant—to impute such an intention to any Jewish community would be an utter absurdity.

Personally, I feel that with a synagogue in Germany, this exceptional history should always be present. The question is: how exactly is this to be achieved?

RD At a different location, we were able to base our project on the existence of a neighboring monument, which made it possible to consistently and unconditionally give priority to the mission of the house as a place for research and mediation and also endow it with a certain monumentality. I am talking about the Mémorial de la Shoah in Drancy [→ Fig. 6] near Paris. In Drancy, French Jews were interned from 1941 to 1944 in the Cité de la Muette, a U-shaped housing estate built between 1932 and 1934, from where they were then deported to the concentration camps. The Shoah Mémorial is across the street. Visitors look at a monument with a railway carriage which was erected in front of the still-inhabited settlement and—without prejudice to its artistic merit—provides information about the history of the place. I don't know, admittedly, whether such a constellation would also be conceivable in connection with a synagogue building.

JS Well, envisioned in the designs for a new building for the Jewish community center in Munich, for example, were exhibition areas—but something of this kind doesn't appear to me to be a necessary component of the spatial program for a synagogue.

RD I agree, in a synagogue it would be somewhat out of place. I don't know how you feel about it, but I find it somehow disquieting to contemplate a reconstruction of the splendid synagogue in Hamburg.

JS Absolutely. And you're reconstructing an image, and this is also an issue, that would no longer appear sustainable today in relation to its original claims and intentions. Ultimately, the aims of a German synagogue in 1906 met with failure in 1938—for this reason alone, in this concrete instance, I regard a reconstruction as problematic. Interestingly, we ascertained that this situation is not perceived in exactly this way by all of the representatives of the Jewish communities. But I'd like to return to your views on synagogue design, as expressed already in the case of Aachen: to what extent can the fragile, the provisional, and the portative which is to say the tent theme, which resonates in this design, nonetheless become a theme for a synagogue that occupies a central location in a large city? I'm not really convinced that such a narrative could be excluded here. In this regard, your design in Aachen is of interest, since it reveals this aspect only at second glance, rather via a characterization of the project. The drawings themselves

6
Mémorial de la Shoah, Drancy
—
Diener & Diener Architekten
2012

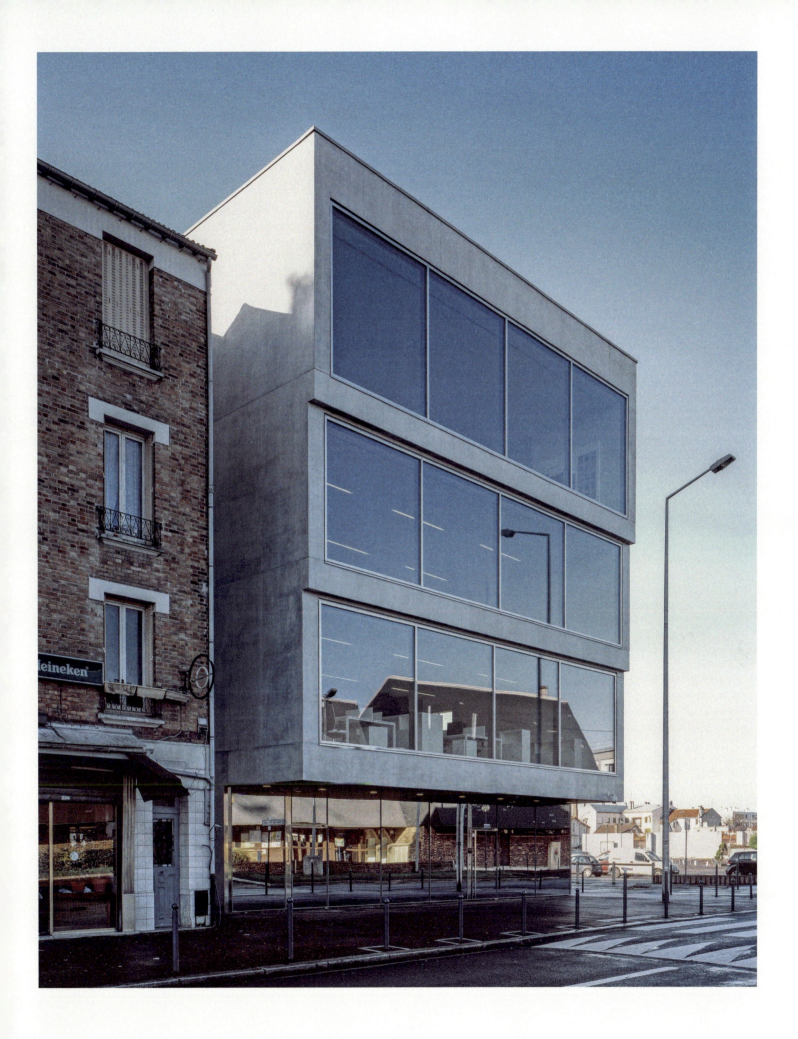

mehr tragfähig erweisen würde. Letztlich ist ja das, was 1906 eine deutsche Synagoge sein wollte, 1938 gescheitert – schon deswegen halte ich das Rekonstruieren in diesem konkreten Fall für problematisch. Interessanterweise haben wir festgestellt, dass dieser Umstand nicht von allen Vertretern der jüdischen Gemeinde genauso gesehen wird. Aber ich würde gerne noch einmal auf Deine Überlegungen zur Gestalt einer Synagoge, die Du bereits vorhin am Beispiel von Aachen geäußert hast, zurückkommen: Also inwieweit kann das Fragile, das Provisorische und auch Portative, also das Zelt-Thema, was bei diesem Entwurf mitschwingt, nicht doch auch Thema einer innerstädtischen und großstädtischen Synagoge sein? Ich bin nicht wirklich überzeugt, dass hier so ein Narrativ auszuschließen wäre. Euer Entwurf in Aachen ist ja auch insofern interessant, als er dieses Moment erst auf den zweiten Blick, eher in der Beschreibung des Projektes, erkennen lässt. Die Zeichnungen an sich zeigen einen sehr kraftvollen Baukörper mit einer symmetrischen Fassade, der zwar zurückgesetzt ist, aber doch eine gewisse Autonomie und ein Gewicht hat. Die Art und Weise, wie er ausgeführt werden sollte, ist das eigentlich Entscheidende – etwas, das sich in den Bleistiftzeichnungen allenfalls in der Art, wie mit feinem Strich gezeichnet wurde, mitteilt und das sich auch in einen gewissen Widerspruch zur Kubatur und ihrer spezifischen Kraft setzt. Möglicherweise könnten vergleichbare Themen doch auch heute noch eine Rolle spielen?

RD Ich denke schon, dass das möglich wäre. Wobei heute ja ein Phänomen existiert, dem wir damals nicht begegnet sind – nämlich, dass mittlerweile eigentlich alles gebaut wird. Die Produktion von Architektur hat sich durch verschiedenste Faktoren in den letzten 30 Jahren multipliziert und die Verwendung von Materialien ist sehr viel simpler und beliebiger geworden. Es ist schwieriger geworden, die Art der Fertigung von Architektur und das Wesen eines Baukörpers in einen eigenen und unverwechselbaren Zusammenhang zu bringen. Daher würde sich bei so einem Vorhaben in jedem Fall auch die Frage stellen, ob es tatsächlich noch gelänge, mit einem Dispositiv wie damals – auch wenn jetzt die Dimensionen andere wären – etwas von dem Grundgedanken der Zeichenhaftigkeit wieder zu entwickeln oder zu bewahren. Aber als Versuch wäre es sicher interessant und auch nicht zwingend zum Scheitern verurteilt.

Mein Eindruck ist, dass vor allem die expressiven Gesten inzwischen zum Gewöhnlichen geworden sind

JS Bei der von Dir angesprochenen Beliebigkeit bin ich mir gar nicht sicher, ob sie tatsächlich so stark auf der Ebene der Verwendung von Materialien eingetreten ist oder ob das nicht vielmehr die Formensprache betrifft. Mein Eindruck ist eher, dass vor allem die sehr expressiven Gesten inzwischen zum Gewöhnlichen geworden sind. Wir beschäftigen uns aktuell mit der Kongresshalle auf dem Nürnberger Reichsparteitagsgelände – dort nimmt man Günther Domenigs «Pfahl» doch heute nurmehr mit einem Schulterzucken zur Kenntnis. Man

display a very powerful volume with a symmetrical facade, which to be sure is set back somewhat, but nonetheless possesses a certain autonomy and weight. The way in which it was to be executed is actually the decisive thing—something conveyed by the pencil drawings at most in the way they are executed using fine strokes, and which generates a certain inconsistency with the cubature and its specific force. Conceivably, comparable themes could nonetheless play a role today as well?

RD I think so, that should be possible. Although today you have to contend with a phenomenon that didn't exist back then—namely, that, meanwhile, everything possible has been built already. Over the past thirty years, the production of architecture has been multiplied by the most diverse factors, and the use of materials has become much simpler and more arbitrary. It has become much more difficult to bring the way architecture is fabricated and the essential aspect of the building into its own, distinctive coherency. For this reason, the question would necessarily arise with such an undertaking of whether you could still really be successful in using a similar approach to the one back then—notwithstanding that different dimensions are involved today—to develop again or maintain these basic ideas concerning symbolic quality. But it would certainly be interesting as an attempt, and not necessarily doomed to failure.

My impression is that such expressive gestures in particular have meanwhile become commonplace

JS With regard to the arbitrariness you mention, I'm not certain whether it emerges so strongly on the level of the use of materials, whether it's instead more strongly related to the form language. My impression is, rather, that it's in particular these highly expressive gestures that have meanwhile become commonplace. We're currently occupied with the Congress Hall on the Nuremberg Nazi Party rally grounds—there, Günther Domenig's "Pfahl" (a diagonal glass and steel passageway) is greeted today with a shrug of the shoulders. You see it, you understand the symbolism and the intention, at which point it has already exhausted itself. In my view, the value of the building, like your synagogue in Aachen, resides in the subtler handling of symbolism, which is then less vulnerable to wearing out. To be sure, it moves on a different level, but nonetheless remains in the sphere of the familiar. Which may be a source of power for such strategies.

RD Since it also doesn't speak of an individual gesture.

JS . . . Although its individuality can hardly be denied.

RD But to begin with, it's simply a building. Whereby the task of building a synagogue is something special and extremely demanding. For Jewish sacred buildings, unlike church building, only a very small number of designs have emerged over time that are truly genuine and of high quality architecturally—and for the most part, these are smaller synagogues.

sieht ihn, man versteht das Zeichen und die Absicht, aber darin erschöpft es sich dann auch. Der Wert eines Hauses wie Deiner Synagoge in Aachen läge meiner Meinung nach darin, dass das Zeichen subtiler argumentiert und deswegen weniger stark einem Verschleiß ausgesetzt ist. Es bewegt sich zwar auf einer anderen Ebene, aber bleibt dennoch im Kreis des Gewohnten. Darin liegt vielleicht auch die Kraft solcher Strategien.

RD Da es auch nicht von einem individuellen Gestus spricht.

JS ...obwohl ihm das Individuelle kaum abzusprechen ist.

RD Aber zunächst ist es doch einfach ein Haus. Hingegen ist die Bauaufgabe einer Synagoge etwas Besonderes und sehr anspruchsvoll. Anders als im Kirchenbau gibt es im jüdischen Sakralbau durch die Zeiten hindurch nur wenige Entwürfe, die tatsächlich genuin und architektonisch hochwertig sind – wenn, dann sind es zumeist kleinere Synagogen.

JS Dieses Thema wurde ja bereits im 19. Jahrhundert, als in Deutschland relativ viele Synagogen neu gebaut wurden, als Problem sichtbar. Hier beginnt ein Prozess, den ich die Suche nach dem Moment des Anderen, des Eigenen nennen würde. Die zentrale Frage damals war, an welche Bildsprache man überhaupt anknüpfen sollte: Waren es diese maurischen Traditionen, die sich auf Spanien beziehen, oder sollte man sich eher auf die Tradition des sephardischen Judentums berufen?

RD Ich glaube, bei Schinkel waren es sogar auch ägyptische Referenzen.

JS Aber wäre das auch heute noch das erklärte Ziel – also: Sollte eine Synagoge dieses Moment des Andersartigen in sich tragen? Ist sie nicht vielmehr Teil der Stadt – oder darf sie das gar nicht mehr sein?

RD Sie muss Teil der Stadt sein. Aber diese Frage nach dem Andersartigen, das ist eine Einschätzung, die uns zu beurteilen nicht ansteht. Zumal ich in so einer Differenzierung auch nicht den geringsten Sinn für unsere heutige Gesellschaft zu erkennen vermag. Wenn ich das richtig erinnere, war die damalige Entwicklung ja auch in gewisser Weise der Verlegenheit der nicht-jüdischen Architekten geschuldet, die, wenn sie mit Synagogen beauftragt wurden, eben nicht den traditionellen Kirchenbau zitieren wollten. Meiner Meinung nach gibt es da also keine Spur, die jetzt wiederaufzunehmen wäre.

JS Lass mich zum Abschluss noch eine Frage stellen: Inwieweit spielt für eine Synagoge in der Stadt das Moment des Pathetischen eine Rolle? Interessanterweise ist Pathos heute für unsere Studenten kein Problem mehr – sie empfinden es tatsächlich eher als legitimes Mittel, um auch die Bedeutung eines solchen Bauwerkes in der Stadt zum Ausdruck zu bringen.

RD Jetzt fehlt uns Martin Steinmann! Aber: Habt ihr nur von Pathos gesprochen oder auch von Monumentalität?

JS This issue was already perceived as a problem in the nineteenth century, when a relatively large number of new synagogues were being built in Germany. Beginning here is a process I would call the search for the other, for one's own identity. Back then, the central question was: which visual language should be invoked? The Moorish tradition, with its connection to Spain, or should one instead link up with the tradition of Sephardic Judaism?

RD With Schinkel, I believe, there were even Egyptian references.

JS But would that still be the explicit aim today? Which is to say: should this aspect of otherness be inherent to a synagogue? Isn't it instead a part of the city? Or should it no longer be that?

RD It has to be a part of the city. But concerning this question of otherness, that's an assessment that isn't ours to make. Particularly since, in such a differentiation, I'm unable to perceive the slightest sense of our contemporary society. If I remember correctly, the development back then was also caused by a sense of embarrassment on the part of non-Jewish architects when accepting commissions for synagogues, the sense that they had to avoid citing traditional church architecture. In my view, there is no track there that could be taken up again now.

JS In concluding, allow me to pose another question: to what extent does the theatrical aspect play a role today for a synagogue in the city? For our students today, interestingly, pathos is no longer a problem—in fact, they regard it as a legitimate resource for endowing the significance of such buildings within the city with expressiveness.

RD If only Martin Steinmann were here now! But: are you speaking only about pathos, or about monumentality as well?

JS About both; you see it right away in the designs. I have to confess, I really do find this aspect of the works difficult to some extent—especially where the monumental is not subject to refraction, and instead remains one-to-one.

I don't believe that an emphatic pathos for a synagogue in a German city would be a comprehensible position

RD No, I also don't believe that an emphatic pathos would be a comprehensible position for a synagogue in a German city. With a sacred building, you're given the task to endow the building with an expression that corresponds to its exceptional purpose—hardly by means of explicit pathos, though.

JS In this regard, synagogues are of course related to churches. In the sense that here, too, the liturgical necessities of the space are given immediate expression in the

JS Von beidem, man sieht es auch gleich bei den Entwürfen. Ich gestehe, dass ich diesen Aspekt in den Arbeiten zum Teil doch schwirig finde – insbesondere dann, wenn das Monumentale keine Brechung erfährt, sondern eineindeutig wird.

Ich glaube, dass ein pointiertes Pathos für eine Synagoge in einer deutschen Stadt keine nachvollziehbare Position wäre

RD Ja, ich glaube auch, dass ein pointiertes Pathos für eine Synagoge in einer deutschen Stadt keine nachvollziehbare Position wäre. Man hat bei einem Sakralbau die Aufgabe, dieser besonderen Bestimmung des Hauses Ausdruck zu verleihen – aber wohl kaum durch ein explizites Pathos.

JS Insofern sind Synagogen ja den Kirchen durchaus verwandt. In dem Sinne, dass auch hier die liturgischen Notwendigkeiten des Raumes unmittelbar Ausdruck in der Gestalt des Bauwerkes finden – somit ist beiden, allein aus ihrer räumlichen Disposition heraus, bereits eine gewisse Monumentalität zu eigen.

RD Es ist allerdings auch so, dass Synagogen, vor allem für orthodoxe Juden, einen ganz selbstverständlichen Platz im Leben einnehmen. Sie gehen jeden Tag zwei Mal, morgens und abends, in die Synagoge und verstehen ihre Arbeit als einen Dienst an Gott. Das ist jetzt alles sehr vereinfacht ausgedrückt – was ich damit meine, ist, dass die Synagoge Teil einer Identität ist, sobald es darum geht, diese Zugehörigkeit zum Judentum zu leben. Dann ist diese Verbindung zum Gebäude der Gemeinde fast alltäglich.

JS Jetzt würde ich Dir gerne einige der Entwürfe zeigen. Interessant ist, dass bei den Projekten tatsächlich alle Spielarten der Präsenz und der Sichtbarkeit vertreten sind: Einerseits gibt es Arbeiten, die durchaus zeichenhaft im Stadtraum stehen, andererseits haben wir Entwürfe, die extrem zurückhaltend bleiben, bis hart ans Verschwinden der Synagoge. Das ist zum Beispiel das Projekt von Ria Roberg, das bei uns in Weimar entstanden ist [→ S. 198–201]. Hier gibt es ein vergleichsweise niedriges Gebäudeensemble, das sich um einen sehr schönen Innenhof gruppiert, aber im Straßenraum, zur Stadt hin, zeigt die Synagoge keine Präsenz.

RD Schön! Sehr schön, muss ich sagen!

JS Janis Kukral dagegen erinnert in seiner Arbeit für den Standort am Berliner Fraenkelufer an das zerstörte neoklassizistische Portal der alten Synagoge [→ S. 76–81]. Er versucht mit einer gewissen Monumentalität, aber in einer zeitgenössischen Formensprache zu argumentieren.

RD Schöne Grundrisse!

JS Um noch eine größere Bandbreite aufzufächern, möchte ich Dir noch das Projekt von Valentin Müller und Malte Wiegand zeigen [→ Abb. 7 & S. 188–193]. Ein

building's design—a certain monumentality is required of both, solely by virtue of their spatial disposition.

RD But it's also the case that synagogues, in particular for Orthodox Jews, occupy an entirely self-evident place in their lives. They enter the synagogue twice daily, mornings and evenings, and understand their work as a service to God. I'm expressing this in a simplified way—what I mean is that the synagogue is part of an identity, as soon as it's a question of living out an affiliation with Judaism. This connection to the building of their community is therefore more of an everyday one.

JS At this point, I'd like to show you a few of the designs. What is interesting is that, with these projects, all conceivable variants of presence and visibility are represented: on the one hand, there are projects that have a strong symbolic impact within the urban environment; on the other hand, there are designs that remain extremely reserved, almost to the point where the synagogue disappears. There is the project by Ria Roberg, for example, that was produced in Weimar [→ pp. 198–201]. Here, we find a relatively low-rise ensemble of buildings, which are grouped around a very lovely inner courtyard, but in relation to the street space, to the town, the synagogue has no real presence.

RD Nice! Very nice, I have to say!

JS In his project for the location on Fraenkelufer in Berlin, in contrast, Janis Kukral recalls the destroyed neoclassical portal of the old synagogue [→ pp. 76–81]. He tends to argue through a certain monumentality, but in a contemporary form language.

RD Beautiful floor plans!

JS And broadening out to an even wider spectrum, I'd like to show you a project by Valentin Müller and Malte Wiegand [→ Fig. 7 & pp. 188–193]. A project that quite explicitly makes the exotic and the symbolic central themes.

RD It's interesting that research in this direction was pursued as well. But in my view, this approach isn't really viable—in the end, even the exotic must convey a certain logic for it to represent a valid solution. But

7
Entwurf Neue Synagoge Bornplatz, Hamburg
Design for the new synagogue, Bornplatz, Hamburg
—
Valentin Müller & Malte Wiegand
2021

Projekt, das ganz explizit das Fremdartige und Zeichenhafte zu seinem zentralen Thema macht.

RD Es ist interessant, dass auch in diese Richtung recherchiert wurde. Aber meines Erachtens ist das eigentlich kein Weg, der möglich wäre – schließlich müsste ja auch das Fremdartige eine Logik in sich tragen, damit es am Ende auch eine berechtigte Lösung darstellt. Aber diese existiert ja hier nicht. Mir persönlich wäre dieser Entwurf dann auch zu spielerisch.

JS Hier in dieser Arbeit von Mahmoud Ghazala Einieh und Sven Petersen gibt es den Versuch, auch die Erinnerung an die alte Synagoge zu transportieren: zum einen in der äußeren Erscheinung mit ihren Anklängen an maurische Formensprachen, aber mehr noch im Inneren, wo der Innenraum der ehemaligen Bornplatzsynagoge rekonstruiert wird – allerdings nicht in seiner ursprünglichen Gestalt, sondern in einer allgemeineren, rohen Form [→ S. 184–187].

RD Das ist ein interessantes Thema, was im Innenraum auch spannend umgesetzt wurde. Außen wirken die Zitate historischer maurischer Architektur unausgewogen, wenn ihre Realisierung den Aufwand übersteigt, der mit einer regulären architektonischen Option verbunden wäre.

JS Ist das für Dich eine Frage des reinen Aufwandes oder nicht vielmehr eine nach der Angemessenheit der Mittel in einem formalen Sinne?

RD Ja, ich meinte letzteres und nicht die finanzielle Ebene. Immer dann, wenn es bei der Wahl der architektonischen Mittel zu einer Übersteigerung dieses Transfers kommt, wird es meines Erachtens unangemessen.

JS Die Schwierigkeit bei solchen Projekten liegt wohl auch darin, dass sie ausschließlich über die Erinnerung an die historische Bauform argumentieren und damit so eindeutig sind. Womit sich dann auch das intendierte Zeichen schnell erschöpft – man hat es erkannt, auf den ersten Blick verstanden und in diesem Moment verliert es bereits an Relevanz. Gerade bei der Auseinandersetzung mit diesen Projekten lerne ich immer mehr, dass die Strategie heute für uns nur eine sein kann, die Erinnerung öffnet und sie nicht auf bestimmte Argumente einschränkt.

RD Und sie auch nicht versteinert. Das würde ich unterschreiben.

here, that's not the case. For me personally, this design seems too playful.

JS Here, in the project by Mahmoud Ghazala Einieh and Sven Petersen, we see an attempt to transport the memory of the old synagogue: first, through its external appearance, with its reminiscences of Moorish forms, but even more so within, where the interior space reconstructs the former Bornplatz Synagogue—not in its original form, but in a more general, rough form [→ pp. 184–187].

RD That's an interesting theme, fascinating as well the way it's implemented in the interior. On the outside, the references to historical Moorish architecture seem rather imbalanced, if their realization exceeds the investment associated with a mainstream architectural option.

JS Is this purely a question of expense for you, or is it not instead a question of the fitness of the means employed in a formal sense?

RD Yes, I was referring to the latter, not the financial issue. Whenever the choice of architectural means involves an exaggeration of this transfer, it becomes disproportionate, in my view.

JS With such projects, the difficulty also resides, presumably, in the fact that they argue exclusively in relation to the memory of a historical building type, and are therefore excessively one-to-one. Which is why the intended signal is exhausted so quickly—it is both recognized and understood at first glance, and at that very moment, has already lost its relevance. It's precisely by examining these projects that I learn, more and more, that the only possible strategy for us today is to try to open up a space for memory, and not to restrict ourselves to specific arguments.

RD Or allowing them to rigidify. I can subscribe to that.

1 Rosamund Diamond und Wilfried Wang (Hg.): *From City to Detail*, London/Berlin 1992, S. 96 ff.
2 Camillo Sitte: *Der Städtebau nach seinen künstlerischen Grundsätzen*, Reprint der 4. Auflage von 1909, Braunschweig 1983, II. Das Freihalten der Mitte, dort S. 29 ff.
3 Vgl. AIT-Architektursalon Hamburg am 18.05.2021, Gespräch moderiert von Olaf Bartels, www.youtube.com/watch?v=nqg-sr_faPc (abgerufen am 26.04.22).

Tempel
Temple
Poolstraße

1
Blick vom Vorhof
auf das Portal,
Gemälde:
undatiert
View of the portal
from the forecourt,
painting:
undated

Tempel Poolstraße
Temple Poolstraße

Poolstraße 11–14, Hamburg
Johann Hinrich Klees-Wülbern
1844 (zerstört/destroyed 1944)

Der sogenannte «Zweite Israelitische Tempel» in der Hamburger Poolstraße – Nachfolger eines Provisoriums («Erster Israelitischer Tempel»)[1] – war eine der ersten gebauten Reformsynagogen der Welt und gilt daher als eine Keimzelle des weltweiten liberalen Judentums, wie es heute vor allem in Nordamerika fortbesteht.

Die Geschichte dieses 1844 errichteten «Zweiten Israelitischen Tempels» nimmt ihre Anfänge in den Emanzipationsbestrebungen, die Ende des 18. Jahrhunderts in Teilen der jüdischen Bevölkerung einsetzten. Mit dem Gebrauch der deutschen Sprache und der Anpassung von Kultvorschriften, Speisegesetzen und Feiertagsgeboten sollte die Sonderstellung der Jüdinnen und Juden in der christlich geprägten Gesellschaft abgebaut werden.[2] In diesem Zusammenhang bildete sich Anfang des 19. Jahrhunderts eine liberale Reformbewegung, die 1817 den «Neuen Israelitischen Tempelverein in Hamburg» hervorbrachte.[3] Die Bewegung suchte eine Annäherung der kultischen Tradition an den Gottesdienst der protestantischen Kirche, was sich auch auf die Gestaltung und Ausstattung der Gotteshäuser auswirkte.[4]

Nach mehreren vergeblichen Versuchen der seit den 1820er-Jahren stetig wachsenden Reformgemeinde, ein Grundstück zum Neubau eines – von der Reformbewegung «Tempel» genannten – Gotteshauses (denn das ausschließliche Ziel, ins Heilige Land zurückzukehren und den Tempel in Jerusalem wiederaufzubauen, war von den Reformern aufgegeben oder zumindest umgedeutet worden)[5] zu erhalten, wurde ihr schließlich 1841 vom Hamburger Rat ein Grundstück im Hinterhof der Häuser Poolstraße 11–14 für einen Neubau zugewiesen.[6]

Die für Synagogen nicht ungewöhnliche Hinterhoflage des für 640 Personen ausgelegten Neubaus[7] wurde damit begründet, «daß es der Gottesverehrung ebenso wenig würdig ist, das ihr gewidmete Haus den Blicken der Menge geflissentlich auszusetzen, als es ihnen sorgsam zu entziehen […], weil wir weder auf das erste Werth legen noch das letztere für nöthig halten […].»[8] Im Typus einer dreischiffigen Basilika auf nahezu quadratischem Grundriss angelegt, orientierte sich der von Hinrich Klees-Wülbern entworfene, weiß verputzte Tempel am damals zeitgenössischen Klassizismus, dem jedoch auch gotische und maurische Bauformen beigemischt wurden. Erstmals wurden an der Fassade auch jüdische Symbole verwendet.[9]

Eine Reihe programmatisch-baulicher Anpassungen im Vergleich zu orthodoxen Vorgängerbauten weisen auf das Reformprogramm des neuen Tempels hin: unmittelbar vor der Apsis und dem Aron Hakodesch waren Kanzel und Lesepult positioniert, so dass keine zentrale Bima mehr vorhanden war

The so-called "Second Israelite Temple" located on Poolstraße in Hamburg—the successor to the provisional "First Israelite Temple"[1]—was built as one of the first Reform synagogues in the world, and is hence regarded as a nucleus of liberal Judaism worldwide, as practiced today in North America in particular.

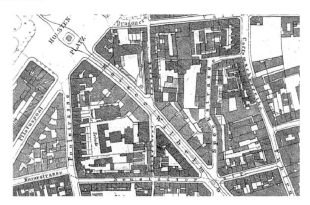

The story of the Second Israelite Temple, erected in 1844, has its origins in the striving for emancipation that emerged in segments of the Jewish population in the late eighteenth century. The use of the German language and the adaptation of cult regulations, dietary laws, and holiday commandments were intended to diminish the exceptional position of Jews within Christian society.[2] It was these tendencies that gave rise to a liberal reform movement in the early nineteenth century, leading to the establishment in 1817 of the "New Israelite Temple Association in Hamburg."[3] The movement sought to bring the cultic tradition closer to the worship service of the Protestant church, and this had an impact on the design and accoutrements of Jewish houses of God as well.[4]

In 1841, following numerous unsuccessful attempts by the Reform community (which had been growing steadily since the 1820s) to acquire a parcel of land for the construction of a new house of God, referred to by the Reform movement as a "temple" (the exclusive goal of returning to the Holy Land and rebuilding the Temple in Jerusalem having been either abandoned altogether or at least reinterpreted by the reformers),[5] Hamburg City Council allocated a parcel, consisting of the rear courtyard of the buildings located at Poolstraße 11–14, for a new synagogue building.[6]

The rear courtyard situation—hardly unusual for synagogues—of the new building, intended for 640 people,[7] was justified with the explanation that "it would be as unworthy for the worship of God to expose the house of worship to the eyes of the crowd as it would be to carefully conceal it from them […],

2
Historischer Lageplan: 1921
Historic site plan: 1921

und das Männergestühl ähnlich einem Kirchenschiff in eine Richtung blickend aufgestellt werden konnte. So schien der sogenannte synagogale Raumkonflikt bezüglich teilweise entgegengesetzter Blickrichtungen bei traditioneller zentraler Anordnung des Almemor inmitten des Gestühls in diesem Raum aufgelöst. Die musikalische Begleitung des Gottesdienstes mittels eines rückwärtig auf einer Empore angeordneten Chores und einer zu diesem Zweck eingebauten Orgel waren aufsehenerregende und sehr umstrittene Neuerungen. Die getrennte Platzierung der Frauen auf einer – wenn auch nunmehr unvergitterten – dreiseitig umlaufenden Empore blieb jedoch weiterhin erhalten.[10]

Die Nutzung des «Zweiten Israelitischen Tempels» durch die jüdische Gemeinde endete bereits 1931[11], wodurch der Tempel – wohl auch durch seine Hinterhoflage – von den Pogromen 1938 verschont blieb. Das Gebäude wurde jedoch bei einem Bombenangriff 1944 bis auf zwei ruinöse Teile zerstört[12] und geriet dann zunehmend in Vergessenheit. Der einstige Standort und Teile der Ruinen wurden zuletzt unter anderem durch eine Autowerkstatt genutzt. Seit 2003 stehen die Gebäudereste unter Denkmalschutz.[13]

Historische Bedeutung hat der Tempel in der Poolstraße insbesondere als erster gebauter Tempel des liberalen Judentums. Die heute weitgehend brachliegenden Ruinen sind die letzten sichtbaren baulichen Überreste jüdischer Geschichte in der Hamburger Innenstadt. Sie werden bei der «Foundation for Jewish Heritage» in London in der insgesamt über 3000 Objekte umfassenden Liste der zwanzig gefährdetsten jüdischen Relikte Europas geführt.

since we attach no importance to the first, and regard the second as unnecessary [...]."[8] Laid out as a basilica with three aisles on a nearly square ground plan, the white-plastered temple, designed by Hinrich Klees-Wülbern, was oriented toward a then contemporary classicism, into which Gothic and Moorish architectural elements were, however, mixed. Jewish symbols appeared on the facade for the first time.[9]

Introduced into the new temple in conformity with the Reform program—and contrasting with more Orthodox predecessors—were a series of programmatic and structural adaptations: positioned immediately in front of the apse and the Aron Hakodesh (Torah Ark) were the pulpit and lectern, so that a central bimah was no longer present, and all of the male pews faced the same direction, as in a church nave. This evidently resolved the so-called synagogal spatial conflict produced by the to some extent opposed viewing directions entailed by the traditional central arrangement of the almemar (or bimah) amidst the pews. Regarded as a sensational and highly controversial reform was the musical accompaniment of the worship service by means of a choir positioned in a rear gallery, along with an organ installed there for this purpose. Preserved, however—although now without any dividing partition—was the separate placement of the women on a continuous three-sided gallery.[10]

The use of the Second Israelite Temple by the Jewish community had terminated in 1931,[11] and the temple was spared the pogroms of 1938—probably due to its rear courtyard situation. Apart from two ruinous sections, the building was however destroyed by an air raid in 1944,[12] and fell increasingly into oblivion. The former location and portions of the ruins have been used, among other things, for an auto repair workshop. The remnants of the building have been under landmarks protection since 2003.[13]

The temple on Poolstraße is historically significant in particular as the first built evidence of liberal Judaism. The ruins, today largely fallow, are the last remaining visible architectural remnants of Jewish history in Hamburg's city center. They were included by the Foundation for Jewish Heritage in London, on its list of more than 3,000 objects, as among the twenty most endangered Jewish relics in Europe.

3
Blick vom Vorhof auf das Portal, Foto: 2021
View of the portal from the forecourt, photo: 2021

4
Blick auf die Überreste der Apsis, Foto: 2021
View of the remains of the apse, photo: 2021

1 Vgl. Aliza Cohen-Mushlin und Harmen H. Thies (Hg.): *Synagogenarchitektur in Deutschland. Dokumentation zur Ausstellung «... und ich wurde ihnen zu einem kleinen Heiligtum ...» – Synagogen in Deutschland,* Petersberg 2008 (Schriftenreihe der Bet Tfila – Forschungsstelle für jüdische Architektur in Europa, Band 5), S. 171.
2 Vgl. Harold Hammer-Schenk: *Synagogen in Deutschland. Geschichte einer Baugattung im 19. und 20. Jahrhundert (1780–1933),* Teil 1, Hamburg 1981 (Hamburger Beiträge zur Geschichte der deutschen Juden, Band VIII), S. 146 f.
3 Vgl. ebd., S. 153, sowie auch: Arno Herzig und Saskia Rohde (Hg.): *Die Juden in Hamburg 1590 bis 1990. Wissenschaftliche Beiträge der Universität Hamburg zu Ausstellung «Vierhundert Jahre Juden in Hamburg»,* Hamburg 1991, S. 149 f.
4 Vgl. ebd., S. 150.
5 Vgl. Harold Hammer-Schenk: *Synagogen in Deutschland,* S. 152.
6 Vgl. ebd., S. 157.
7 Vgl. ebd.
8 Ebd., zitiert nach Kurt Goldenberg: *Der Kultus- und Profanbau der Juden erläutert an Hand von Hamburg-Altona-Wandsbek,* Diss. Dresden o. J. (um 1924), S. 56.
9 Vgl. Arno Herzig und Saskia Rohde (Hg.): *Die Juden in Hamburg 1590 bis 1990,* S. 151.
10 Vgl. ebd., S. 152.
11 Vgl. Aliza Cohen-Mushlin und Harmen H. Thies (Hg.): *Synagogenarchitektur in Deutschland,* S. 172.
12 Vgl. ebd.
13 Denkmalliste der Hansestadt Hamburg nach § 6 Absatz 1 Hamburgisches Denkmalschutzgesetz vom 5. April 2013 (HmbGVBl, S. 142), Stand 28.03.2022, Objekt 13698.

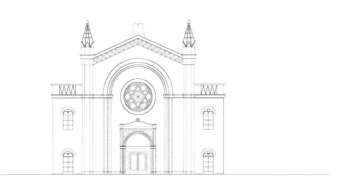
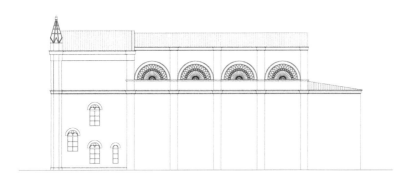
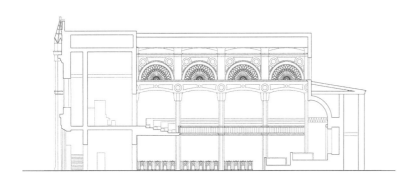
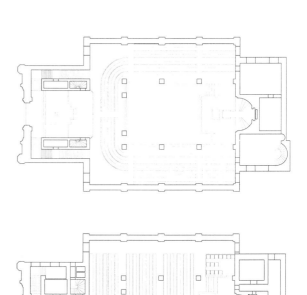

5
Ansicht zum Hof
View toward the courtyard

6
Seitenansicht
Elevation

7
Längsschnitt
Longitudinal section

8
1. Obergeschoss
First floor

9
Erdgeschoss
Ground floor

10
Eröffnungsfeier, Lithografie: um 1844
Opening ceremony, lithograph: ca. 1844

Felix Balling

Bauhaus-Universität Weimar
Prof. Jörg Springer

Durch das Zusammenspiel von bebautem Raum und Freiraum entsteht eine atmosphärische Dichte und dennoch eine selbstverständliche Choreografie, die im Gebetsraum ihren bildmächtigen Höhepunkt findet. Der Blick zum Himmel, zenitales Licht und die besondere, aus Ziegeln gemauerte Kegelform unterstreichen die Entrücktheit dieses Raumes. Durch die Setzung neuer und durch das Einbinden noch bestehender Gebäudeteile wird der frühere Gebetssaal zeichenhaft freigehalten. In der Enge der Hofbebauungen bildet dieser Freiraum als kontemplativer Garten den ideellen Mittelpunkt der Anlage.

Emerging through the interplay between built and open space is an atmospheric density, but also a self-evident choreography that finds its visually powerful high point in the prayer room. The view of the heavens, the zenithal light, and the special conical shape in brick masonry underscore the otherworldliness of the space. Through the introduction of the new and the integration of surviving parts of the building, the original prayer hall is preserved symbolically as an open space. As a contemplative garden, this open space within the narrow courtyard forms the conceptual center of the complex.

1
Lageplan
Site plan

2
Garten mit historischer Wand
Garden with historic wall

—
1:1500

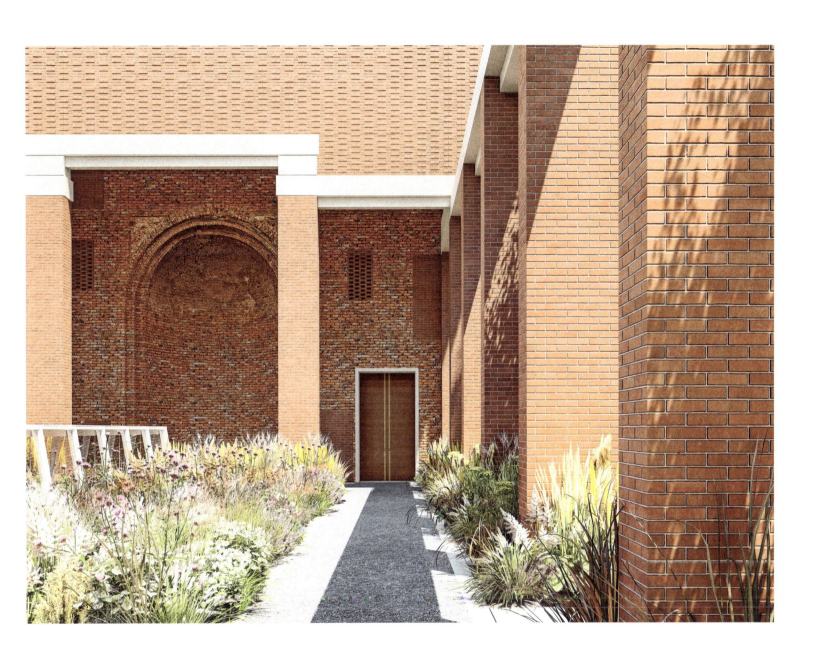

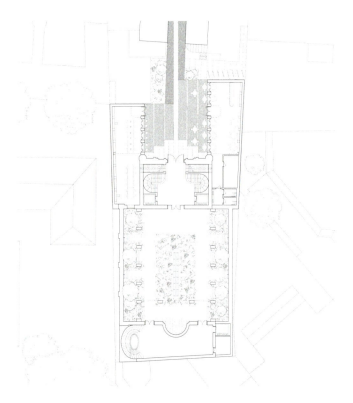

3
Hof mit
umgestalteter
Bestandsfassade
Courtyard with
remodeled
existing facade

4
Erdgeschoss
Ground floor

—
1:1750

5
Querschnitt
Hof
Cross section
through courtyard

6
Querschnitt
mit Salon
Cross section
with salon

7
Salon mit Blick auf
historische Apsis
Salon with view
of historic apse

—
1:750

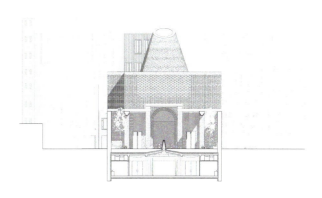

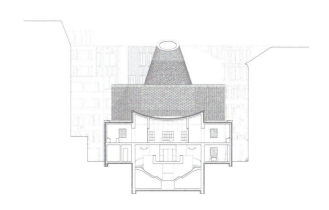

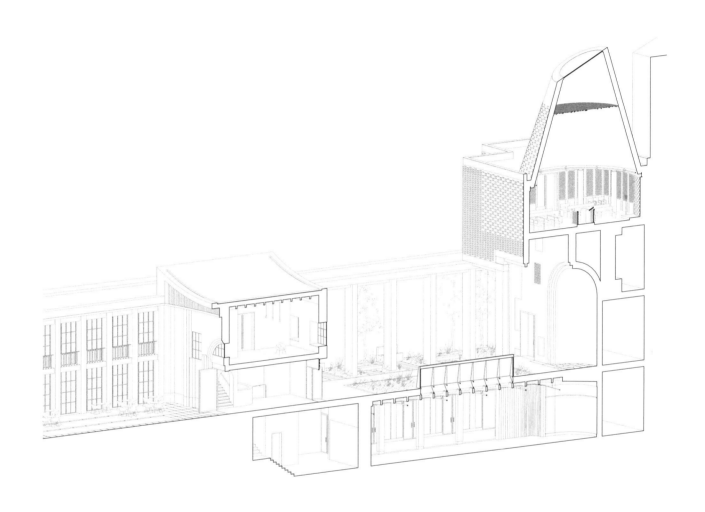

8
Schnitt-
axonometrie
Axonometric
section
—
1:500

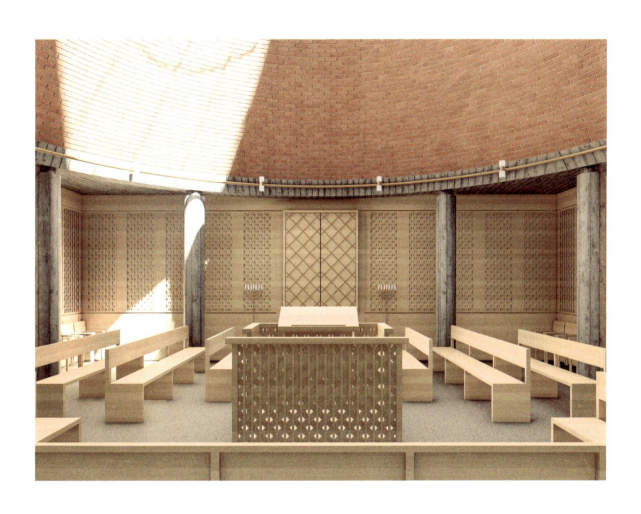

9
Gebetsraum
Prayer room

Velat Bilgili & Max Kreese

Technische Universität Dresden
Prof. Ivan Reimann, Prof. Thomas Müller

Ein komprimierter Baukörper ersetzt den historischen Vorgängerbau und formuliert eine neue Zugangssituation im Hof. Kernidee ist die Freistellung des neuen Gebetsraumes als eigenständigen Baukörper und die Anordnung der weiteren Programmbereiche in einem neuen Kopfbau, der die Ruinenreste des ehemaligen Eingangsgebäudes ersetzt. Ein durchgestecktes, räumlich komplexes Foyer im Neubau erschließt die Gemeinderäume und den Festsaal. Die Überreste der Apsis werden in den neuen Gebetsraum integriert, der von der dreigeschossigen Bibliothek im Norden und einem Hof im Süden eingefasst ist. Eine diffuse Belichtung über den zeltartigen Deckeneinbau bestimmt die Raumatmosphäre des Gebetsraumes. Die lebendige Gestaltung der Westfassade mit kolossalen Arkaden zeugt einerseits von einem neuen Selbstbewusstsein jüdischen Lebens, zugleich tritt sie in Interaktion mit der neogotisch-klassizistischen Formensprache.

The historical predecessor building is replaced by a compact structure that brings about a new entrance arrangement in the courtyard. The core concept is the independence of the prayer room, which now becomes a freestanding building, and the configuration of the other programmatic areas in a building with new frontage that supplants the surviving remnants of the former entrance structure. In the new building, a front-to-back, spatially complex foyer provides access to the community rooms and the banquet hall. The remains of the apse are integrated into the new prayer room, which is framed by the three-story library to the north and a courtyard to the south. The spatial atmosphere of the prayer room is shaped by diffuse lighting that enters via the tent-style ceiling installation. The lively design of the west facade, with its colossal arcades, testifies to a new self-confidence in Jewish life while engaging in dialogue with the neo-Gothic, classicist form language.

1
Lageplan
Site plan

2
Fassade mit
Bestandswand
zum Hof
Facade with
existing wall facing
the courtyard

—
1:1500

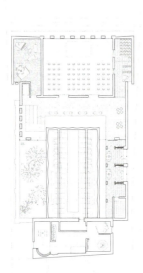

3
Gebetsraum
Prayer room

4
2. Obergeschoss
Second floor

5
Erdgeschoss
Ground floor

—
1:750

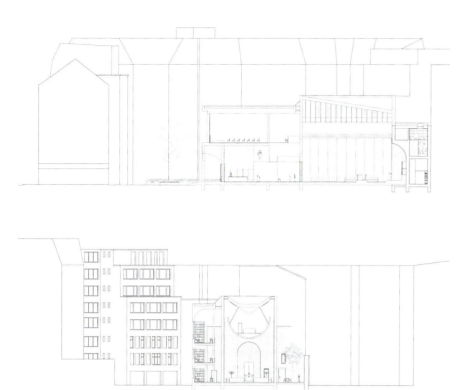

6
Längsschnitt
Longitudinal
section

7
Querschnitt
Cross section

8
Schwellenraum
Threshold space

—
1:750

Arthur Helmecke

Bauhaus-Universität Weimar
Prof. Jörg Springer

Mittels dreier aufgesetzter Laternen aus Weißbeton deutet der Entwurf die baulichen Überreste des Tempels zu einer neuen volumetrischen Komposition um. Die nach außen fensterlosen Laternen überhöhen das Gebäude an seinen Rändern, während sie in ihrer Mitte ein Walmdach verbergen. Wo im Äußeren nur ein Bronzerelief an der Schaufassade zum Hof die Funktion und Bedeutung des Gebäudes baukünstlerisch kommuniziert, wird den Besuchenden im Inneren eine komplexe Sequenz durchgestalteter Räume unterbreitet, die durch Auswölbungen, Treppenschnecken und Lufträume in sich bedingende, voneinander nicht mehr lösbare Beziehung zueinander gesetzt werden. Der Gebetssaal entwickelt sich aus den Überresten der historischen Apsis, ist aber in Geometrie, Raumwirkung und Belichtung neu gedacht. Die aufgesetzten Laternen und die Gauben des unter sich alle Räume vereinenden Walmdachs lassen zenitales Licht diffus durch das ganze Gebäude fallen und verleihen den Räumen ihre sakrale Stimmung. Gekrönt wird die Raumfolge von einem lapidaren Dachboden für informelle Zusammenkünfte. Er verleiht der fein justierten Gestimmtheit des Hauses eine alltägliche Lockerheit.

Surmounted by a trio of white concrete lanterns, the design interprets the structural remnants of the temple to generate a new volumetric composition. Toward the outside, the lanterns are windowless; they elevate the building along the edges while concealing a centrally positioned hip roof. Outside, only a bronze relief on the main facade facing the courtyard conveys the building's function and significance, while entering visitors are presented with a complex sequence of carefully designed rooms, each positioned in relation to the others through convex shapes, spiral shell staircases, and airspaces, so that they become interdependent, mutually inseparable elements. Reconceived in terms of geometry, spatial effect, and illumination, the prayer hall is developed from the remains of the historic apse. The surmounting lanterns and the dormers of the hip roof, which unifies all of the rooms set beneath it, allow zenithal light to diffuse throughout the building, endowing the various spaces with a sacred atmosphere. The spatial sequence is crowned by a lapidary attic level for informal gatherings. This space gives the carefully calibrated mood of the building a casual, everyday feel.

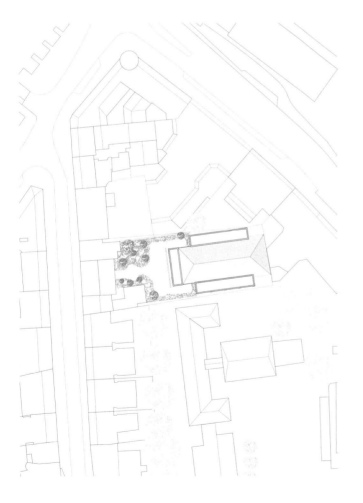

1
Lageplan
Site plan

2
Dachboden
Attic

—
1:1500

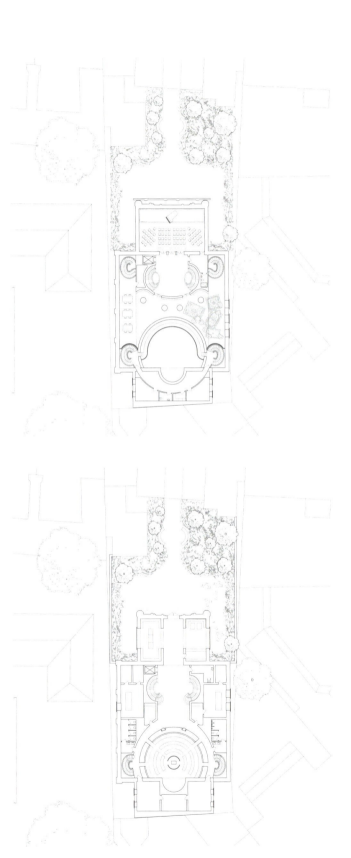

3
Schaufassade
zum Hof
Representative
facade facing
the courtyard

4
1. Obergeschoss
First floor

5
Erdgeschoss
Ground floor

—
1:750

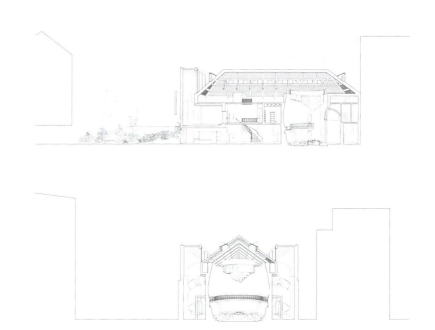

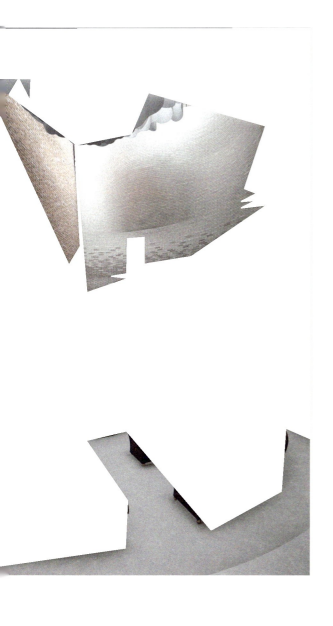

6
Längsschnitt
Longitudinal section

7
Querschnitt
Cross section

8
Gebetsraum
Prayer room

—
1:750

Lea Marzinzik & Leonard Weber

Bauhaus-Universität Weimar
Prof. Jörg Springer

Der Entwurf fügt dem Ort zunächst ein Raster an Stützen hinzu, das sich in seinem Rhythmus an den baulichen Überresten des zerstörten Tempels orientiert. Über das gesamte Grundstück und die Toreinfahrt bis zur Straße gezogen, «trägt» das Raster den Entwurf im wörtlichen Sinne – das eigentliche Gebäude scheint über sich selbst hinaus zu vibrieren. Während im Äußeren eine nüchterne Kubatur und Fassadengestalt die baulichen Überreste in den Vordergrund rücken, wird im Inneren eine unerwartete, eigene Welt erzeugt: Eine von oben belichtete Stahlkonstruktion ist allseitig mit Gussglasplatten bekleidet und bildet den diffus leuchtenden Kern des Gebäudes, dessen Herzstück, mit fast schon barockem Formwillen, der Gebetsraum darstellt. Die erhaltene Apsis mit dem Toraschrein ist das zentrale Element, an dem der Rhythmus der Stützen endet.

To begin with, the design superimposes a grid of supports—which is oriented toward the rhythm and structural remains of the destroyed temple—onto the location. Extending across the entire site and the gated entrance up to the street, the grid "carries" the design in a literal sense: the actual building seems to vibrate beyond its boundaries. While outwardly a sober cubature and facade design shift the architectural remains into the foreground, an autonomous, unexpected world is generated within: a steel construction, illuminated from above, is clad on all sides with cast glass panels, forming the diffusely glowing core of the building, whose centerpiece is the prayer room, which is characterized by an almost baroque formal impulse. The central element is the surviving apse with the Torah shrine; the rhythm of supports terminates here.

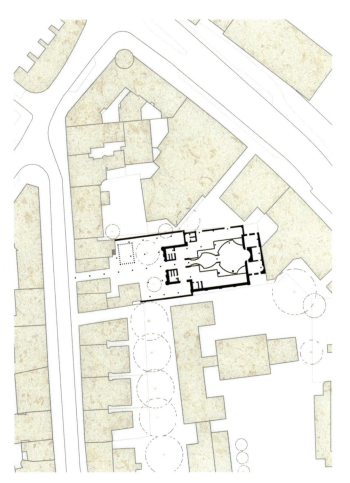

1
Lageplan
Site plan

2
Hof mit
Bestandsfassade
Courtyard with
existing facade

—
1:1500

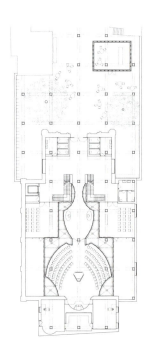
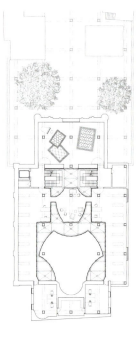

3
Salon

4
Erdgeschoss
Ground floor

5
1. Obergeschoss
First floor

6
2. Obergeschoss
Second floor

—
1:750

7
Längsschnitt
Longitudinal
section

8
Querschnitt
Cross section

9
Ansicht zum Hof
Courtyard view

10
Entrée
Entrance

—
1:750

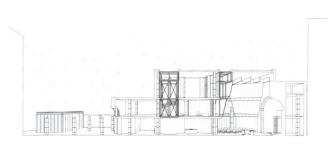

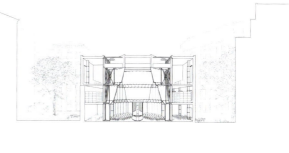

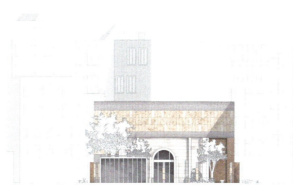

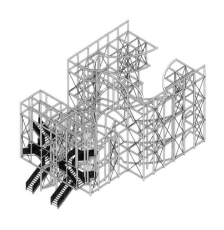
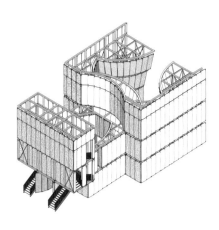
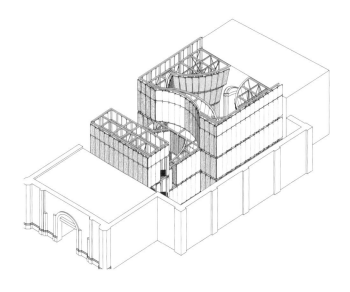

11
Aufbau des
Hauses
Structure of
the building
—
1:750

12
Gebetsraum
Prayer room

Franz-Josef Höing & Philipp Stricharz
im Gespräch mit
in conversation with
Wolfgang Lorch, Ivan Reimann, Jörg Springer & Gesine Weinmiller

Philipp Stricharz hat sich in den ersten Monaten des Streits um den Wiederaufbau der Bornplatzsynagoge sehr engagiert für eine Rekonstruktion ausgesprochen und ist dafür von vielen Seiten angegriffen worden – bis hin zum Vorwurf, die Geschichte ungeschehen machen zu wollen. Gerade weil seine Position für uns nicht die nächstliegende ist, haben uns seine Argumente nachdenklich gemacht. In seiner gut begründeten Haltung erkennen wir auch die grundsätzlichere Frage nach den Grenzen unserer Ausdrucksfähigkeit als Architekten – Anlass und Gegenstand des Synagogen-Projekts. Das Gespräch findet gemeinsam mit Hamburgs Oberbaudirektor Franz-Josef Höing statt. Gut zwei Jahre nach der Entscheidung für den Wiederaufbau und im Wissen um die notwendigen konkreten Weichenstellungen, an denen beide gemeinsam arbeiten, wird der Diskurs differenzierter.

GW Zu Beginn unseres Gesprächs möchte ich uns gerne auf die städtebaulichen Themen, die am Joseph-Carlebach-Platz wichtig sind, einstimmen. Zunächst einmal war interessant, dass – zumindest in Hamburg – alle Studierenden mit der Prämisse angefangen haben, dass der Bunker «gesetzt» ist – und dass er auch nicht abgerissen werden sollte, weil er vor Kurzem erst renoviert wurde. Allerdings haben sie dann im Laufe der Arbeit doch schnell gemerkt, dass es unglaublich schwierig ist, beides, also Synagoge und Bunker, miteinander zu denken – zumal der Bunker [→ Abb. 1] den Nationalsozialisten zur Zementierung der städtebaulichen Situation diente und verhindern sollte, dass an dieser Stelle jemals ein Wiederaufbau der Bornplatzsynagoge stattfinden könnte. Er ist also durchaus als gezielte städtebauliche Aggression zu verstehen. Trotz allem gibt es auch Entwürfe, die den Bunker beibehalten haben: zum einen die Arbeit von Lei Zhang, welche ihn gewissermaßen für die jüdische Gemeinde vereinnahmt und als Sockel für den Neubau benutzt. Im Städtebaulichen sähe es dann so aus, dass das Bodenmosaik sowie die alte stadträumliche Ordnung der Synagoge nicht mehr vorhanden sind und auch nicht an diese erinnert wird. Vielmehr ist der Bunker, der deutlich überformt wird, dann das zentrale Element. In der Arbeit von Ina Lafrentz und Samuel Pahlke zeigt

During the initial months of the controversy concerning the rebuilding of the Bornplatz Synagogue, Philipp Stricharz strongly advocated a historical reconstruction, a position for which he was attacked from various quarters—some going as far as accusing him of attempting to "undo" history. Precisely because this option hardly seemed the obvious choice for us, his arguments gave us pause and prompted us to reflect. His well-reasoned stance also touched upon the fundamental question of the limits of the expressive capacity of architecture—the very occasion and object of the Synagogue Project itself. Also participating in our conversation was Franz-Josef Höing, Hamburg's chief planning officer. A good two years after the decision to rebuild, and in awareness of the specific constraints and priorities shaping the joint work of these two men, the discussion has become more differentiated.

GW To begin with, I'd like to highlight some of the urban planning themes that are important for Joseph-Carlebach-Platz. First of all, it was of interest that—at least in Hamburg—all of the students began with the premise that the bunker is "a given," that it is not to be demolished, having been renovated only recently. As their work progressed, admittedly, they soon realized that it's incredibly difficult to conceive of the two—the synagogue and the bunker—together, particularly since the bunker [→ Fig. 1] allowed the National Socialists to consolidate the urbanistic situation, deliberately frustrating any future attempt to rebuild the Bornplatz Synagogue at this location. It is hence definitely interpretable as a deliberate act of urbanistic aggression. Despite all of this, some of the designs retain the bunker: first, there is the project by Lei Zhang, which in a sense appropriates it for the Jewish community, using it as the pedestal for a new building. In urbanistic terms, it would bring about a situation where the pavement mosaic as well as the earlier urbanistic arrangement of the synagogue would simply cease to exist, nor would their memory be perpetuated. The project by Ina Lafrentz and Samuel Pahlke is based on a very similar approach [→ Fig. 2]. These are the only two designs, however, that worked with the bunker as an element of the existing architectural

sich eine ganz ähnliche Herangehensweise [→ Abb. 2]. Allerdings sind das auch die beiden einzigen Entwürfe, die überhaupt mit dem Bunker als Bestand gearbeitet haben – daher meine Frage an Sie: Wie stehen Sie eigentlich zu dem Bunker?

Man muss sich die Freiheit nehmen, den Bunker auch wegzudenken

FJH Ich denke, dass man sich gerade an der Hochschule alle Freiheiten nehmen und jede Art von Entwurfsübung auch dazu benutzen sollte, einmal auszuloten, was alles gehen würde. Man muss also nicht sklavisch am Bunker festhalten, nur weil er gerade frisch gestrichen ist oder weil der Denkmalschutz der Meinung war, dass man ihn unter Schutz stellen sollte. Die eigentliche Aufgabe handelt ja davon, der Frage nachzugehen, wie sich so ein Neubau einer Synagoge in den Stadtraum einfügen und als Mehrwert dieses Quartier beleben kann? Insofern stellt sich für mich gar nicht so sehr die Frage «Bleibt der Bunker stehen oder nicht?», sondern eher «Wie viele Freiheiten nimmt man sich, um das dortige Potenzial wachzurütteln?». Auch beim Allende-Platz, der zwar im Moment mit spärlichen Mitteln vom Bezirk hergerichtet wird, hat man aktuell nicht unbedingt das Gefühl, dass er immer so bleiben müsste – dort schlummern ebenso Potenziale. Man sollte also nicht nur über eine Architektur nachdenken, die mal geometrischer oder mal ein bisschen freier ist, sondern sich auch fragen: Was ist das für ein Projekt und welche Bestandteile muss es haben, damit es eine Art Transmissionsriemen für die Stadtentwicklung ist? Also muss man sich auch die Freiheit nehmen, über diesen Bunker nachzudenken – und ihn auch wegzudenken, wenn man mit einem starken Konzept nachweisen kann, dass das einen Mehrwert erzeugt. Aber den Bunker mit ein paar Blumen an der Fassade zu dekorieren, wie in einem der Entwürfe vorgeschlagen, überzeugt mich nicht.

PS Also ich finde die Entwürfe interessant, und es ist auch erfrischend, Varianten zu sehen, die wir in dieser Form nicht überlegt haben und auch nicht überlegt hätten. Mir fällt allerdings zu den beiden Projekten ganz banal ein: Wenn man die Synagoge auf den Bunker setzt, wie kommt man eigentlich in den Betsaal, der dann im letzten Geschoss des Gebäudes liegt? Man weiß ja, dass am Schabbat Technik für uns Tabu ist, insofern wäre das ein rein praktisches Erschließungsproblem. Zwar kann man über solche Dinge wie den sogenannten «Schabbat-Fahrstuhl» nachdenken, der bestimmt in Ihren Gesprächen auch eine Rolle spielte. Aber auch diese Variante wäre schon nicht mehr für alle verträglich, einige würden solch eine Notlösung nicht benutzen wollen. Abgesehen davon ist der Bunker, so wie er jetzt am Joseph-Carlebach-Platz steht, natürlich ein städtebaulicher Gewaltakt. Auch wenn wir in der heutigen Runde nicht über Politik reden wollen, so liegt sie doch bei allen Aspekten dieses Projekts immer auch mit auf der Hand. Bei diesen beiden Entwürfen waren es zum Beispiel sicherlich der Wunsch und die Aussage: Man zeigt es den Nationalsozialisten noch einmal

inventory. Hence my question to all of you: what is your attitude toward the bunker?

You need to take the freedom to simply remove the bunker

FJH I believe that, especially in the university context, there should be total freedom, and that every type of design exercise should be employed in order to explore the realm of the possible. There is no need to adhere slavishly to the bunker, simply because it was just freshly painted, or because the authorities responsible for historic preservation adopted the view that it should be placed under protection. The actual task here is to investigate the question: how could a new synagogue building be integrated into the urban environment, and how could it moreover enliven the surrounding district as an added value? So for me, the question isn't really: "Should the bunker remain or not?," and is instead: "How much freedom should be taken in order to activate the potential that exists there?" At Allende-Platz as well, which is currently being refurbished by the district with meager resources, you don't really have the feeling that things need to stay like that forever—a certain potential is slumbering there as well. We need to think not just about a certain type of architecture, whether it should be geometric or perhaps a bit freer, but to also consider the question: what kind of project is this, and which components should it have if it is to serve as a kind of transmission belt for urban development? Which also means the freedom to consider the bunker—and to simply remove it, provided you can demonstrate a powerful concept that generates added value through its elimination. But to simply decorate the bunker by adding a few flowers to the facade, as proposed by one design, doesn't convince me.

PS Well, I find the designs interesting, and it's refreshing to see variants that we never considered in this form, and would not in fact have considered. The prosaic thought that occurs to me concerning the bunker is: if you set the synagogue on top of the bunker, how would you enter the prayer hall, which would then occupy the uppermost story of the building? On Shabbat, as you know, technology is taboo for us, so there's a purely practical problem of access. In such situations, of course, you could consider the so-called "Shabbat elevator," which must have played a role in your

1
Ehemaliger Bunker am Joseph-Carlebach-Platz, Hamburg, Foto: 2012
Former bunker on Joseph-Carlebach-Platz in Hamburg, photo: 2012

hinterher. Der Bunker ist jetzt eine Synagoge und sieht auch aus wie eine solche! Zumal der zweite Entwurf auch eine Kuppel vorsieht und von der Anmutung durchaus an die ehemalige Bornplatzsynagoge erinnert. Interessanterweise kann man alle diese Erwägungen aber auch immer in ihr Gegenteil verkehren: Denn auf der anderen Seite wären solche Entwürfe ja auch gleichzeitig eine weitere Manifestierung des Bunkers. Ich meine, auch wenn man ihn in diesen Arbeiten umbaut, wäre er als solches damit für die nächsten Jahrzehnte existent und endgültig gesetzt. Das war es, was mir durch den Kopf ging.

Sollen die Bedingungen für einen Wiederaufbau von einem architektonischen Gewaltakt diktiert werden?

IR Aus meiner Sicht ist die Frage nach dem Umgang mit dem Bunker auch keine, die man aus einer rein städtebaulichen Perspektive entscheiden sollte. Man muss hier vielmehr überlegen, ob man sich die Bedingungen für den Wiederaufbau der Synagoge von einem architektonischen Gewaltakt diktieren lassen sollte, der dazu bestimmt war, einen ebensolchen Wiederaufbau für alle Zeit zu verhindern. Daher ist es auch keine politische Problematik im Sinne der Tagespolitik. Es ist eher eine Entscheidung, ob und wie man diesen Teil der Geschichte für die weitere Entwicklung des jüdischen Lebens an diesem Standort akzeptieren will – oder inwieweit es notwendig ist, hier eine Tabula rasa zu machen.

JS Wir fokussieren alle immer sehr stark auf den Bunker, eben weil er diese gewaltsame Setzung war. Aber sobald wir ihn einmal wegdenken, gerät ebenso in den Blick, dass künftig auch die Bauten der Universität, die dort in gepflegter Ignoranz errichtet wurden, die Wirkung der Bornplatzsynagoge im Stadtraum beeinträchtigen werden – und das in gravierendem Ausmaß. Das heißt: Wenn man die Präsenz der Bornplatzsynagoge an diesem Ort in der Stadt wieder erreichen möchte, wird man mit Blick auf den Stadtraum über mehr als nur den Bunker nachdenken müssen. Das ist jedoch eine Erkenntnis, die man erst dann erlangt, wenn man für diesen Ort zu entwerfen beginnt – weshalb sie auch in der allgemeinen und öffentlichen Diskussion bisher keine Rolle spielte.

FJH Ja, aber das ist keine neue Erkenntnis – und keine, aus der man automatisch folgern muss, dass man auch noch Hand an die Gebäude der Universität legen müsste. Es ist eher die Frage, mit welcher Kraft man dort eine neue Synagoge denkt und wo sie positioniert ist, welches Volumen sie einnimmt und welche Form sie hat. Es mag ja sein, dass sich die Hochschule gegenüber diesem Raum ein bisschen ignorant verhält, aber die nötige Prägnanz bekommt man mit einem Entwurf schon hin.

WL Allerdings muss man sich bei der Betrachtung der städtebaulichen Situation auch immer im Klaren sein, dass nicht nur die Hochbauten nicht mehr existent sind, sondern dass auch der damalige Stadtgrundriss nicht mehr gegeben ist. Das heißt, diese Extrapositionierung, welche die Bornplatzsynagoge dort einmal einnehmen

conversations. But even this variant wouldn't be acceptable to everyone—some people would decline to use such an expedient. Apart from that, the bunker, as it now stands on Joseph-Carlebach-Platz, is of course an act of urbanistic violence. And although we weren't planning to talk about politics in today's panel, it nonetheless touches, always, on all aspects of this project. With both of these designs, for example, you clearly encounter a desire and the message: let's show the National Socialists once again, after-the-fact. Now, the bunker is a synagogue, and looks like one too! Especially since the second design includes a cupola, and the impression it makes is quite reminiscent of the former Bornplatz Synagogue. Interestingly, it's also possible to reverse all of these considerations into their contraries: on the other side, such designs would also be a further manifestation of the bunker. What I mean is, even though it is modified in these designs, it would nonetheless exist during the coming decades, acquiring a certain permanence. These are some of the things that went through my mind.

Should the conditions for a reconstruction be dictated by an act of architectural violence?

IR From my perspective, the question of how to deal with the bunker is not something that can be decided from a purely urbanistic perspective. Instead, you need to ask yourself whether you're going to allow the conditions for the reconstruction of the synagogue to be dictated by an act of architectural violence, one that was intended to interfere precisely with such a reconstruction for the foreseeable future. Which is also why this is not a political issue in the sense of day-to-day politics. It's instead a question of deciding whether and how this part of history is going to be accepted for the further development of Jewish life at this location—or whether it's necessary instead to begin with a tabula rasa.

JS We're all still focusing quite insistently on the bunker, precisely because its placement was such an act of violence. But as soon as we think it away, we realize that in the future, the university buildings too, all of them erected in a kind of studied ignorance, will interfere with the impact of the Bornplatz Synagogue on the surrounding urban space—and moreover severely. Which means: if the former presence of the synagogue is to be recreated in this spot in the city, then with regard to

2
Entwurf Neue Synagoge Bornplatz, Hamburg
Design for the new synagogue, Bornplatz, Hamburg
—
Ina Lafrentz & Samuel Pahlke
2021

konnte und eingenommen hat, ist in dieser Form nicht mehr möglich, da schlichtweg die räumliche Disposition an dieser Stelle nicht mehr dieselbe ist [→ Abb. 3].

GW Genau diese Frage nach dem verlorengegangenen Stadtgrundriss und einer möglichen Interpretation desselben verhandelt vor allem die Arbeit von Clara Poursedighi sehr schön [→ S.194–197]. Der Entwurf arbeitet mit dem Bodenmosaik als Innenhof, welches als Abbild der Leere beibehalten wird, wo einst die Synagoge stand – und rundherum entwickelt sich wieder ein Ensemble des jüdischen Lebens. Was halten Sie davon?

FJH Ich glaube, dieser Ansatz kann eine Denkrichtung sein. Also zu sagen, man lässt die Mitte frei, respektiert das Mosaik und entwickelt drumherum ein kleines Quartier. Ob das jetzt schon formal richtig gut gemacht ist, ist eine andere Frage. Im Moment hat die Anordnung der Baukörper noch etwas Angestrengtes – auch mit dieser quadratischen Fläche, an der die ebenfalls quadratische Synagoge dransitzt. Ich würde nicht sagen, dass mich das betört. Aber die Mitte freizulassen und daraus dann etwas zu machen mit einer ganz anderen Bedeutung, finde ich als Grundidee und Entwurfsansatz auch nicht uninteressant.

Diskutiert man abstrakt über Städtebau oder über die Zeichen, die man mit diesem Projekt setzt?

PS Für mich stellt sich hierbei immer ganz grundsätzlich die Frage: Diskutiert man abstrakt über Städtebau, also losgelöst vom spezifischen Ort und von den Zeichen, die man mit diesem Projekt setzt – oder führt man die Diskussion mit dem Ziel der Zusammenführung der politischen, gedenkpolitischen, aber auch zukunftsorientierten Aspekte? Der Entwurf, den wir gerade gesehen haben, ist meiner Meinung nach eine Arbeit, die sehr stark die Leerstelle mit dem Bodenmosaik zelebriert und in den Mittelpunkt stellt. Was mir bei solchen Ansätzen immer etwas zu kurz kommt, ist der Gedanke: Was löst eigentlich so ein Gebäude nicht nur in der Stadtbevölkerung aus – hier läge der Schwerpunkt auf der Gedenkpolitik –, und insbesondere: Was löst dieses Zeichen, das man dort setzt, bei einem jüdischen Kind aus, das nebenan in die Schule geht? Was sich vielleicht auch schon fragt, ob es später selbst mit seiner Familie in Hamburg leben möchte. So ein Entwurf, der sich hier meiner Meinung nach eher wie eine Gedenkstätte darstellt, ist weniger das Zeichen: Hier ist der Ort deiner Zukunft und der Zukunft deiner Kinder und Enkelkinder. Er vermittelt eher die Aussage: Du bist hier an einem Ort, der vielen Jüdinnen und Juden das Leben gekostet hat, überlege es dir gut.

GW Erinnerung und Zeichenhaftigkeit sind gute Stichworte, die uns direkt zu einer Frage, die Jörg Springer kürzlich aufgebracht hat, führen – nämlich, ob ein Neu- oder Wiederaufbau der Bornplatzsynagoge eigentlich ohne die direkten Bezüge zur Shoah denkbar ist. Also: Ist es möglich, das Weiterleben der nächsten Generationen nicht nur unter dem Diktum der Shoah zu sehen? Und: Wie kann die neue Synagoge dazu einen Beitrag leisten?

the urban environment, we will need to reconsider more than the bunker itself. This realization arrives, however, only when you begin to create a design for this location—which is why it has played no role in general and public discussions to date.

FJH Yes, but that's not a new realization—nor does it automatically lead to the conclusion that you'd need to interfere with the university buildings. It is instead a question of the force with which the new synagogue is conceived, where it's positioned, which volumes it occupies, and what form it takes. It may indeed be that the university behaves with a degree of ignorance in relation to this space, but the necessary incisiveness can nonetheless be achieved through the design.

WL When considering the urbanistic situation, however, it's important to be clear about the fact that not only do the high-rise buildings no longer exist, but the former urban layout is no longer present either. Which means that the extraposition formerly occupied by the Bornplatz Synagogue is no longer possible in this form, given that the spatial disposition of the site is simply no longer what it was [→ Fig. 3].

GW Precisely this question of the now-vanished urban layout and a possible interpretation of it is dealt with very beautifully in particular in the project by Clara Poursedighi [→ pp.194–197]. Her design works with the pavement mosaic as an inner courtyard, which hence maintains an image of the empty space where the synagogue once stood—developed around it, once again, is an ensemble for Jewish life. What do you think of it?

FJH I think this approach is a possible line of thought. Which is to say, the center is left free, the mosaic is respected, and a little quarter is developed around it. Whether it's done well in formal terms is a different question. At the moment, the configuration of the building still seems somehow strained—also with a square surface, upon which an equally square synagogue sits. I wouldn't say I find it captivating. But as a basic idea, as a design approach, leaving the center free and creating something around it with a very different meaning, could certainly be interesting.

Do we discuss urban planning abstractly, or instead talk about the signal the project strives to send?

PS For me, this poses the fundamental question: should we be discussing urban planning in abstract terms, which is to say, detached from the specific location and from the signal to be given by the project—or should the discussion strive to integrate the political and the commemorative, but also future-oriented aspects? In my view, the design we have just seen strongly celebrates the empty space marked out by the floor mosaic, positioning it at the center. For me, what always falls short with such approaches is the idea: what does such a building trigger, and not just in the urban population? Here, the emphasis would be on a politics of commemoration. And in particular: what does the

Wir haben nicht die Aufgabe, der ganzen Stadt als Platzhalter für das Bedürfnis nach Schuldbewältigung zu dienen

PS Ich finde, das sind ganz wichtige Themen, die auch die aktuelle Diskussion um die Rekonstruktion stark geprägt haben. Hier stellen sich dann vor allem die Fragen: Hängt die Erinnerung an die Shoah an diesem Ort, an der Bornplatzsynagoge? Und: Ist der Ort, der den Juden weggenommen wurde und bis heute von den Naziverbrechen geprägt ist, überhaupt der adäquate Platz dafür? Dazu kann ich Ihnen als Anekdote ein Beispiel geben: Wir haben im Foyer der Talmud-Tora-Schule an der Decke ein Kunstwerk aus Scherben, das uns einmal zugedacht wurde und die ermordeten Kinder, die dort zur Schule gingen, symbolisieren soll. Das heißt: Alle Schülerinnen und Schüler gehen morgens zuallererst unter diesem Mahnmal hindurch. Jetzt stellen Sie sich einmal vor, Ihr sechs, sieben Jahre altes Kind fragt: Was ist eigentlich mit diesen Scherben dort oben an der Decke? Was soll man darauf antworten? Niemand würde so etwas seinen Kindern jeden Tag zumuten wollen – bei uns wird es völlig selbstverständlich und als wohlmeinendes Geschenk angesehen! Dasselbe gilt auch für den Joseph-Carlebach-Platz. Es ist ein Platz, der uns weggenommen wurde. Wir haben nicht die Aufgabe, der ganzen Stadt als Platzhalter für das Bedürfnis nach Schuldbewältigung zu dienen. Auf der anderen Seite haben wir natürlich ein eigenes Bedürfnis, unserer ermordeten Familien zu gedenken – was allerdings ganz erheblich gestört wird, weil von außen sehr stark versucht wird, uns vorzuschreiben, wie so ein Gedenken auszusehen habe. Aber eines kann ich sagen: Auf keinen Fall darf dieser Ort eine Shoah-Gedenkstätte werden – er muss ein Ort des Lebens und der Zukunft sein. Ein Ort, an dem auf keinen Fall die Verbrechen vertuscht und überschrieben werden – im Gegenteil: Wir bauen die Bornplatzsynagoge ja deswegen wieder auf. Man wird ja allein aufgrund der Universitätsgebäude und des Stadtgrundrisses immer sehen, dass es nicht mehr das ist, was es einmal war. Aber wir bauen hier

signal being sent here trigger in a Jewish child who goes to school next door? Who may already be asking him or herself whether he or she wants to live in Hamburg later with his or her own family. Such a design, which, in my opinion, takes the form of a kind of memorial, fails to say: "This should be a place for your future and the future of your children and grandchildren." Instead, it conveys the message: "You find yourself in a place where many Jews lost their lives, so you need to ponder that carefully."

GW Memory and symbolism are good keywords that bring us directly to a question raised recently by Jörg Springer, namely whether a new or reconstructed building for the Bornplatz Synagogue is conceivable without a direct reference to the Shoah. Which is to say: is it possible to avoid seeing the continued existence of the coming generations under the dictum of the Shoah? And how can the new synagogue make a contribution here?

It is not our task to serve the entire city as a placeholder for the need to come to terms with guilt

PS I believe these are very important topics, which have also strongly shaped current discussions about reconstruction. This raises, in particular, the question: is the memory of the Shoah connected to this location, to the Bornplatz Synagogue? And: is this place, which was taken away from the Jews, and is still characterized by Nazi crimes up to the present, really the adequate place for it? I offer the following anecdote as an example. Suspended on the ceiling in the foyer of the Talmud Torah School is a work of art consisting of shards: it was intended for us, and is designed to symbolize the murdered children who once went to school here. Which means: all of the students start the day by passing beneath this memorial. Now, just imagine your six- or seven-year-old child asking you: what are they all about, these shards on the ceiling? What is your answer? No one would want to inflict this on their own children every day—with us, it's simply taken for granted, and regarded as a well-intended gift! The same thing is true for Joseph-Carlebach-Platz. This place was taken from us. It's not our task to serve the entire city as a placeholder for the need to come to terms with guilt. On the other hand, of course, we need to commemorate our murdered families—which is, however, somewhat disrupted, since there are aggressive attempts from the outside to dictate to us how such a remembrance should take place. But I will say one thing: this place simply can't be allowed to become a Shoah memorial— it needs to be a place for life and for the future. A place where this crime should by no means be concealed or overwritten—on the contrary: that's precisely why we're rebuilding the Bornplatz Synagogue. Simply by virtue of the university buildings and the urban layout, you will always see that it's no longer what it once was. But we're not constructing a memorial to the Shoah here, something the city has perhaps long needed at a different location—that's simply not the aim of this undertaking as a whole.

3
Blick vom Bornplatz, Hamburg, Foto: um 1914
View from Bornplatz, photo: ca. 1914

keine Gedenkstätte für die Shoah, welche die Stadt vielleicht an anderer Stelle schon längst gebraucht hätte – das ist nicht das Ziel dieses ganzen Vorhabens.

JS Das ist ein guter Anknüpfungspunkt: Herr Stricharz, Sie selbst haben diese Argumentation auch bereits in der öffentlichen Diskussion gebraucht, als Sie sich gegen den Vorwurf gewandt haben, ein Wiederaufbau der Synagoge würde Geschichte verfälschen. Ich meine, dem ist wenig entgegenzusetzen – also, wenn Sie sagen, die Erinnerung an die Zerstörung ist eine Aufgabe der nicht-jüdischen Gesellschaft und keine Aufgabe der jüdischen Gemeinde und insofern auch nicht Gegenstand dieses Projektes. Allein der Vorwurf, eine jüdische Gemeinde könnte hier die Geschichte vergessen, ist schlichtweg grotesk und beinahe karikaturhaft. Aber dieser Gedankengang hin zur gezielten Entscheidung für eine Rekonstruktion hat mich auch als Architekt fasziniert. Wir sind ja gegenüber Wiederaufbauten immer relativ skeptisch, ob sie auch wirklich adäquate Lösungen darstellen können. Daher hat mich hier vor allem der explizite Wunsch interessiert, die historische Bornplatzsynagoge tatsächlich so, wie sie einmal war, wiederaufzubauen. Das ist ein Gedanke, der in der deutschen Nachkriegsgeschichte beinahe einzigartig wäre. Wobei allein die Aussage «Ja, wir als Gemeinde können uns heute vorstellen, die alte Synagoge tatsächlich als mögliche und richtige Antwort wiederaufzubauen» an sich bereits zeichenhaft ist. Daher: Was sind für Sie die Beweggründe und Bezugspunkte aus der Gemeinde heraus, die diese Überlegung tragen?

Wir möchten schlichtweg die Freiheit haben, unsere Synagoge auch als Rekonstruktion zu denken

PS Es ist zunächst einmal so, dass wir als Gemeinde uns immer ausbedungen haben, dass es kein Denkverbot gegenüber einer Rekonstruktion geben darf. Zumal auch bislang niemand stichhaltig begründen konnte, warum so etwas nicht gehen soll. Allein in den 1950er-Jahren wurden so viele andere historische Gebäude mit einer großen Selbstverständlichkeit rekonstruiert, ohne dass man dabei, schon aus rein zeitlichen Aspekten, überhaupt in die Nähe einer Wiederaufbaudebatte gekommen wäre. Wir möchten also schlichtweg die Freiheit haben, unsere Synagoge, die uns weggenommen und auch nicht wiederaufgebaut wurde, auch als Rekonstruktion zu denken. Ich kann jetzt die vielfältigen Meinungen nur sehr subjektiv wiedergeben, aber in unserer Gemeinde sieht man die Synagoge ebenso als stolzes Zeichen und auch als einen Teil des gefühlten Zwillingsensembles zusammen mit der Talmud-Tora-Schule [→ Abb. 4]. Zumal die Schule auch ein Projekt ist, das uns überaus stolz macht. Hier haben wir es – ich sage es jetzt einmal sehr plakativ – in diesem alten Gebäude geschafft, die Nazis zu überwinden: Wir sind wieder dort und man hört wieder jüdische Kinder spielen und toben. Allein schon der akustische Eindruck ist für mich jedes Mal ein wahnsinniges Glücksgefühl – vor allem, weil dort vor 20 Jahren noch Stille war! Nebenan am Joseph-Carlebach-Platz haben wir dagegen die Leerstelle. Bei jedem Vorbeigehen springt uns dort der

JS That's a good point of connection: Herr Stricharz, you've already had recourse in public discussions to this argument when resisting the objection that a reconstruction of the synagogue would falsify history. I mean, there isn't much to say in opposition to it—to you saying that to commemorate this destruction is a task for non-Jewish society, not a task for the Jewish community, and to this extent, not an aspect of this project. The very notion, the rebuke, that the Jewish community could forget the history of this place is simply grotesque, almost a caricature. But as an architect, the way this train of thought leads toward a decision for a reconstruction fascinates me. We're always somewhat skeptical of reconstructions, we tend to doubt that they can represent genuinely adequate solutions. Which is why I found the explicit desire to reconstruct the Bornplatz Synagogue in its original form to be so interesting. This is an idea that is virtually unique within German postwar history. The very statement, "Yes, we as a community can conceive of rebuilding the old synagogue as a possible and correct solution," is already emblematic. Hence my question: from your point of view, what are the motivations and points of reference emerging from within the community that support consideration of this idea?

We simply want the freedom to imagine our synagogue as a reconstruction

PS As a community, to begin with, we've always agreed that there can't be any taboo against the idea of a historical reconstruction. Especially since, to date, no one has provided us with cogent reasons why it isn't a viable approach. During the 1950s alone, many historic buildings were reconstructed faithfully simply as a matter of course, as though it were perfectly natural, without anything even remotely resembling a debate about reconstructions arising, if only for chronological reasons. We simply want the freedom to imagine our synagogue—which was taken from us, and has never been rebuilt—as a reconstruction as well. I can only characterize the diverse points of view in a very subjective way, but in our community, the synagogue is seen as a proud symbol, but also perceived as a twin forming an ensemble together with the Talmud Torah School [→ Fig. 4]. Particularly since the school is also a project of which we are extremely proud. Here, in this building, we have succeeded—to state it rather audaciously—in overcoming the Nazis: we are here once again, and you can hear Jewish children playing and romping. For me, the acoustic impression alone is a source of tremendous feelings of joy every time—all the more so since it was still quiet there just twenty years ago! Next door, on Joseph-Carlebach-Platz, in contrast, we have this blank space. And every time you walk by, the bunker catches your eye—yet we all know what could stand there, what could belong to the Talmud Torah School, characterizing the townscape again in a completely self-evident way. Not for nothing has this building been depicted for many years now on the Torah cabinet in the Hohe Weide Synagogue. We see this image again and again, it sits before our eyes every day. This yearning to be a

Bunker ins Auge – aber wir wissen, was dort stehen könnte, was dort eigentlich zur Talmud-Tora-Schule gehören würde und auch einmal ganz selbstverständlich das Stadtbild prägte. Nicht umsonst ist dieses Gebäude seit vielen Jahren in der Synagoge Hohe Weide auf dem Tora-Schrank abgebildet. Wir sehen dieses Bild also immer wieder, wir haben es jeden Tag vor Augen. Diese Sehnsucht, gesellschaftlich sowie auch mit einem eigenen Gebäude wieder ein Teil der Stadtmitte zu sein, wieder normal zu sein und auch einmal mit einer Kippa auf die Straße zu gehen, ohne dass sich alle umdrehen – das alles ist in diesem Bild der Bornplatzsynagoge kumuliert. Ich glaube, all diese Sehnsüchte und dieses Verlangen nach Normalität spiegeln sich auch in dem Wunsch nach Rekonstruktion wider. Natürlich spielt auch der Fakt eine Rolle, dass man nach dem Krieg ganz gezielt hintertrieben hatte, dieses Areal wieder in jüdische Hände zu übertragen und auch die Synagoge wiederaufzubauen. All das drückt sich in diesem Wunsch nach einem Wiederaufbau aus. Es ist aber keineswegs so, dass in unseren Gesprächen, die wir im Rahmen der Machbarkeitsstudie sehr intensiv führen und auch vorher geführt haben, diese Rekonstruktion unser eiserner Wunsch ist und alle, die dem etwas entgegensetzen, «böse» sind. Im Gegenteil: Die Rekonstruktion ist eine Variante, mit der wir uns gegen Denkverbote wehren, aber es stehen durchaus viele Dinge im Raum, die sich immer weiter weg von der Vollrekonstruktion bewegen – zumal eine solche aus verschiedenen, vor allem praktischen Erwägungen heraus wenig Sinn machen würde. Es wird von «Durchschimmern» gesprochen oder vom Wiederaufbau als klar abzugrenzendem Begriff. Da gibt es also eine große Bandbreite.

JS Wenn ich dazu als Randbemerkung ergänzen darf: Auch unsere Projekte sehen bislang ausschließlich Neubauten vor. Mit dieser Prämisse sind wir einmal gestartet, was vielleicht auch mit unserer fachlichen Disposition zu tun hat. Allerdings schaut man sich das Ganze am Ende so an und muss feststellen, dass der Wiederaufbau eigentlich der «Elefant im Raum» und die große Lücke ist. Daher arbeiten wir zurzeit mit einer sehr kleinen Gruppe von Studierenden in Weimar an einem Projekt, in dem der Wiederaufbau der historischen Synagoge gesetzter Ausgangspunkt der Entwürfe ist [→ S. 212–215].

PS Darauf bin ich gespannt.

FJH Herr Springer, Sie haben gesagt, dass jetzt ein Entwurfsprojekt zur Rekonstruktion realisiert wird, nachdem Sie diese Variante bislang immer ausgeschlossen hatten. Aber warum haben Sie das denn nicht jetzt schon offensiv als Aufgabe gestellt? Genau das interessiert uns ja: Existiert so eine dritte Variante – also gibt es so eine Art Rekonstruktion und ist es trotzdem etwas Neues? Dazu hätte man sich ja auch von den Studierenden anregen lassen, was das hätte sein können.

part of the city center again, socially, as well as with our own building, to be normal again, to walk down the street wearing a kippah again without everyone turning around to look—all of these things are aggregated in this image of the Bornplatz Synagogue. I believe that all of these yearnings, all of these aspirations toward normality, are mirrored as well in the desire for a reconstruction. Playing a role as well, of course, is the fact that, after the war, attempts to return the site to Jewish hands, and to rebuild the synagogue, were deliberately thwarted. All of these things are expressed in the desire for a reconstruction. But it's by no means the case that in our discussions, which we have conducted very intensively in the framework of feasibility studies, and conducted earlier as well, that we're absolutely determined to have a reconstruction, and that everything opposed to it is seen as "bad." On the contrary: a reconstruction is one variant with which we defend ourselves against thought taboos, but there are certainly many ideas in the room that move further and further away from the idea of a full reconstruction—especially since, for various reasons, mainly practical ones, it wouldn't really make much sense. There is talk of a "shining through" of the former synagogue, or instead of a historical reconstruction as a clearly defined concept. So there's a wide spectrum.

JS If I could just add something as a marginal note: up to this point, our projects, too, have involved new buildings exclusively. This premise was our point of departure, which may have something to do with our professional disposition. Nonetheless, when you consider the issue as a whole, you have to concede, finally, that a reconstruction is, so to speak, the "elephant in the room," that it represents an enormous gap. Which is why we are currently working on a project in Weimar with a small group of students for which the reconstruction of historic synagogues serves as the point of departure for their designs [→ pp. 212–215].

PS I look forward to it.

FJH Herr Springer, you say that now a design project devoted to reconstructions is being conducted, although this variant has been consistently excluded up to this point. But why didn't you set this as a task quite explicitly at the outset? That's exactly what we are interested in: does a third variant exist—which is to say, is there a type of reconstruction that nonetheless involves something new? Here, too, you might have encouraged the students to speculate about how that might look.

The aspiration for a symbolic presence in the city is something new

JS To respond to the question that was addressed to me directly: expressed in the desire to reconstruct the Bornplatz Synagogue is mainly an explicit interest in the symbolic value of this building within the city [→ Fig. 5]. Up to now, such an aspiration has not arisen in this form with regard to other planned synagogue reconstructions. What interests us here is the question of whether

Das Zeichenhafte in der Stadt ist ein neuer Anspruch

JS Um die direkte Frage an mich zu beantworten: In dem Wunsch, die Bornplatzsynagoge zu rekonstruieren, kommt ja vor allem auch ein explizites Interesse an der Zeichenhaftigkeit dieses Bauwerks in der Stadt zum Ausdruck [→ Abb. 5]. Das ist ein Anspruch, der in dieser Form an andere wiederaufzubauende Synagogen bislang nicht gestellt wurde. Was uns hierbei interessiert hat, ist, ob wir auch mit zeitgenössischen Mitteln unserer Disziplin einem solchen Anspruch gerecht werden könnten. Das war eigentlich die Frage an unsere Studierenden. In der Tat gibt es auch, vor allem am Hamburger Lehrstuhl, einige Projekte, die Teile der alten Synagoge wiederherstellen und diese dann zum Ausgangspunkt der weiteren Überlegungen machen. Das geht nicht so weit, das ganze Bauwerk in seiner Wirkung im Stadtraum zu rekonstruieren – sondern es ist vielmehr ein tastendes Probieren und Austarieren, um dem Anspruch an die Zeichenhaftigkeit dessen, was da neu entsteht, gerecht zu werden.

GW Diesen Aspekt der teilweisen Wiederherstellung behandelt auch die Arbeit von Mahmoud Ghazala Einieh und Sven Petersen, welche den Gebetsraum 1:1 in seiner ursprünglichen Größe, Form und Gliederung wiederaufbaut [→ S. 184–187]. Somit soll der räumliche Eindruck der alten Synagoge erhalten werden, während die ganze restliche Kubatur neu formuliert und mit anderen Nutzungen gefüllt wird. Hierbei war die Frage, ob man mit solch einer Herangehensweise, die das gesamte jüdische Leben in einem Bauwerk unterbringt und mit einer architektonischen Kraft und Ausdrucksstärke nach außen trägt, nicht viel mehr erreichen könnte als mit einer einfachen Rekonstruktion.

IR Genau solche Fragen haben wir auch mit der Gemeinde am Fraenkelufer andiskutiert. Im Gespräch hat sich gezeigt, dass der Synagogen-Innenraum – also der eigentliche Gebetsraum – rein proportional eine ganz andere Bedeutung hat und dass sehr viele weitere Aspekte und Räume eine sehr viel größere Bedeutung haben als früher. Insofern haben wir uns auch gefragt, ob überhaupt der Name «Synagogen-Projekt» für den Entwurfskurs richtig gewählt ist. Aber die Frage ist: Wenn das heutige jüdische Leben anders aussieht, ist es nicht für den Neuanfang und die Zukunft sogar zwingend notwendig, sich von dem alten Bild zu lösen? Also ist es, wenn man den Ort der Zukunft schaffen will, nicht kontraproduktiv, sich an die Erinnerung zu klammern? – Obwohl ich die Gründe, die Sie dafür nennen, trotzdem sehr gut nachvollziehen kann.

Das Gebäude darf ausdrücken, dass man hier keinen Neuanfang macht – denn es ist schließlich keiner

PS Einige Punkte, die jetzt genannt wurden, wie zum Beispiel die Größe des Synagogen-Innenraums, treiben uns genauso um. Einen Betsaal in dieser Größe brauchen wir, ganz offen gesagt, so nicht mehr. Wir benötigen keine 1400 Plätze – an den hohen Feiertagen rechnen wir auch in den nächsten Jahrzehnten

4
Talmud-Tora-Schule, Hamburg, Foto: 1914
The Talmud Torah School, Hamburg, photo: 1914
—
Ernst Friedheim 1911

we might be able to do justice to this aspiration using the current resources of our discipline. That's the question we addressed to our students. In fact, there exist a number of projects, in particular in Hamburg, that restore parts of old synagogues, which then become points of departure for further deliberations. Not to the extent of reconstructing entire buildings or recreating their impact within the urban environment—instead, it's a question of a tentative testing and balancing in order to do justice to the aspiration for symbolic value in a new building.

GW This aspect of a partial reconstruction is dealt with as well in the project by Mahmoud Ghazala Einieh and Sven Petersen, which recreates the prayer room on a 1:1 scale, restoring its original size, shape, and configuration [→ pp. 184–187]. This preserves the spatial volume of the old synagogue, while the remaining portion of the volume is reformulated and designed to accommodate other utilizations. Here the question is whether such an approach, which accommodates Jewish life as a whole in a single building, displaying architectural power and expressive force outwardly, might not be capable of achieving far more than a straightforward reconstruction.

IR We touched on precisely these questions with the Fraenkelufer community. In conversation, it emerged that, purely in proportional terms, the interior space of the synagogue—which is to say, the actual prayer room—had a very different significance, and that many other aspects and spaces had far greater significance than had been the case earlier. To that extent, we also asked whether the name "Synagogue Project" for the design course was chosen correctly. But the question remains: if contemporary Jewish life looks very different, isn't it absolutely necessary to detach yourself from this earlier image in order to make a new beginning? Which is to say: when it comes to creating a place for the future, isn't it counterproductive to cling to a memory? Although I can certainly understand the reasons you've given quite well.

It's fine for the building to express the fact that no new beginning is being made—because no such thing is taking place here

PS A number of points mentioned here, for example the size of the synagogue interior, preoccupy us as well. To be quite frank, a prayer hall with these dimensions isn't really needed any longer. We don't need 400 places —on High Holidays, even in the coming decades, we expect around 500 or 600 people. In the building, and on the premises as a whole, exactly as you've said, you need an entire series of additional facilities and utilizations—precisely because the school, with the kindergarten and youth center, are directly adjacent—if Jewish life is to take place there. There, I agree with you completely. But to your second question, I would reply: no, a reconstruction is not counterproductive. It's fine for the building to express the fact that no new beginning is being made—because no such thing is taking place

mit 500 bis 600 Menschen. Genau wie Sie gesagt haben, braucht man in dem Gebäude und auch auf dem Areal – gerade, weil die Schule mit Kindergarten und Jugendzentrum direkt angrenzen – eine ganze Reihe an anderen Einrichtungen und Nutzungen, damit sich das jüdische Leben dort abspielen kann. Also da bin ich ganz bei Ihnen. Aber zu Ihrer zweiten Frage würde ich sagen: Nein, eine Rekonstruktion ist nicht kontraproduktiv. Das Gebäude darf ruhig ausdrücken, dass man hier keinen Neuanfang macht – denn es ist schließlich keiner. Wir Juden und Jüdinnen sind seit langer Zeit ein zentraler, prägender Teil der Stadt – und ich denke, das muss dort auch zum Ausdruck kommen. Das heißt jetzt nicht, dass man völlig rückwärtsgewandt bauen sollte, aber man sollte eben auch nicht das Gegenteil tun, also gezielt versuchen, nicht an die Vergangenheit zu erinnern – damit meine ich sowohl die seinerzeitige Anmutung als auch den Zwischenzeitraum. Das darf eben auch nicht vertuscht werden, dass die Synagoge eine Zeit lang dort nicht mehr stand – und dafür ist es, meiner Meinung nach, zwingend, in irgendeiner Form daran zu erinnern, was dort früher einmal stand. So sehe ich es, das ist meine persönliche Meinung.

GW Dann kommen wir zum nächsten Thema, nämlich: Wie sieht ganz grundsätzlich ein Sakralraum für eine jüdische Gemeinde heute, im Jahr 2022, in Hamburg aus? Dazu ist zu sagen, dass solche Themen aktuell in der Lehre unterrepräsentiert sind: Ich habe selbst noch in den 80er-Jahren bei Friedrich Kurrent, der einen Lehrstuhl für Sakralbau innehatte, studiert – heute gibt es leider in ganz Deutschland keine einzige Professur mit dieser Spezialisierung mehr. Auch hatte in unserem Entwurfskurs bislang niemand eine Synagoge besucht und auch nur die wenigsten waren schon einmal in einer Kirche. Die einzigen aktiv Gläubigen sind die Muslimas und Muslime, die sich daher sehr fruchtbringend in den Kurs eingebracht haben. Daher gab es zur Frage nach der Gestalt und dem Charakter des Gebäudes auch erst einmal eine spannende Grundsatzdiskussion innerhalb des Entwurfskurses. Hier schließt sich dann auch die Frage an, wie viel Zeichenhaftigkeit man nach außen in den Stadtraum zeigen will – oder ob man eher ein zurückhaltendes städtebauliches Ensemble formulieren möchte, das dann seine Kraft nach innen hin entwickelt. Hier haben wir, wenn Sie sich die Arbeiten anschauen, eine sehr große Bandbreite an architektonischen Varianten. Ich persönlich glaube, dass es an diesem Ort wichtig ist, auch mit Kraft zu argumentieren – gerade weil der Vorgängerbau, ganz egal, was man über seine architektonischen Qualitäten denken mag, eben auch städtebaulich ein sehr deutliches Zeichen setzte.

FJH Ja, hier kann es jede Menge Kraft vertragen. Die Aufgabe ist es, auszuloten, was das konkret für diesen Ort heißt: Das hat etwas mit dem Standort an sich, aber auch mit dem Verhältnis des Hauses zur umgebenden Bebauung zu tun. Ich glaube, der Neubau kann auch ein kräftiges Volumen haben, zumal drumherum ziemlich große, offene Flächen sind und man eher aufpassen muss, dass das Ganze nicht zu klein wird. Dann muss man sich aber auch mit Blick auf den Stadtraum fragen:

5
Kuppel Bornplatzsynagoge, Hamburg, Foto: 1906
Cupola of the Bornplatz Synagogue, Hamburg, photo: 1906

here. We Jews have been a central, formative element of the city for a long time now—and I believe this too must be expressed there. That doesn't mean the need to build in a way that is entirely backward-looking, but nor should you do the reverse, deliberately avoid recalling the past—by which I mean both the building's original appearance, as well as the intervening period. Nor should it be covered up that, for a period of time, the synagogue no longer stood there—in my opinion, it's imperative that the building that formerly occupied the site be remembered in some form. That's how I see things, that's my personal view.

GW Let's move on now to our next topic: in principle, what should a sacred space for a Jewish community look like today, in the year 2022, in Hamburg? It must be said that, currently, such topics are underrepresented in teaching curricula: I myself studied in the 1980s with Friedrich Kurrent, who held a professorship in sacred architecture—today, there is no longer a single professorship with that specialization. And in our design course, no one had visited a synagogue up to that point, and very few had ever been in a church. The only active believers are the Muslims, who hence made highly fruitful contributions to the course. To begin with, therefore, there was a basic discussion within the design course on the question of the building's design and character. Following from this is the question of how much symbolic value should be displayed in relation to the urban environment—whether it's better to formulate a restrained urbanistic ensemble whose force is developed within. When we review the projects, we find an enormous spectrum of architectural variants. Personally, I believe that at this location it's important to argue with force—all the more since the predecessor building, regardless of one's view of its architectural qualities, made a powerful urbanistic statement.

Ist das jetzt zu viel oder genau richtig dimensioniert? Hat es einen überzeugenden architektonischen Ausdruck? Hier hätte ich mir bei einigen Entwürfen eine stärkere, eigenständige architektonische Antwort gewünscht.

GW Ich denke, dass mit den Arbeiten der Studierenden doch sehr schön ein weites Feld von potenziellen architektonischen Handlungsansätzen abgedeckt wurde: Einerseits haben wir Entwürfe, die sich möglichst nah an der Rekonstruktion orientieren, andererseits gibt es ganz freie Arbeiten, die keine formalen Rückbezüge suchen. An allen Lehrstühlen sieht man da sehr gelungene Ergebnisse, wobei man besonders in Weimar und Darmstadt auch die Affinität zum Kirchenbau herausspürt.

Es ist die einzige entscheidende Gelegenheit, in Hamburg einmal deutlich jüdische Präsenz zu zeigen

PS Um noch einmal auf die ursprüngliche Frage nach der Zeichenhaftigkeit zurückzukommen: Ich sehe es ähnlich, dass hier mit Kraft und Sichtbarkeit argumentiert werden sollte. Man muss schließlich auch daran denken, dass dieser Ort am Joseph-Carlebach-Platz die einzige entscheidende Gelegenheit in Hamburg ist, einmal ganz deutlich jüdische Präsenz zu zeigen. Da muss dieses Zeichen auch augenfällig sein. Ein Ziel des Projektes ist es, dass Menschen – und zwar einschließlich auch Antisemiten – in Zukunft gewissermaßen gar nicht darum herumkommen, dass Jüdinnen und Juden im Hamburg präsent sind. Daher: Wenn das in diesem Projekt nicht gelänge, hätte man eine große Chance vertan.

FJH Yes, this place can support a great deal of force. The task is to gauge, concretely, what that means for this site: which has something to do with the location itself, but also with the relationship between the building and the architectural surroundings. I believe the new building can have a powerful volume, since it's surrounded by rather large, open areas, and the danger instead is that the new ensemble might be too small. Then you have to ask, with an eye towards the urban environment: is it too much, or are the dimensions just right? Is the architectural expression persuasive? With some of the designs, I would have hoped for a more powerful, independent architectural response.

GW It seems to me that the student projects actually did a nice job of covering a broad field of possible architectural approaches: first, there are designs that are oriented as closely as possible toward a reconstruction, and on the other hand, conceptions that are wholly unencumbered, devoid of formal references. With all of the professorships, we find successful results, although, in Weimar and Darmstadt in particular, one senses a certain affinity with church building.

This is the sole substantive opportunity to clearly display a Jewish presence in Hamburg

PS To return once more to the original question of symbolic value or symbolism: I agree that it's necessary to argue here with force and visibility. Finally, it has to be considered as well that this location at Joseph-Carlebach-Platz represents the sole substantive opportunity to clearly display a Jewish presence in Hamburg. The signal given needs to be quite prominent. One aim of the project is to ensure that in the future, people—and that includes anti-Semites—can't get around the fact that there is still a Jewish presence in Hamburg. If this project fails to do that, an enormous opportunity will have been wasted.

Mirjam Wenzel
im Gespräch mit
in conversation with
Wolfgang Lorch &
Jörg Springer

Im Wintersemester 2020/21 war Mirjam Wenzel Bauhaus-Gastprofessorin in Weimar. Ihre Rolle als Direktorin des Jüdischen Museums in Frankfurt am Main versteht sie als einen aktiven Beitrag zur Gesellschaft, in der sie lebt. Es geht ihr nicht nur darum, zu bewahren und Dinge zu zeigen – sie will wirken. Dennoch hat sie auf unsere Anfrage, sich am Synagogen-Projekt zu beteiligen, zunächst sehr zurückhaltend reagiert. Zur Architektur könne sie nichts sagen, davon verstünde sie nichts. Was folgte, waren dann doch zwei sehr anregende Tage mit den Studierenden in Weimar und mehrere engagierte Gespräche, die unseren Blick auf das Bauen von Synagogen in Deutschland heute geweitet haben.

JS Ich möchte unser Gespräch heute gerne mit der sehr allgemeinen Frage einleiten, in welcher – möglicherweise besonderen – Form Erinnerungen für den Neubau einer Synagoge eine Rolle spielen.

> **MW** Das hängt, meiner Ansicht nach, zunächst einmal vom Ort und dessen Geschichte ab – wird ein neuer Ort geschaffen oder hat er einen historischen Vorgänger? Letzteres ist ja in Deutschland in der Regel der Fall, weil Synagogen heute zumeist in Städten gebaut werden und es hier gemeinhin schon einmal ein jüdisches Gotteshaus gab, das dann 1938 zerstört und niedergebrannt wurde. Die Leerstelle, die dadurch entstanden ist, wurde im Laufe der Jahre häufig in irgendeiner Form besetzt – sei es durch eine Erinnerungsinitiative, eine Gedenkstätte oder ein Denkmal. Daher geht es auch beim Neubau einer Synagoge am angestammten Platz um den Bezug auf das, was konkret an diesem Ort oder auch ganz allgemein einmal an jüdischer Kultur vor Ort existierte.

WL Was ist Deiner Meinung nach dann hierbei der Übertrag auf den Ort, also worauf bezöge man sich bei einem Neuanfang? Nimmt man die Zwischenzeitschicht, welche seit dem Bruch der Shoah vergangen ist, in den Blick oder versucht man eine Wiederholung dessen, was einmal war?

During winter semester 2020/21, Mirjam Wenzel was a guest professor at the Bauhaus Universität Weimar. As director of the Jewish Museum in Frankfurt am Main, she strives to make an active contribution to the society of which she is a part. For her, it is not just a question of preserving and displaying objects—she wants to have a real impact. Initially, all the same, she responded with hesitation when invited to participate in our Synagogue Project. She understood nothing about architecture, she remarked, and hence could say nothing about it. Nonetheless, her participation resulted in two stimulating days with the students in Weimar, and a number of lively discussions that broadened our perspective concerning the topic of synagogue building in Germany.

JS I'd like to begin our discussion today with a rather general question. In what form—and perhaps in a highly particular one—does memory play a role in the construction of a new synagogue?

> **MW** To begin with, in my view, that depends on the location and its history. Is a new place being created, or are there historical predecessors? In Germany, the latter is of course the rule, since for the most part synagogues are being built today in cities, most of which had Jewish houses of God previously, which were destroyed and burned down in 1938. In the postwar years, the voids in the city spaces were often occupied in one form or another—whether through an initiative devoted to memory, or as a historic site or memorial. When it comes to building a new synagogue at a historical Jewish location, therefore, it's a question of what references are being made to the former presence of Jewish culture at that site in general.

WL In your view, what should be carried over to the location? Which is to say: what references are appropriate to such a new beginning? Do you take the intervening period of time into account, the one that has passed since the radical break of the Shoah, or do you instead attempt to recreate what formerly existed?

Der Wunsch, sich auf die prachtvolle deutsch-jüdische Kultur zurückzubeziehen, ist Ausdruck einer Wiederentdeckung von Tradition

MW Das wandelt sich immer wieder, deshalb muss man diese Frage im historischen Kontext beantworten. Zunächst einmal war es nach 1945 für die meisten Jüdinnen und Juden, die die Shoah überlebt hatten und sich in den Displaced Persons Camps der US Army versammelten, unvorstellbar, dauerhaft unter den Mördern ihrer Familien zu leben. Zudem standen die neu gegründeten jüdischen Gemeinden erheblich unter Druck, sich wieder aufzulösen – und bauten dennoch bald wieder Synagogen auf. Diese ersten Gotteshäuser trotzten also dem Druck, der vonseiten internationaler jüdischer Organisationen auf die neu oder wieder gegründeten Gemeinden ausgeübt wurde, und dienten zugleich als Schutzräume vor der postnationalsozialistischen deutschen Gesellschaft. Sie waren daher meist inwendige Räume, die keinerlei Repräsentanz in die Öffentlichkeit anstrebten. Erst seit den 1990er-Jahren findet wieder eine nennenswerte Symbolisierung nach außen statt, mit der die jüdischen Gemeinden als relativ neue Tendenz auch wieder vermehrt historische Rückbezüge artikulieren. Das ist eine keinesfalls selbstverständliche Entwicklung. Ein Großteil der jüdischen Gemeinschaft, insbesondere in der Bundesrepublik Deutschland, waren osteuropäische Überlebende und deren Nachkommen, die in ihren Familienbiografien schlichtweg keinen Bezug zum deutschen Judentum hatten. Heute besteht die jüdische Gemeinschaft mehrheitlich aus postsowjetischen Jüdinnen und Juden. Der Wunsch, sich auf die bedeutende und prachtvolle deutsch-jüdische Kultur zurückzubeziehen, ist also nicht in familiären Traditionen begründet. Er ist vielmehr Ausdruck einer Wiederentdeckung von Tradition, oder auch einer Art jüdischen Renaissance. In diesem Zusammenhang spielen die alten Synagogen, die hier einmal standen, heute eine ganz andere, wichtige Rolle. Wie gesagt: Wenn man über Erinnerungen und Rückbezüge spricht, muss man diese zunächst einmal in ihrer historischen Entwicklung betrachten, denn was heute vorstellbar ist und gewünscht wird, wäre noch vor 30, 40 Jahren nicht einmal annäherungsweise denkbar gewesen.

JS Es ist interessant, dass Du hier sofort den ganz großen Schritt zur Erinnerung an die Zeit vor 1933 zurückgehst. Diese Frage nach den Rückbezügen und Erinnerungen hatte sich ja zunächst einmal aus der Rekonstruktionsdebatte entwickelt, in der es immer wieder den Vorwurf gibt, dass man mit dem Wiederaufbau einer Synagoge einen Teil der Geschichte auslöschen würde. Worauf ein Teil der jüdischen Community antwortet: Es ist nicht unsere Aufgabe, Geschichte sichtbar zu machen, wenn überhaupt, wäre das eine Angelegenheit der uns umgebenden Gesellschaft, keine der Gemeinden. Aber ist es nicht dennoch möglicherweise Thema einer heute in Deutschland neu zu bauenden Synagoge, die Geschichte der Shoah auch mit zu transportieren?

The desire to refer back to a glorious German-Jewish culture is an expression of the rediscovery of tradition

MW That changes constantly, hence your question leads to an elaboration on historical developments. After 1945, to start with, it seemed unimaginable for most of the Jews who had survived the Shoah, and had been gathered in the US Army's camps for displaced persons, to live permanently among the people who had murdered their families. Moreover, the newly established Jewish communities stood under considerable pressure to dissolve themselves once again—nonetheless, they soon began building synagogues again. These first houses of God therefore defied the pressure experienced by the newly founded communities from international Jewish organizations, and at the same time served as protective spaces in relation to a post-National-Socialist German society. For the most part, they were inward-looking spaces that made no attempt to fulfill public or representative functions. Only beginning in the 1990s does a significant symbolization begin to take place again, with a tendency for Jewish communities to articulate historical references to an increasing degree. This development should by no means be taken for granted. The greater part of the Jewish community, in particular in the Federal Republic of Germany, consisted of survivors from Eastern Europe and their descendants, whose family biographies simply had no connection to German Jewry. Today, due to Jewish immigration in the 1990s, post-Soviet Jews are the majority within the Jewish community in Germany. The desire to refer back to a significant and glorious German-Jewish culture is therefore not grounded in family traditions. It is instead an expression of the rediscovery of tradition, or else of a kind of Jewish renaissance. In this context, the former synagogues that have been destroyed are playing a crucial role. As I've said: when we speak about memory and historical references, these must be regarded in relation to historical developments, since what seems conceivable or desirable today might have been simply unimaginable thirty or forty years ago.

JS It's interesting that you immediately take the enormous step toward the memory of the historical period before 1933. To begin with, this question of historical references and memory emerged in the context of debates about historical reconstruction, which consistently gave rise to the allegation that synagogue reconstructions would erase part of history. To which one segment of the Jewish community responds: "It's not our task to make history visible; at most, that would be the business of the surrounding society, not of our communities." All the same, isn't it conceivable for a new synagogue building in Germany to take up the theme of the Shoah and to convey its significance?

Must a synagogue also have a symbolic form that positions it in relation to the Shoah?

MW I reflect on the question of responsibility in the same way. Jews are conscious of the fact that they live in Germany, which is to say the country that organized

Muss eine Synagoge zugleich auch eine symbolische Form haben, die sich ins Verhältnis zur Shoah setzt?

MW Die Frage nach der Zuständigkeit sehe ich genauso. Jüdinnen und Juden sind sich dessen gewahr, dass sie in Deutschland, also dem Land, welches die Shoah organisierte, leben. Dieser Fakt ist bei einer Mehrheit nach wie vor Bestandteil der eigenen Familiengeschichte und damit auch im Bewusstsein präsent – sehr viel präsenter als bei den meisten nicht-jüdischen Deutschen. Zudem begegnen viele Jüdinnen und Juden in ihrem Alltag judenfeindlichen Projektionen und Aggressionen. Die Frage ist nun: Muss eine Synagoge, die ja Versammlungs- und Studienort, aber auch der Raum des Betens ist, zugleich auch eine symbolische Form haben, die sich ins Verhältnis zur Shoah setzt? Diese Frage stellt sich nicht nur bei dem Bau jeder neuen Synagoge in Deutschland, sie hat auch für die jüdische Gemeinde eine ganz andere Bedeutung als für die nicht-jüdische Gesellschaft.

WL Eine Synagoge ist ja kein Mahnmal und kein Denkmal. Das ist das eine. Aber eine Synagoge ist in Deutschland ebenso ohne die Shoah nicht zu denken – die Gemeinden wurden vernichtet, die Gebäude zerstört. Wobei es aktuell auch einen Paradigmenwechsel gibt und man wieder Bezüge zu weiter zurückliegenden Epochen sucht, sodass man also nicht mehr sagt: Der Bruch durch die Shoah war so groß, es ist nur ein völliger Neuanfang denkbar. Diese Haltung war ja lange der Status quo und der Grund dafür, dass seit den 1950er-Jahren eine ganze Reihe von Synagogen andere Wurzeln gesucht haben, wie man auch in den verschiedenen baulichen Umsetzungen jener Zeit sieht. Heute stehen wir durch diesen Wandel wieder vor einer neuen Fragestellung. Daher: Welche Rolle spielen diese rund 100 Jahre Reformjudentum, die in den Synagogen davor zum Ausdruck kamen – und wenn man heute an diese Epoche anknüpfen will, auf was bezieht man sich dabei?

Die Bornplatzsynagoge war Ausdruck des Selbstbewusstseins des Reformjudentums

MW Das sind erst einmal ganz verschiedene Fragen. Zum einen muss man sagen: Es existieren ja noch alte Synagogen – hier in der Westend-Synagoge wurden die Innenräume zerstört, das Gebäude an sich ist aber erhalten geblieben [→ Abb. 2]. Brisant wird es, wenn wir an Orte wie die Bornplatzsynagoge oder die Synagoge in der Oranienburger Straße [→ Abb. 1] denken. Sie waren schon damals hochsymbolischer Ausdruck des Selbstbewusstseins des Reformjudentums und wurden auch auf eine bestimmte Art und Weise bespielt und genutzt, wie es heute sicherlich nicht mehr der Fall sein kann. Einerseits sind die Gemeinden nicht mehr so groß, andererseits existiert diese Form eines selbstverständlichen, breitenwirksamen, liberalen Judentums nurmehr in den USA und ein wenig noch in London und Paris. Das heißt, hier ist mit der Shoah auch eine Kultur zerstört worden, die mit einer Praxis und einem bestimmten Selbstverständnis zu tun hatte, an welches die liberale Strömung

the Shoah. For a majority of them, as mentioned earlier, this fact is a part of their own family histories, and hence very present in their consciousness—far more so than for most non-Jewish Germans. Moreover, many Jews encounter anti-Semitic projections and forms of aggression in everyday life. The question is: must a synagogue, a place for gathering and study, but also a space for prayer, have a symbolic form that positions it in relation to the Shoah? Not only does this question arise whenever a new synagogue is constructed in Germany, it also has an utterly different significance for the Jewish community than it does for non-Jewish society.

WL A synagogue is neither a monument nor a memorial. That's the first thing. At the same time, a synagogue in Germany is unimaginable without reference to the Shoah—the community was annihilated, its buildings destroyed. Whereby we're also passing through a paradigm shift; it's now becoming possible to refer to historical periods that lie further in the past, so you can no longer say: the radical break of the Shoah was so enormous that only a completely new beginning is conceivable. This attitude was the status quo for a long time, and it's the reason a large number of synagogues sought out different roots during the 1950s, as manifested in the diverse architectural results dating from that period. Today, due to this shift, we're confronting a new problematic. Therefore, the question: what role is played by the Reform Judaism, now roughly a century old, that found expression in the synagogues from that era? And regarding attempts to create connections to that era, what exactly is being referred to?

The Bornplatz Synagogue was an expression of the self-confidence of Reform Judaism

MW To begin with, these are very different questions. First, it has to be said that certain older synagogues do still exist—here in the Westend Synagogue, the interiors were destroyed, but the building nonetheless remained intact [→ Fig. 2]. Things become controversial when it comes to places like the Bornplatz Synagogue or the synagogue on Oranienburger Straße [→ Fig. 1]. When originally built, they were already highly symbolic expressions of the self-confidence of Reform Judaism, and were enjoyed and used in ways that cannot possibly still be the case today. On the one hand, the communities are no longer as large as they once had been, and on the other, this kind of taken-for-granted liberal Judaism does only exist in the United States and to some extent in London and Paris today, but not in Germany any more. The liberal culture that evolved in German-Jewish communities in the nineteenth century and the feeling of belonging that once was its basis were destroyed in the Shoah—even if there is a considerable attempt to renew Reform Judaism within Germany today. Therefore, it's interesting that Jewish communities, when it comes to constructing new synagogues in Germany today, articulate a desire to link up with the type of symbolization that is associated with Reform Judaism. In particular since, currently, the specific places where these debates are taking

in der jüdischen Gemeinschaft in Deutschland seit den 1990er-Jahren zwar anzuknüpfen sucht, die als solche aber viel weniger selbstverständlich ist. Deswegen ist es interessant, wenn heute von jüdischen Gemeinden der Wunsch artikuliert wird, in dem Neubau von Synagogen an diese Art von Symbolisierung des Reformjudentums anzuschließen. Vor allem auch, weil die Orte, an denen die Debatte konkret stattfindet, aktuell nicht der liberalen Strömung in der jüdischen Gemeinschaft angehören – es aber auch nicht so wahrgenommen wird, dass die Synagogen, die hier dereinst standen, dies taten.

JS Wir kommen hier sofort in eine Diskussion über die Angemessenheit der Form für die Gemeinde. Mit der Frage, ob tatsächlich eine Erinnerung an die Zerstörung der Synagogen noch ein Thema von Neubauten sein sollte, halten wir uns offensichtlich gar nicht mehr auf.

MW Ich finde, dieses Thema war lange sehr präsent. Im Moment geht es eher um ein wiedererstarkendes Selbstbewusstsein, eine Rückbesinnung auf etwas, das zwar zerstört wurde, aber jetzt ebenso mit seinem eigenen Potenzial wiederentdeckt und großgeschrieben wird. Das ist etwas, was vor allem für jüngere Menschen eine Rolle spielt – gerade auch in der Paradoxie unserer Gegenwart, in der wir einerseits mit zunehmendem Antisemitismus zu tun haben, auf der anderen Seite aber dieses Selbstbewusstsein, der Wunsch nach Selbstbestimmung und auch das Einfordern derselben immer stärker werden.

WL Was ich vor Kurzem gelernt habe: Nach dem Krieg gab es eigentlich nurmehr die Einheitsgemeinde, in der sich alle unter einem Dach versammelten und trotz ihrer Vielfältigkeit zusammenfanden, weil sie in den einzelnen Konfessionsgruppen schlichtweg zu wenige gewesen wären. Diese Zugehörigkeit zu den einzelnen Strömungen wird heute an vielen Stellen stärker ausdifferenziert, was auch dahin führt, dass das Gebet und Gemeindeleben nicht mehr in einem gemeinsamen Haus stattfinden. Ist das auch Teil der aktuellen Debatte?

MW Ja, das ist auch Bestandteil der Ausdifferenzierung, die gerade stattfindet. Es ist in der Praxis tatsächlich nur selten der Fall, dass die verschiedenen Strömungen in einem gemeinsamen Haus zusammenfinden, da die innerjüdischen Konflikte nicht gerade geringfügig sind. Das sogenannte Frankfurter Modell der Westend-Synagoge bildet da eine Ausnahme: Hier beten sowohl die orthodoxe Mehrheitsgemeinde wie auch der Egalitäre Minjan unter einem Dach – wenn auch, aufgrund der verschiedenen Liturgien und Praktiken, in verschiedenen Räumen.

Es gibt ein neues Interesse an Zeichen in der Architektur

JS Es ist bei diesem Thema ja auch bemerkenswert, dass aktuell doch gerne die falschen Hüllen in Anspruch genommen werden und plötzlich eine konfessionell ganz anders orientierte Gemeinde eine Reformsynagoge place aren't associated with the liberal Jewish communities—nor does it seem to play a crucial role that the synagogues that once stood there formerly were.

JS We're already getting into the topic of the suitability of certain architectural forms for the community. Evidently, we're not really dwelling on the question of whether the memory of the destruction of the synagogues should still be a theme for new constructions.

MW I believe, however, that this topic was present for a long time. At the moment, it's a question of a reinvigorated self-confidence, a return to something that was destroyed, but whose intrinsic potential is now being rediscovered and written out in capital letters. This plays a role in particular for younger people—all the more so in the current situation, with all of its paradoxes: on the one hand, we're dealing with increasing anti-Semitism, but on the other, we're seeing a growing self-confidence, as well as a growing desire for self-determination.

WL Something I learned about only recently: after the war, there was only a single unified community, which gathered together under a single roof, coming together despite all of its diversity, because the individual confessional groups were simply too small on their own. In many places, this affiliation with individualized tendencies is becoming more differentiated today, with the result that prayer and community life no longer take place in a single building. Is that an aspect of the current debate?

MW Yes, that's also one component of the differentiation now taking place. In practice, it's actually rare for the various tendencies to come together in a single building, given that conflicts within the community are not exactly minor. The so-called "Frankfurt model" of the Westend Synagogue is an exception: here, the Orthodox majority community prays along with the Egalitarian Minyan community under a single roof—albeit in different rooms, due to divergent liturgies and practices.

There is a new interest in architectural symbolism

JS It seems remarkable that currently, a kind of false raiment is being claimed, that a community with a quite different orientation in confessional terms would perceive a Reform synagogue as an appropriate habitat. This is especially striking in Hamburg. It could also be said that, evidently, something originally conceived as a built symbol functions now very differently on the symbolic level, even within the Jewish community, or perhaps so feebly that the original intention has become virtually imperceptible.

WL In Hamburg, it's also noticeable that the Chabad-Lubavitch movement has profiled itself within the larger community, saying: "We're occupying this place exclusively, and no one else can coexist here, not even with separate entrances." Despite attempts to integrate the whole into a unified community, you nonetheless have something resembling a claim to sole representation.

1
Synagoge Oranienburger Straße, Berlin, Stich: 1866
Synagogue on Oranienburger Straße, Berlin, engraving: 1866
—
Eduard Knoblauch & Friedrich August Stüler
1866

als die richtige Behausung empfindet. In Hamburg ist es besonders prägnant. Man kann also sagen: Was dereinst als gebautes Zeichen gedacht wurde, funktioniert auf der symbolischen Ebene augenscheinlich selbst innerhalb der jüdischen Gemeinschaft nun anders oder nurmehr so schwach, dass das, was mal das Anliegen war, kaum noch wahrgenommen wird.

WL In Hamburg ist es ja auch beachtlich, dass sich Chabad/Lubawitsch innerhalb der Einheitsgemeinde profiliert und sagt: Wir besetzen diesen Ort allein und alles andere darf hier auch nicht mit getrennten Zugängen koexistieren. Man versucht das Ganze zwar noch in die Einheitsgemeinde zu integrieren, aber letztlich entsteht da so etwas wie ein Alleinvertretungsanspruch.

MW Ja, Chabad, also der Lubawitscher Chassidismus, ist eine Strömung, die aktuell viel Zulauf hat und dementsprechend auch relativ machtvoll agiert. Allerdings sind die von ihnen vertretene Orthodoxie und das Reformjudentum wirklich grundverschiedene Strömungen, die ganz woanders herkommen, andere Praktiken und auch ein unterschiedliches Verständnis der Tradition haben. Dass Chabad nun die Bornplatzsynagoge, also einen symbolischen Ort des Reformjudentums, für sich reklamiert, ist schon interessant.

JS Das ist ja auch für uns als Architekten interessant, weil damit natürlich sofort Fragen nach den baulichen Zeichen aufgeworfen werden: inwieweit diese auch heute noch in gleicher Weise gelesen werden, ob sie überhaupt eindeutig sind, inwiefern sie das je waren – oder

2
Westend-Synagoge, Frankfurt am Main, Foto: 2010
Westend Synagogue, Frankfurt am Main, photo: 2010
—
Franz Roeckle 1910 (beschädigt/damaged 1938/44)
—
Max Kemper & Werner Hebebrand 1950 (Neugestaltung/redesign)
—
Henryk Isenburg 1994 (Neugestaltung Innenraum/interior redesign)

MW Yes, the Chabad movement, which is to say Lubavitch Chassidism, is a tendency that has a lot of momentum at the moment, and a corresponding degree of power. But the Orthodox tendency they represent is fundamentally different from Reform Judaism—they come from very different places, cultivate different practices, and have a different understanding of tradition. The fact that the Chabad group is now staking a claim to the Bornplatz Synagogue, which is to say a symbolic place of Reform Judaism, is quite interesting.

JS And it's also interesting for us as architects, because, of course, questions concerning the architectural signals are raised immediately. To what extent are these legible today in the same way, are they at all unambiguous, to what extent were they ever unambiguous? And what form should they take today? When we turn toward the student projects, we see that Mahmoud Ghazala Einieh and Sven Petersen, for example, attempt to recall the form of the old synagogue in the interior, albeit in a somewhat abstract form [→ pp. 184–187]. There are very few designs that move in this direction. The question is whether such principles are at all viable.

MW What I find so remarkable about the projects is their gestures. I thought postmodernism in architecture was already history. Am I mistaken? Or are we seeing a kind of continuation of the postmodernist citation here?

JS Yes. We're certainly seeing a fondness for form and for forms that seek out historical references with a great sense of nonchalance.

MW But as citations?

WL Work is being carried out, I believe, with direct transfers, but the elements are viewed rather as fragments. Often, postmodernism didn't simply work with fragments, but also subjected them to a process of translation. Observing recent developments, it seems to me that it resembles working with spolia—something old is taken up and positioned as a citation within the total composition.

JS In this context, the term spolia may not be far off the mark. There is certainly a new interest in symbolism in architecture, and this can be seen in the current debate. Resonating, consistently, in the desire for a reconstruction, not least of all, is a desire to communicate something through the architectural image. In a sense, the building in its totality is handled and read as a symbol. Playing a role on this level, again, is the topic of ambivalence and otherness—which is to say, an attempt to distinguish the synagogue from a Christian church, at the same time treating it as part of the city, adapting it to the logic of the urban fabric. This was an important aspect for the Hamburg synagogue, a freestanding building that occupied the square like a church. Interesting in our context are the connections to the city in particular, which is to say: to what extent are synagogues, too—and the aspect of foreignness—interpreted as self-evident components of the city? Or aren't they?

welcher Art sie heute sein müssten. Wenn wir uns einmal die Entwürfe der Studierenden anschauen, so versuchen zum Beispiel Mahmoud Ghazala Einieh und Sven Petersen im Innenraum, wenn auch abstrahiert, an die Formen der alten Synagoge zu erinnern [→ S.184–187]. Es gibt nur wenige Entwürfe, die diesen Weg gehen. Die Frage ist hierbei, ob solche Prinzipien überhaupt tragfähig sind.

MW Also, was ich bemerkenswert an den Entwürfen finde, sind ihre Gesten. Ich dachte, die Postmoderne in der Architektur wäre bereits Geschichte. Liege ich da falsch oder findet da so eine Art Fortschreibung postmoderner Zitate statt?

JS Ja. Es gibt durchaus schon wieder eine Liebe zur Form und eine Liebe zu Formen, die in großer Gelassenheit Rückbezüge suchen.

MW Aber als Zitat?

WL Ich denke, man arbeitet tatsächlich mit direkten Überträgen, aber sieht die Dinge eher als Fragmente. Die Postmoderne hat ja oftmals nicht nur mit Fragmenten gearbeitet, sondern diese noch einmal übersetzt. Wenn ich die neue Entwicklung sehe, kommt mir das manchmal wie ein Arbeiten mit Spolien vor – man nimmt etwas Altes und setzt es wie ein Zitat in die Gesamtkomposition ein.

JS Der Begriff der Spolie ist möglicherweise in diesem Zusammenhang gar nicht so verkehrt. Es gibt ja auch ein neues Interesse an Zeichen in der Architektur, was sich ebenfalls in der aktuellen Debatte zeigt. Nicht zuletzt schwingt in diesem Wunsch nach einer Rekonstruktion immer das Bedürfnis mit, etwas durch dieses architektonische Bild zu vermitteln. Das Gebäude wird gewissermaßen in seiner Gesamtheit als Symbol behandelt und gelesen. Auf dieser Ebene spielt auch wieder das angesprochene Thema der Ambivalenz und Andersartigkeit eine Rolle – also jener Versuch, die Synagoge von einer christlichen Kirche zu unterscheiden, sie aber dennoch als Teil der Stadt zu behandeln und in die Logik des urbanen Gefüges einzupassen. Für die Hamburger Synagoge, die ja wie eine Kirche frei auf dem Platz stand, war das ein wichtiger Aspekt. In unserem Kontext sind hier vor allem die Bezüge zur Stadt interessant, also: Inwieweit werden die Synagogen auch – und da spielt dieses Moment der Fremdartigkeit mit hinein – als selbstverständliche Teile der Städte interpretiert oder eben nicht?

Wenn man an etwas anschließt, was einmal existent war, dann geht es nicht um Fremdheit

MW Ebenso: Sind sie als Teile der Städte geplant? Dieses ganze Thema des Inkludiert- und Bestandteil-Seins hängt ja auch mit Deiner ersten Frage nach der Fortsetzung über den Bruch hinweg zusammen. Jüdischerseits gibt es heute oft den Wunsch und das Selbstverständnis, Teil dieser Gesellschaft zu sein und nicht als Projektionsfläche für diverse Dinge zu dienen. Allerdings

When you create a connection with something that existed formerly, it's no longer a question of foreignness

MW And likewise: are they planned as integral parts of the city? This entire topic of inclusion, of functioning as a constituent part, is also related to your initial question concerning continuity across a radical break. From a Jewish perspective, there is often a desire to be a self-evident part of society, not to serve as a projection surface for a variety of things. Which is, at the same time, counteracted by the experience of its impossibility. Which is why I'm caught up short when you speak of foreignness. What I mean is that when the desire arises to create a connection with something that existed formerly, then viewed historically, it's no longer a question of foreignness. Even the putatively exotic appearance of the Reform synagogues, which presented themselves, with their to some extent Orientalizing forms, as grand and self-confident, did not want, back then, to inscribe an alien cultural tradition into the modern city, but were instead emblems of self-affirmation and thereby made references to a time that was often perceived as a golden age of coexistence. At that time, this harking back to the Sephardic cultural realm was a form of distinction, and marked off the synagogue from the church. It signified a conceptual point of contact with an epoch during which scholars like Maimonides or Nachmanides developed rabbinic Judaism further in decisive ways, while at the same time living in a non-Jewish society. It was a highly educated, flourishing time. But the question that arises from this today is: if these forms seem so appealing again, then what exactly is it that we find so attractive about them? Is this a kind of self-exoticization? Is it a question of reconnecting with history? Or of the self-confidence that comes to expression here: to be a part of society, yet at the same time to remain different? Or all of these things at the same time?

JS I don't believe it can be defined unequivocally. Many of the things that functioned visually around 1920 wouldn't be understood at all today. Something that was perceived back then as exotic, as marking it off from a church, would seem perfectly natural today. So the question is posed anew: what does this architectural language stand for today, especially since the stylistic programs of the synagogues in Berlin and Hamburg are very different from one another, and how might they be readable today?

WL Actually, it's quite simple: to begin with, in purely formal terms, the buildings of the Reform synagogues are legible as churches, with the Christian image programs, which could of course not have been adopted, replaced now by a different form of ornamentation. To some extent, these modifications are visible outwardly as well, as on Oranienburger Straße, with the decorated dome, but are often more visible in the interior, in the architectural decoration and the articulation of the surfaces. But then again, the transitions are fluid, and that makes it difficult, because when it came to the

wird dieser zugleich von der Erfahrung konterkariert, dass das unmöglich ist. Ich muss deshalb auch stutzen, wenn Du von Fremdartigkeit sprichst. Ich meine, wenn der Wunsch aufkommt, wieder an etwas anzuschließen, was einmal existent war, dann geht es ja historisch gesehen nicht um Fremdheit. Auch das vermeintlich fremde Erscheinungsbild der Reformsynagogen, die sich mit ihren teils orientalisierten Formen groß und selbstbewusst zeigten, war damals ja kein Einschreiben einer andersartigen Kulturtradition in die moderne Stadt, sondern hatte mit einer Selbstvergewisserung und Rückbesinnung auf eine Zeit zu tun, die oft als das goldene Zeitalter der Koexistenz wahrgenommen wurde. Dieser Rückbezug auf den sephardischen Kulturraum war in seiner Zeit ja auch eine Distinktion und unterschied die Synagoge von der Kirche. Es war ein gedanklicher Anschluss an eine Epoche, in der Gelehrte wie Maimonides oder Nachmanides das rabbinische Judentum entscheidend weiterentwickelten und zugleich in einer nicht-jüdischen Gesellschaft lebten, es war eine hochgebildete, florierende Zeit. Aber die Frage, die sich aktuell daraus ergibt, ist ja: Wenn heute diese Formen wieder so reizvoll sind, was genau erscheint uns daran attraktiv? Ist es eine Art Selbstexotisierung? Ist es die Geschichte, an die man anschließen will? Ist es das Selbstbewusstsein, das darin zum Ausdruck kommt: Teil einer Stadt zu sein, aber doch anders zu sein? Ist es alles zusammen?

JS Ich denke, man kann es nicht eindeutig bestimmen. Vieles von dem, was 1920 noch als Bild funktioniert hat, würde heute gar nicht mehr verstanden werden. Was damals im Unterschied zu einer Kirche noch als exotisch wahrgenommen wurde, wäre heutzutage selbstverständlich. Also stellt sich die Frage wieder neu: Wofür stehen diese Architektursprachen, zumal bei den Synagogen in Berlin und in Hamburg die stilistischen Programme auch noch sehr unterschiedlich sind, und wie würden sie heute wieder gelesen werden?

WL Eigentlich wäre es ja ganz simpel: Zunächst kann man die Gebäude der Reformsynagogen auch rein von der Form her als Kirche lesen, bei der lediglich die eingeschriebenen christlichen Bildprogramme, die man zweifelsohne nicht übernehmen konnte, durch eine andere Ornamentik ersetzt wurden. Diese Abwandlung zeigte sich teilweise auch nach außen, wie in der Oranienburger Straße mit dem verzierten Turmhelm, oftmals spielte sie sich aber mehr im Innenraum, beim

configuration of the interior, there was again an orientation toward church types, since the principle of a central reading was not pursued, and everything was instead oriented strongly toward the front. The basic type of the church was taken up and a few things adapted, while other things couldn't be modified in this way, or there was no desire to [→ Fig. 3].[1] Or is that a misinterpretation?

A harking back to a past time that was a source of pride

MW That was the basic tendency, yes. The notion that Judaism is a religion is actually an outcome of Jewish emancipation, and evolved in the course of the nineteenth century. Before that, Judaism was a practice: it was how you lived, how you organized your day; a tradition that told you how things were to be done. This enormous shift resonates in synagogue building as well, because, for the first time, it raised the question of how Judaism as a religion related to other religions. At that point, of course, synagogues had already existed for centuries, which is to say as gathering places where you prayed, studied, and celebrated, but the development toward a representative building within a non-Jewish public environment nonetheless has to do mainly with the idea of Judaism as a religion. The requirement for representation was differentiated depending upon how much splendor and solemnity characterized the religious services. Only in this era of equality, when religious affiliation no longer shaped daily life, did the question of distinctiveness or of references arise. Back then, interestingly, the idea emerged in Reform Judaism, for instance, of referring to synagogues and temples, or of furnishing them with Moorish stylistic elements. In my view, such references to Jerusalem, to the Mediterranean region, and to medieval Spain and its culture, are expressions of Jewish memory culture, a harking back to a past time that was a source of pride.

WL But is this assimilation not, at the same time, an expression of the desire on the part of Jews to be German in Germany? On the one hand, there is the cultural harking back to the roots, clearly. But didn't a desire emerge together with the gain in freedom beginning in 1830, and with the strengthening of Reform Judaism, to be anchored in German culture? Or is this erroneous?

MW I think it's false. I prefer to regard Jews on the territory of contemporary Germany as a distinctive group with particular traditions who already lived here before the idea of a Holy Roman Empire of the German Nation ever arose. It's been documented that Jews settled in this region since the year 321. They helped to shape the culture that evolved here. In retrospect, the fact that, in the nineteenth century, they understood themselves as a part of German society may seem a kind of illusion. In cultural terms, however, it was an expression of a cultural affiliation that existed regardless. For this reason, I'd prefer to speak of acculturation rather than assimilation.

WL But we are in agreement to the extent that this kind of acculturation was misguided.

3
Synagoge Hannover,
Postkarte: um 1905
Hanover Synagogue,
postcard: ca. 1905
—
Edwin Oppler
1870 (zerstört/destroyed 1938)

Bauschmuck und der Ausgestaltung der Oberflächen, ab. Aber dann sind die Übergänge wieder fließend und das macht es schwierig, weil man sich bei der Situierung im Inneren dagegen wieder an den Kirchen orientierte, indem man nicht das Prinzip der zentralen Lesung verfolgte, sondern alles stark nach vorne ausrichtete. Man hat also den Grundtypus der Kirche verwendet und einige Dinge adaptiert, aber andere konnte und wollte man nicht anpassen [→ Abb. 3].[1] Oder ist das eine Fehlinterpretation?

Ein Rückbezug auf eine vergangene Zeit, die stolz macht

MW Tendenziell ja. Die Auffassung, dass das Judentum eine Religion sei, ist ja eine Folge der jüdischen Emanzipation, entwickelte sich also erst im 19. Jahrhundert. Vorher war Judentum eine Praxis, wie man lebte und seinen Tag gestaltete; eine Tradition, die einem sagte, wie Dinge zu tun waren. Dieser große Wandel schwingt auch beim Synagogenbau mit, weil erst durch ihn die Frage aufgeworfen wurde, wie sich das Judentum als Religion zu anderen Religionen verhält. Natürlich gab es zu diesem Zeitpunkt bereits seit Jahrhunderten Synagogen, also Versammlungsorte, in denen gebetet, gelernt und gefeiert wurde, aber die Entwicklung hin zum repräsentativen Gebäude in einer nicht-jüdischen Öffentlichkeit hat doch vor allem mit der Idee vom Judentum als Religion zu tun. Je nachdem wie prächtig und feierlich der Gottesdienst zelebriert wurde, differenzierte sich dann auch das Repräsentationsbedürfnis aus. Erst in dieser Zeit der Gleichberechtigung, als die Glaubenszugehörigkeit nicht mehr den Alltag bestimmte, stellte sich dann auch die Frage der Unterscheidung ebenso wie der Bezüge. Interessanterweise kam man damals zum Beispiel auch im Reformjudentum auf die Idee, Synagogen als Tempel zu bezeichnen oder eben mit maurischen Stilelementen zu versehen. Meiner Meinung nach ist dieser Bezug auf Jerusalem, den Mittelmeerraum oder das mittelalterliche Spanien und dessen Kultur auch ein Ausdruck der jüdischen Erinnerungskultur, ein Rückbezug auf eine vergangene Zeit, die stolz macht.

WL Aber ist diese Assimilation nicht gleichzeitig auch ein Ausdruck des Deutsch-Sein-Wollens der Juden in Deutschland? Das eine ist der kulturelle Rückbezug auf die Wurzeln, das ist klar. Ist aber mit der Freizügigkeit ab 1830 und dem Erstarken des Reformjudentums nicht auch gleichzeitig ein Wunsch entstanden, sich in der deutschen Kultur zu verankern? Oder ist der Gedanke falsch?

MW Ich finde das falsch. Ich würde Jüdinnen und Juden auf dem Territorium des heutigen Deutschlands stets auch als indigene Bevölkerungsgruppe sehen, die hier schon lebte, bevor die Idee eines Heiligen Römischen Reichs Deutscher Nation entstand. Nachweislich leben Jüdinnen und Juden seit 321 auf diesem Gebiet. Sie prägten die Kultur, die sich hier entwickelte, mit. Dass sie sich im 19. Jahrhundert als Teil der deutschen Gesellschaft verstanden, mag im Nachhinein wie eine

For me, it's important to see nineteenth-century German-Jewish history in all of its potential

MW I don't see it as misguided at all—on this point, we're certainly not in agreement! In my view, it's important to see this period in its own right—and non-Jewish society must also ask itself: what would have needed to happen to prevent things from moving in the direction they did? Solely because of National Socialism, we regard the trust placed by many Jews in German society at that time as an error. But what needed to occur for this trust to endure? It's extremely important, in my view, to avoid considering the extraordinary history of German-Jewish modernity from its endpoint, to instead perceive the potential that existed at that time on its own terms. Back then, the Jews weren't naive, the anti-Semitic parties were all already in place. This trust was bestowed upon a society that had still said, just a hundred years earlier: "You are different, and therefore don't have the same rights and opportunities, you can't practice the same occupations, and you'll only be permitted to live in restricted zones, and by no means to take up residence among us in an unregulated way." For me, it's important that German-Jewish history—this extraordinary readiness on the part of German Jews to invest in education, science, culture, and business, and to contribute to shaping developments in these areas—be regarded as a leap of faith in relation to German society, and that it be seen in all of its potential.

JS Our initial question was: what does this mean for us today? How much difference is desirable, how much is necessary? When we consider the Bornplatz Synagogue, you have to concede that, from a contemporary perspective, its otherness, is barely discernible, which is not the case with the synagogue on Oranienburger Straße.

MW Absolutely. But can we think about the question of difference in the context of a diverse society, which is to say beyond the German-Jewish neurosis? In general, this is an extremely important and a thoroughly political topic. For this reason, of course, it's also fascinating to consider a reconstruction from this perspective—then, with an object that is as present as the Bornplatz Synagogue, it would also be a question of creating a central place with a historical reference, a place where questions of difference and belonging could also be negotiated.

A return to a central place of Jewish life

WL Which brings us to the question of presence—that a return and a reoccupation take place, and moreover at a site that was long central to Jewish life in Hamburg. Where the synagogue sat, somehow isolated, but also self-confidently at a prominent corner. Of course, very few people who passed the synagogue actually entered the building—which is beside the point, since the question of presence is not a question of the interior, but instead of the building's outward appearance within the city. But, of course, this urbanistic situation no longer exists today.

Illusion wirken. Es war in historischer Hinsicht jedoch vor allem Ausdruck einer kulturellen Zugehörigkeit, die ohnehin bestand. Ich würde daher auch nicht von Assimilation, sondern von Akkulturation sprechen.

WL Wir sind aber insofern einig, dass diese Art von Akkulturation ein Irrweg war.

Es ist wichtig, die deutsch-jüdische Geschichte des 19. Jahrhunderts in ihrem ganzen Potenzial zu sehen

MW Ich sehe das überhaupt nicht als Irrweg – und das ist ein Punkt, in dem wir uns gar nicht einig sind! Ich bin der Ansicht, dass man diese Zeit in ihrer eigenen Berechtigung sehen muss – und die nicht-jüdische Gesellschaft ebenso fragen muss: Was hätte denn geschehen müssen, damit nicht geschehen wäre, was geschehen ist? Wir bewerten das damalige Vertrauen vieler Jüdinnen und Juden in die deutsche Gesellschaft heute allein aufgrund der Nationalsozialisten als Irrtum. Aber was hätte passieren müssen, damit dieses Vertrauen Bestand gehabt hätte? Ich finde es wirklich wichtig, die außergewöhnliche Geschichte der deutsch-jüdischen Moderne nicht vom Ende her zu denken, sondern deren damaliges Potenzial als solches zu sehen. Jüdinnen und Juden waren auch damals nicht naiv, die antisemitischen Parteien waren alle schon da. Es war ein geschenktes Vertrauen gegenüber einer Gesellschaft, die noch 100 Jahre zuvor gesagt hatte: Ihr seid anders, deshalb habt ihr nicht dieselben Rechte, keine Möglichkeit auf die gleichen Berufe und könnt allenfalls in abgegrenzten Bezirken wohnen, euch aber keinesfalls unkontrolliert irgendwo unter uns niederlassen. Es ist mir wichtig, die deutsch-jüdische Geschichte des 19. Jahrhunderts, diese außergewöhnliche Bereitschaft von deutschen Juden, in Bildung, Wissenschaft, Kultur und Wirtschaft zu investieren und die Entwicklungen in diesem Bereich maßgeblich mitzugestalten, als Vertrauensvorschuss in die deutsche Gesellschaft und in ihrem ganzen Potenzial zu sehen.

JS Unsere Ausgangsfrage war ja: Was heißt das für uns heute? Wie viel Differenz ist wünschenswert und muss auch sein? Wenn man sich die Bornplatzsynagoge anschaut, muss man feststellen, dass die Andersartigkeit aus heutiger Perspektive kaum noch auszumachen ist, was bei der Synagoge in der Oranienburger Straße nicht der Fall ist.

MW Durchaus. Aber können wir die Frage nach der Differenz im Kontext einer diversen Gesellschaft, also jenseits der deutsch-jüdischen Neurose, denken? Es ist ja auch ganz allgemein ein wichtiges und durchaus politisches Thema. Daher wäre es natürlich ebenfalls reizvoll, die Rekonstruktion einmal unter diesem Blickpunkt zu betrachten – dann ginge es gerade bei so einem präsenten Objekt wie der Bornplatzsynagoge ebenso darum, einen zentralen Ort mit historischem Rückbezug zu schaffen, an dem auch solche Fragen nach Differenz und Zugehörigkeit verhandelt werden würden.

MW Especially since most of these places were then occupied by bunkers.

JS In Hamburg, it's even more extreme, because the bunker was only the initial form of the active destruction of urban space; arriving later was the astonishing lack of comprehension on the part of the university itself. Examining the urban layout today, you see that the impact of the synagogue would be impaired not just by the bunker, but also, and very substantially, by the university buildings as well. And it's this circumstance, too, that makes a reconstruction so difficult.

WL Although there's nothing singular about a bunker being built directly on the site of a destroyed synagogue. In Hamburg, however, we have the remarkable case of the bunker itself being granted historic preservation status—but that's a question of the value of temporal strata, I don't want to dwell on that now.

JS It's interesting that a strong consensus exists today, which includes the non-Jewish urban society of Hamburg, for reconstructing the synagogue at this location as a kind of signal. Or is that just how it seems?

MW I'm not at all certain that this consensus exists today—after the attack in Halle, the German public was ready to pay a contribution to Jewish life. Consequently, the reconstruction project in Hamburg was pushed sucessfully—with an aggressive campaign that proposed the reconstruction as a signal of opposition to anti-Semitism, which made it difficult to oppose it. In the non-Jewish world, there existed and exists a strong desire to do something to oppose the resurgence of anti-Semitism. It remains unclear, however, exactly what that should be.

JS But can the signal that is sent there be effective? To be perfectly frank, I'm skeptical about a neo-Romanesque synagogue being at all suitable for sending such a signal; about whether it will actually be understood, whether it wouldn't simply be one reconstruction among many. Which brings us again to the question of intelligibility and legibility.

WL You're asking not just about the presence of a synagogue that occupies a prominent location, about a certain public perception, but about its iconology. Which is to say: what does this form convey? What does it say?

MW I can certainly understand your question, Jörg, and I believe it's necessary to continue discussing it. What exactly is it that arises there? Is the need for symbolic presence redeemed through the reconstruction—or is it a question of the site, the building's presence?

JS Mirjam, we've learned a lot from you about the motives that led to a reconstruction being conceivable in the first place. To summarize, you could probably say that, here, the motivations are quite different, that in this context, many lines of argument that are deployed elsewhere as pros and cons are completely irrelevant.

Eine Rückkehr an den zentralen Ort jüdischen Lebens

WL Womit wir bei der Frage nach der Präsenz sind – dass man wieder sichtbar wird, dass eine Rückkehr und keine Wiederbesetzung stattfindet, und zwar an einem Ort, welcher lange Zeit der zentrale Punkt des jüdischen Lebens in Hamburg war. Wo die Synagoge zwar irgendwie einsam, aber auch selbstbewusst an einer prominenten Ecke saß. Zwar haben nur die Wenigsten, die dort entlanggegangen sind, das Gebäude auch betreten – aber das spielt ja keine Rolle, weil die Frage der Präsenz keine Frage des Innenraums, sondern eine der äußeren Erscheinung in die Stadt hinein ist. Aber allein diese städtebauliche Situation gäbe es ja heute nicht mehr.

MW Zumal die meisten Orte ja dann noch einmal durch Bunker besetzt wurden.

JS In Hamburg ist es noch extremer, weil der Bunker ja nur die erste, aktive Zerstörung des Raumes war, danach gab es ein erstaunliches Unverständnis bei der Universität selbst. Wenn man sich heute den Stadtgrundriss anschaut, wäre die Wirkung der Synagoge ja nicht nur durch den Bunker beeinträchtigt, sondern auch ganz erheblich durch die Bauten der Universität. Auch dieser Umstand macht ja eine Rekonstruktion so schwierig.

WL Wobei es ja nichts Singuläres ist, dass direkt auf den Grundstücken der zerstörten Synagogen Bunker gebaut wurden. In Hamburg ist es allerdings der bemerkenswerte Fall, dass nun der Bunker an sich auch unter Denkmalschutz steht – aber das ist eine Frage der Wertigkeit von Zeitschichten, an der ich mich jetzt auch nicht aufhalten würde.

JS Es ist interessant, dass es heute auch in der nicht-jüdischen Stadtgesellschaft Hamburgs durchaus einen Konsens gibt, die wiederaufgebaute Synagoge als Zeichen an diesem Platz haben zu wollen. Oder scheint das nur so?

MW Ich bin mir nicht sicher, ob es diesen Konsens heute gibt – nach dem Anschlag von Halle gab es den Wunsch, ein Zeichen zu setzen. Infolgedessen wurde auch das Rekonstruktionsvorhaben in Hamburg durchgesetzt – mit einer aggressiven Kampagne, die die Rekonstruktion als Zeichen gegen Antisemitismus postulierte und es schwer gemacht hat, dagegen zu sein. In der nicht-jüdischen Welt gab und gibt es den großen Wunsch, etwas gegen das Wiedererstarken des Antisemitismus zu tun. Nur weiß man gemeinhin nicht so genau, was.

JS Aber soll das Zeichen, das dort entsteht, vermitteln? Ganz offen gestanden: Ich bin skeptisch, ob die Wiederherstellung einer neoromanischen Synagoge überhaupt geeignet wäre, ein solches Zeichen zu sein; ob es tatsächlich so verstanden würde, oder ob es nicht einfach eine Rekonstruktion unter vielen wäre. Damit sind wir wieder bei der Frage der Verständlichkeit und Lesbarkeit.

But evidently, the aims of those who are pushing today for reconstruction are not at all identical with the aims of the people who built these synagogues in the first place, since there seems to be a fundamentally different iconographic understanding between these two groups. For us as architects, this is to begin with a frustrating realization—perhaps also a sensitive problem, with misunderstandings immediately arising when a building that was constructed as a Reform synagogue is taken into service now in line with a completely traditional understanding. But concerning the preceding question as well: "How much difference should we actually seek, and how much contrariety can our society tolerate at such a location?," is one that I regard, in perspective, as essential—and one, I fear, that will be discussed for years to come.

The radical break is already present in a fundamental way, and need not be narrated or further symbolized

MW In contrast to other reconstructions, the narrative here is probably this: in the absence of this radical break, the necessity for reconstructing a synagogue wouldn't arise. It is therefore present in a fundamental way, and need not be narrated, further symbolized, or thought through. And there is something else I take seriously within the current debates: the post-Soviet Jews in particular regard themselves as the descendants of the people who defeated Hitler—and wouldn't a reconstructed synagogue at this central site be the most powerful possible symbol of the defeat of National Socialism?

JS Philipp Stricharz argues similarly: not to rebuild the synagogue would means Hitler was right.

MW There is something in that, and the desire for such a gesture should be taken very seriously. Developing now, in this generation, with things such as defensive capabilities and resistance, is a new Jewish perspective on history, one that doesn't align with the victim narrative, but has instead to do with pride.

WL I'd like to touch again on the topic of memory: during this debate, I always think of the Frauenkirche in Dresden [→ Fig. 4], whose reconstruction, with its tremendous aura, was like a national symbol of rebuilding. The difficulty here is that, while you can still see that the church was constructed from old and new pieces of stone, in less than a generation this won't be as evident. It will merge with the urban environment, acquiring a patina, so that perhaps only the remains of the portal, set in front like the dome fragment of the old Frauenkirche in Dresden, will serve as reminders. People will walk by without realizing that anything happened here, and the surroundings too will be lovelier than ever. Here, it's not a question of Jewish history in particular, and instead an exemplification of the history that is told by the city through its main buildings.

JS I'm not sure history will really be forgotten so easily, although this argument is consistently deployed in

WL Du fragst also nicht nur nach der Präsenz, also dass die Synagoge einen prominenten Ort besetzt und eine bestimmte Außenwirkung hat, sondern nach der Ikonologie. Also: Was vermittelt, was spricht diese Form?

MW Ich kann Deine Frage, Jörg, vollkommen nachvollziehen und ich glaube, es ist die Aufgabe, hierüber auch weiterhin im Gespräch zu sein. Also: Was ist es denn eigentlich, was dort entsteht? Ist dieses Bedürfnis der Zeichenhaftigkeit mit der Rekonstruktion eingelöst – oder geht es doch eher um den Ort, geht es um die Präsenz?

JS Wir haben von Dir, Mirjam, viel gelernt über Motive, die eine Rekonstruktion überhaupt denkbar machen. Zusammenfassend kann man wohl sagen, dass hier die Beweggründe ganz andere sind und somit viele Argumentationsstränge, die sonst als Für und Wider ins Feld geführt werden, in diesem Kontext völlig irrelevant werden. Aber augenscheinlich sind auch die Ziele derjenigen, die heute den Wiederaufbau forcieren, gar nicht identisch mit den Zielen derer, die diese Synagoge dereinst gebaut haben, es gibt offensichtlich ein ganz anderes Verständnis desselben Bildprogramms. Das ist für uns als Architekten erst einmal ein Stück weit eine frustrierende Erkenntnis – und möglicherweise auch ein empfindliches Problem, weil plötzlich solche Missverständnisse entstehen, also dass etwas, was einmal als Reformsynagoge gebaut wurde, nun für ein ganz traditionelles Verständnis in den Dienst genommen werden kann. Aber auch die vorangegangene Frage «Wie viel Differenz sollten wir eigentlich suchen und wie viel Gegensätzlichkeit hält unsere Gesellschaft heute an einem solchen Ort aus?» halte ich perspektivisch für einen wesentlichen Punkt – über den man, fürchte ich, wohl noch einige Jahre diskutieren wird.

Der Bruch ist von Grund auf gegenwärtig, er muss nicht miterzählt oder zusätzlich symbolisiert werden

MW Was wohl das wesentliche Narrativ im Unterschied zu anderen Rekonstruktionen ist: Die Notwendigkeit zum Wiederaufbau einer Synagoge wäre ja ohne den Bruch nicht gegeben. Er ist somit schon von Grund auf präsent und muss nicht miterzählt, zusätzlich symbolisiert oder mitgedacht werden. Und auch das nehme ich in den aktuellen Debatten ernst: Gerade postsowjetische Jüdinnen und Juden verstehen sich als Nachfahren derjenigen, die einst Hitler besiegt haben – und wäre nicht eine rekonstruierte Synagoge an diesem zentralen Ort das größtmögliche Zeichen des Sieges über den Nationalsozialismus?

JS So argumentiert ja auch Philipp Stricharz: Die Synagoge nicht wiederaufzubauen, hieße Hitler Recht geben.

MW Da ist etwas dran und auch den Wunsch nach so einer Geste nehme ich sehr ernst. Gerade jetzt in dieser Generation entwickelt sich mit Themen wie Wehrhaftigkeit und Widerstand eine neue jüdische Perspektive auf die Geschichte, die nicht über das Opfernarrativ funktioniert, sondern mit Stolz zu tun hat.

4
Alte und neue Steine, Fassade der 2005 wiederaufgebauten Frauenkirche, Dresden, Foto: 2008
Old and new stone blocks, facade of the Frauenkirche in Dresden, reconstructed in 2005, photo: 2008

opposition to historic reconstructions. In Cracow, standing along the Ring, are these apparently old buildings, but it is precisely an awareness of the achievement represented by this reconstruction that has become an important aspect of the city's identity today. Things are similar in Dresden. Although I'm not really sure it was a good idea to rebuild the Frauenkirche—there was a nationwide debate about it in Germany. In Hamburg, no such discussion is taking place, which brings us back to the German-Jewish neuroses. However, would a discussion about reconstruction involve the larger public, or should it instead be led to begin with by the Jewish community?

MW Definitely the latter, I would say. Ultimately, we're talking about a synagogue—about a place where members of a Jewish community come together in order to meet, learn, study, and worship God. Furthermore, community members need to articulate their needs when it comes to the construction of new buildings—it's only then that topics such as the building's relationship to the surroundings, to history, and to non-Jewish society play a role. So, to begin with, we're talking about an internal process of negotiation.

A unity between external appearance and interior

JS Up to this point, our discussion has barely touched upon how the character of the location will actually be shaped. Mirjam, you've argued in a very conciliatory way in relation to the advocates of historic reconstruction.

WL Jetzt muss ich noch einmal das Thema der Erinnerung anreißen: Bei dieser Debatte denke ich immer an die Dresdener Frauenkirche [→ Abb. 4], deren Rekonstruktion mit ihrer großen Strahlkraft ja wie ein nationales Aufbausymbol war. Das Schwierige hierbei ist: Momentan erkennt man noch, dass sie aus alten und neuen Steinen zusammengesetzt ist, aber in weniger als einer Generation wird dem nicht mehr so sein. Sie wird stadträumlich eingewachsen und derart patiniert sein, dass möglicherweise nur der Rest des Portals, welcher als Stolperstein davor liegt, erinnernd wirkt. Man wird da vorbeigehen und nicht merken, dass dort irgendetwas geschehen ist und auch die Umgebung ist so schön, wie sie niemals war. Es geht jetzt nicht um jüdische Geschichte, sondern eher exemplarisch um die Geschichte, die eine Stadt mit ihrem zentralen Bauwerk erzählt.

JS Ich bin mir nicht so sicher, dass Geschichte tatsächlich so leicht vergessen wird, wie das immer als klassisches Argument gegen jede Rekonstruktion vorgebracht wird. In Krakau am Ring stehen auch diese nur scheinbar alten Häuser und gerade das Wissen um die Wiederaufbauleistung ist heute ein wichtiger Teil der Identität dieser Stadt. In Dresden ist das ähnlich. Wobei ich gar nicht weiß, ob es tatsächlich gut war, die Frauenkirche wiederaufzubauen – hierzu gab es ja auch eine breite, deutschlandweite Debatte. In Hamburg gibt es eine solche Diskussion nicht, womit wir wieder bei den deutsch-jüdischen Neurosen wären. Aber: Wäre die Wiederaufbaudiskussion überhaupt eine der großen Allgemeinheit oder nicht eine, die zunächst einmal die jüdische Gemeinschaft führen müsste?

 MW Ich würde sagen: ganz klar letzteres. Schließlich geht es um eine Synagoge – den Ort, an dem sich die jüdische Gemeinschaft trifft, ihre Gottesdienste abhält, lernt und studiert. Es geht ja auch darum, hier als Gemeinde neue Bedürfnisse zu artikulieren – erst danach spielen solche Themen wie die Bezugsverhältnisse zur Umgebung, zur Geschichte, zur nicht-jüdischen Gesellschaft eine Rolle. Das wäre also erst einmal ein interner Aushandlungsprozess.

Die Einheit von äußerer Erscheinung und Innenraum

JS In unserer Diskussion haben wir das, was später den eigentlichen Charakter des Ortes ausmachen wird, bislang immer nur gestreift. Du, Mirjam, hast ja durchaus konziliant gegenüber den Rekonstruktionsbefürwortern argumentiert. Aber was hieße so eine Entscheidung eigentlich für den Raum, der dabei wieder neu entstünde? In Berlin argumentiert man ja völlig offen und sagt: Wir wollen diese Fassade rekonstruieren, was dahinter passiert, kann irgendetwas sein. Sähe man das in Hamburg genauso? Ich meine, wir als Architekten denken natürlich über eine gewisse Identität von äußerer Erscheinung und Raum nach. Daher kann ich mir kaum vorstellen, dass man die Bornplatzsynagoge an ebendieser Stelle wiedererrichtet und gleichzeitig sagt: Mir ist der eigentliche Synagogenraum gleichgültig. Müsste also auch der wiederhergestellte Innenraum

But what would such a decision mean for the spatial situation that would reemerge in the process? In Berlin, it's being said quite openly: we want to reconstruct the facade, but what happens behind it remains an open question. Does this perspective exist in Hamburg as well? Which is to say that, as architects, we of course think in terms of an identity of sorts between outward appearance and internal space. So for me, it's almost inconceivable that you could reconstruct the Bornplatz Synagogue on this very spot, and at the same time say: the actual space of the synagogue is a matter of indifference to me. Wouldn't the reconstructed interior have to be characterized in a specific way as well? Wouldn't this entail a conflict between the ambitions of today's protagonists and what the space formerly was?

 MW I would say so, since today's community is much smaller than the one that gathered here formerly.

JS That always takes me by surprise. The size of the community is always discussed in a way that suggests that the design of a synagogue is a functional question.

 MW But here in Frankfurt, for example, it's a current and thoroughly concrete topic—there is a community center and a large synagogue, but at the moment, space is being sought for the family center. So, actually, the space for religious services plays only a subordinate role in the needs of the community. Positioned in the foreground instead are components such as the kindergarten, the family center, the kosher kitchen. Since a synagogue is a place where people meet, these aspects have to be taken into account when building a new, massive building such as the Bornplatz Synagogue. Nevertheless, a synagogue is not a community center but a place of religous service. Therefore, its architecture needs to have certain components. In Jewish tradition, light plays an important role, the positioning of the Aron HaKodesh and of the Bimah are important aspects of the synagogue architecture. In particular, it's important that a synagogue be conceived in a way that is fundamentally different from a church. The synagogue is the place where the Torah is preserved as a sacred object. Which means that the architecture needs to somehow concentrate on things that are related to the Torah, on what touches and surrounds it. But apart from these formal elements, I believe the atmosphere of the synagogue is shaped by use, by memory, and by time.

The most important element cannot be allowed to appear as the least important

JS What I find interesting is: what do we actually expect from the interior of a newly constructed synagogue? That, meanwhile, there are also other demands, has become clear from your answer, Mirjam—which however also enter into conflict with the demand for symbolic value. This can be seen quite clearly, I believe, in our projects. In a number of designs, for example the one by Robin Thomä from Darmstadt, the synagogue is actually construed as a community center [→ pp. 202–207]. Both in relation to the urban environment as well as in

in einer bestimmten Art und Weise charakterisiert sein? Und gäbe es dabei einen Konflikt zwischen den Ambitionen der heutigen Handelnden und dem, was der Raum früher war?

MW Das denke ich schon, weil die Gemeinde heute ja viel kleiner ist als diejenige, die sich hier einst traf.

JS Das wundert mich immer. Man diskutiert immer die Größe der Gemeinde, als sei die Gestalt einer Synagoge eine funktionale Frage.

MW Aber hier in Frankfurt ist das zum Beispiel ein aktuelles und durchaus konkretes Thema – es gibt ein Gemeindezentrum und eine große Synagoge, aber zurzeit wird nach neuen Räumen für das Familienzentrum gesucht. Daher: Der Raum für den Gottesdienst spielt eigentlich nur eine nachgeordnete Rolle. Vielmehr stehen der Kindergarten, das Familienzentrum, die koschere Küche, all so etwas im Vordergrund, zumal eine Synagoge ja auch ein Ort ist, an dem man sich verabredet und trifft. Das sind Punkte, die auch in den späteren Entwürfen berücksichtigt werden müssten. Die Frage nach einer spezifischen Atmosphäre in Synagogen kann ich aus architektonischer Sicht dagegen nur schwer beurteilen. Sicherlich spielt Licht als wesentliches Element der jüdischen Tradition eine große Rolle, die Positionierung des Aron ha-Kodesch ist ein wichtiger Punkt. Vor allem ist es sehr wichtig, eine Synagoge von Grund auf anders als eine Kirche zu denken. Sie ist der Ort, an dem die Tora als der heilige Text aufbewahrt wird. Daher konzentriert sich alles auf das, was mit der Tora zu tun hat, was sie berührt und umgibt – und diesen Gedanken muss das Gebäude auch irgendwie widerspiegeln. Aber fernab dieser formalen Punkte glaube ich, dass sich eine Atmosphäre auch mit der Nutzung, der Erinnerung und der Zeit herstellt.

Die bedeutendste Sache darf nicht als unwichtigste erscheinen

JS Was mich interessiert, ist: Was erwarten wir eigentlich heute von einem Innenraum einer Synagoge, wenn wir sie neu bauen? Dass es mittlerweile auch andere Ansprüche sind, ist in Deiner Antwort, Mirjam, deutlich geworden – aber die geraten dann ja auch mit dem Anspruch an eine Zeichenhaftigkeit in Konflikt. Ich glaube, das sieht man auch ganz deutlich in unseren Projekten. Wir haben einige Entwürfe, wie den von Robin Thomä aus Darmstadt, in denen die Synagoge tatsächlich als Gemeindezentrum aufgefasst wird [→ S. 202–207]. Sowohl im Stadtraum als auch in der Gestalt werden die Gebäude enorm zurückhaltend präsentiert. Hier, bei dem Projekt von Ria Roberg, ist es noch augenfälliger: Die Synagoge verschwindet fast hinter der Talmud-Tora-Schule [→ Abb. 5 & S. 198–201]. Das sind beides Arbeiten, die dem Anspruch an eine Selbstverständlichkeit vielleicht eher entsprechen, bei denen sich dann allerdings auch die Frage nach der Angemessenheit stellt.

WL Der Entwurf von Ria Roberg könnte auch auf einer Wiese sitzen. Formal ganz schön, aber es sieht doch

5
Entwurf
Neue Synagoge
Bornplatz,
Hamburg
Design for a new synagogue,
Bornplatz,
Hamburg
—
Ria Roberg
2021

its design, the building presents itself in an enormously restrained way. Here, with the project by Ria Roberg, this is even more striking: the synagogue almost disappears behind the Talmud Torah School [→ Fig. 5 & pp. 198–201]. Both projects correspond perhaps to the demand for a kind of self-evident presence, but also necessarily bring up the question of appropriateness.

WL The design by Ria Roberg could also sit on a meadow. Quite lovely in formal terms, but it looks more like an ancillary building. Necessary apart from the formal aspect is an appropriate positioning, so that the significance of the synagogue within the larger ensemble becomes visible. The most important element cannot be allowed to appear as the least important, it must assume its rightful place, and not get lost in relation to the school or the community center, whose volumes are multiply larger. Which isn't always easy, since significance and scale are not necessarily proportionate to one another.

JS Which is exactly what these designs have shown. In the project by Valentin Müller and Malte Wiegand, and for this very reason, albeit in a way that is not entirely practical, they positioned the actual synagogue space in a corner of the third floor—only in this way could this rather small space fulfill its task of having a real presence within the city, which moreover has a very different scale here, in the neighborhood of the university buildings [→ pp. 188–193].

WL The project by Nadine Kreth dealt with this problem quite effectively by creating a kind of forum and positioning the synagogue in front of it as a freestanding

eher wie ein Nebenbau aus. Es ist ja auch jenseits vom Formalen immer eine entsprechende Positionierung nötig, damit die Wertigkeit innerhalb eines Ensembles sichtbar wird. Die bedeutendste Sache darf nicht als unwichtigste erscheinen, sie muss ihren richtigen Platz bekommen und nicht gegenüber der Schule oder dem Gemeindezentrum untergehen, deren Volumina um ein Vielfaches größer sind. Wobei das nicht immer leicht ist, weil Bedeutung und Größe nun eben nicht proportional zueinander stehen.

JS Genau das haben diese Entwürfe ja gezeigt. In der Arbeit von Valentin Müller und Malte Wiegand setzen sie aus ebendiesem Grund, was nur mäßig praktikabel ist, den eigentlichen Synagogenraum ins dritte Obergeschoss auf die Ecke – nur damit dieser recht kleine Raum die Last der Präsenz in die Stadt zu tragen vermag, die in der Nachbarschaft der Universitätsgebäude hier auch noch einen ganz anderen Maßstab aufweist [→ S.188–193].

WL Die Arbeit von Nadine Kreth ist mit diesem Problem ganz gut umgegangen, indem sie eine Art Forum geschaffen und die Synagoge dann freigestellt und davor positioniert hat [→ S.180–183]. Man könnte um der Präsenz willen auch eine große leere Hülle konstruieren und diese dann irgendwie auffüllen, aber das wäre ja wiederum ein Zeichen.

JS Jede Geste wird immer eine Bedeutung bekommen, egal was du tust. Selbst, wenn du vorgibst nichts zu tun. Und zu sagen: Ich rekonstruiere eine Hülle und tue dort drin etwas anderes – auch das wäre ein Zeichen.

MW Das stimmt. Hierzu fällt mir immer die Dresdener Synagoge ein, weil da gefühlt irgendwie ein Missverhältnis zwischen der Größe und Form der Synagoge und der Größe der Gemeinde existiert [→ Abb.6]. Die Wahl der richtigen Zeichen hängt ja auch von der Frage ab, wie sich die Gemeinde heute und wo sie sich in Zukunft sieht. So gibt es in Frankfurt gerade einen großen Bedarf an Funktionsräumen, weil diese sozialen Funktionen des Gemeindelebens mittlerweile eine größere Rolle spielen, was ja auch eine aktuelle Entwicklung ist. Also: Wo sieht sich die Hamburger Gemeinde in zwanzig Jahren?

structure [→ pp.180–183]. For the sake of presence, you could construct a large empty shell, and then fill it in one way or another, but that too would be a signal.

JS Every gesture acquires meaning, no matter what you do. Even when you profess to do nothing: and to say: "I'm reconstructing a shell and doing something else on the inside"—that, too, would be a signal.

MW That's true. Here, I always think of the Dresden Synagogue, because there, you somehow sense an imbalance between the size and form of the synagogue and the size of the community [→ Fig.6]. The choice of the right signal depends as well on the question of where the community sees itself today, and where it expects to be in the future. In Frankfurt, there is a great need for functional spaces, since social functions play an increasingly important role in community life, which is also a current development. Hence the question: how does the Hamburg community see itself in twenty years?

If presence is the aim, can pathos be a means for achieving it?

WL On this question, Charlotte Knobloch recently remarked to Philipp Stricharz: "A synagogue is a symbol, but the other elements, such as the school or kindergarten, are the future of the community, and also the precondition for the synagogue being filled. Build a small synagogue, that always suffices—you need to allow the area around it to grow." I found that astonishing. I mean, it's true, of course. In Hamburg, approaching things in purely pragmatic terms, the task would be to build a school, a community center, and a kindergarten. But this isn't a debate about function.

JS Exactly. Which brings us right back to the symbolic—the decisive signal would drop out, and it would be exchangeable. But we won't succeed in resolving this dilemma today in our discussion. Perhaps we ought to take another look at the larger aspects that emerge from it—namely presence and pathos. If presence is the aim, can pathos be a means for achieving it? This tendency is certainly observable at the moment; it resonates as well in the desire for a reconstruction, and is represented in many of the student projects. Although I'm not sure whether it's really desirable, whether a different type of symbolism would be more appropriate. Or is pathos also an aspect of the thematic positioning of the community, and hence necessary in this instance?

MW Well, actually, pathos is a component of the rhetorical doctrine of Greek antiquity—not an element of Jewish tradition. But is the religious practice of communal prayer, reading, and singing conceivable without pathos? Put differently: isn't the emotive aspect a universal component of religious practices, simply because it's a question of turning toward a power that isn't present as an individual, and which therefore has all the more weight?

6
Neue Synagoge, Dresden
New synagogue, Dresden
—
Andrea Wandel, Dr. Rena Wandel-Hoefer, Andreas Hoefer, Wolfgang Lorch, Nikolaus Hirsch
2001

Wenn Präsenz das Ziel ist, kann Pathos ein Mittel sein?

WL Hierzu meinte zuletzt Charlotte Knobloch gegenüber Philip Stricharz: «Synagoge ist Symbol, aber die anderen Sachen wie Schule oder Kindergarten sind jetzt die Zukunft der Gemeinde und die Voraussetzung, dass die Synagoge auch gefüllt wird. Baut eine kleine Synagoge, die reicht allemal – ihr müsst das Außenherum wachsen lassen.» Das fand ich erstaunlich. Ich meine, es stimmt ja. Wenn man in Hamburg rein pragmatisch denken würde, läge die Aufgabe darin, vor allem eine Schule, ein Gemeindezentrum und einen Kindergarten zu bauen. Aber es ist nun mal keine Funktionsdebatte.

JS Genau, denn damit wäre man sofort wieder beim Punkt des Symbolischen – das entscheidende Zeichen fiele weg und es würde austauschbar werden. Wir werden dieses Dilemma heute in dieser Runde auch nicht auflösen können. Aber vielleicht sollten wir noch einmal die allgemeinen Aspekte, die sich hieraus ergeben, in den Blick nehmen – nämlich Präsenz und Pathos. Also, wenn Präsenz das Ziel ist, kann Pathos ein Mittel sein? Diese Tendenz ist ja im Moment zu beobachten, sie schwingt auch im Wunsch nach Rekonstruktion mit und sie ist ebenso in vielen Arbeiten der Studenten vertreten. Wobei ich mir nicht sicher bin, ob das tatsächlich wünschenswert ist oder ob nicht eine andere Art der Zeichenhaftigkeit angemessener wäre. Oder ist das Pathos auch ein Teil der inhaltlichen Positionierung der Gemeinde und in diesem Fall dann notwendig?

MW Nun, eigentlich ist Pathos ja Bestandteil der rhetorischen Lehre der griechischen Antike – also kein Element der jüdischen Tradition. Aber kann man die religiöse Praxis des gemeinsamen Betens, Lesens und Singens überhaupt jenseits von Pathos denken? Anders gesagt, ist das Pathetische nicht vielleicht allgemeiner Bestandteil von religiösen Praktiken – ganz einfach, weil es hier darum geht, sich an eine Macht zu wenden, die nicht als Person gegenwärtig ist, aber umso mehr Gewicht hat?

JS Das würde ich nicht sagen. Nicht zwangsläufig. Man kann einen sakralen Raum denken, der in vergleichsweise geringem Maße pathetisch ist. Eines meiner Lieblingsbeispiele dafür wäre Rudolf Schwarz' Kirche in Düren [→ Abb. 7].

Die Synagoge ist eine ideelle Heimat

MW Gut, gegen Rudolf Schwarz' Schlichtheit lässt sich natürlich nur schwer argumentieren, wenngleich seine Kirchen natürlich zutiefst protestantisch sind ... Daher lasst uns lieber noch einen anderen wichtigen Begriff in den Blick nehmen, nämlich den der Heimat. Das ist ja ein bedeutendes Thema der jüdischen Kulturgeschichte, das in den letzten Jahren wieder zu einem starken Bezugspunkt geworden ist – und zwar mit all seinen Facetten: die Unmöglichkeit und Gebrochenheit von Heimat bei gleichzeitigem Festhalten an der Sehnsucht nach einem ebensolchen Ort. Wobei man sich ja letztlich nicht wirklich vorstellen kann, in der Diaspora

JS I wouldn't say that. Not necessarily. It's conceivable for a sacred space to be emotive on a relatively small scale. One of my favorite examples is Rudolf Schwarz's church in Düren [→ Fig. 7].

The synagogue is a spiritual homeland

MW All right, it's difficult to argue against Rudolf Schwarz's simplicity, of course, although his churches are profoundly Protestant ... : Let's instead examine another important concept, namely that of Heimat (home/homeland). That's an important theme in Jewish cultural history, and has become an important point of reference again in recent years—and moreover in all of its facets: the impossibility and brokenness of the homeland, and at the same time, a cherishing and longing for precisely such a place. Although, ultimately, it's inconceivable that you would actually find a homeland in the diaspora—apart from what Heinrich Heine referred to as the "portable fatherland," which is to say the Torah. With synagogue buildings, this concept of homeland plays an enormous role, since a synagogue is the container and repository of the Torah, and hence of that which is sacred in Judaism. It is also a place where you are lifted up, where you're at home, a spiritual homeland. And developing oftentimes centrifugally around the synagogue, not least of all, is a Jewish quarter, with its corresponding infrastructure.

WL That's the case in Hamburg, with a substantial part of the community living in the Grindelviertel, where there are many Jewish institutions, whether it's

7
Innenraum Pfarrkirche St. Anna, Düren
Interior of the parish church of St. Anna in Düren
—
Rudolf Schwarz
1956

eine Heimat zu finden – außer mit Blick auf das, was Heinrich Heine das «portative Vaterland» genannt hat, also die Tora. Bei Synagogenbauten spielt dieser Begriff von Heimat eine große Rolle, denn sie sind die Hülle und der Aufbewahrungsort der Tora und damit dessen, was im Judentum heilig ist. Sie sind darüber hinaus Orte des Aufgehoben- und Zuhause-Seins, gewissermaßen eine ideelle Heimat. Nicht zuletzt entwickelt sich ja auch zentrifugal um die Synagoge herum oftmals ein jüdisches Viertel mit einer entsprechenden Infrastruktur.

WL In Hamburg ist das ja auch so, wo ein beträchtlicher Teil der Community im Grindelviertel wohnt und es dort auch viele jüdische Einrichtungen, sei es die Talmud-Tora-Schule oder das Café Leonar, gibt. Hier existiert also schon eine kritische Masse und zwar nicht nur gefühlt, sondern auch eindeutig sichtbar. Wenn es einen Punkt jüdischen Lebens in Hamburg gibt, dann ist es dort und das muss nicht musealisiert werden. Da wird gelebt – auch das ist Restitution und Rückübertragung.

MW Ja, das stimmt. Ich glaube, dass es jüdischerseits undenkbar ist, Deutschland heute «Heimatland» zu nennen – aber es ist möglich, den Ort, an dem ich lebe, und die Synagoge, die ich besuche, als ein Zuhause zu empfinden. Das ist denkbar und das ist auch eine Sehnsucht – eben in aller Gebrochenheit.

the Talmud Torah School or the Café Leonar. Found here, then, is a critical mass, and not only subjectively, but in a way that's clearly visible. When there is a focal point for Jewish life in Hamburg, then it's here, and it needn't be musealized. It's a place for life—that, too, is a form of restitution and repatriation.

MW Yes, that's true. From a Jewish perspective, I believe it's inconceivable to refer to Germany as a "homeland"—but it is possible to perceive the place where I live, and the synagogue I visit, as a kind of home. That is conceivable, and is a kind of longing—despite all brokenness.

1 Unter anderem die Pfarrkirche St. Augustin in Paris (Victor Batlard, 1871) und der Dom St. Peter zu Worms (unbekannt, 1181) gelten als Vorbilder des Entwurfs von Edwind Oppler für die Neue Synagoge Hannover, die 1870 eingeweiht und in der Reichpogromnacht 1938 zerstört wurde.

Synagoge Bornplatz Synagogue

1
Blick von Südwesten,
Foto: 1906
View from
the southwest,
photo: 1906

Synagoge Bornplatz
　Bornplatz Synagogue

Joseph-Carlebach-Platz
(früher/formerly Bornplatz), Hamburg
Semmy Engel & Ernst Friedheim
1906 (zerstört/destroyed 1938/40)

Die von 1904 bis 1906 errichtete Bornplatzsynagoge im Hamburger Grindelviertel war die erste vollkommen freistehende Synagoge Hamburgs[1] und diente der deutsch-israelitischen Gemeinde als Hauptsynagoge. Der weithin sichtbare kuppelbekrönte, monumentale Bau in exponierter Lage zeugte von der um die Jahrhundertwende erlangten Anerkennung der jüdischen Gemeinde in der Hansestadt und brachte auch deren Identifikation mit der deutschen Nation zum Ausdruck. In unmittelbarer Nähe zur Synagoge am Bornplatz wurde am Grindelhof bis 1911 auch die Talmud-Tora-Schule errichtet.[2]

Durch die infolge der bürgerlichen Revolution 1848/49 erreichte, in der Hamburger Verfassung 1860 verkündete, weitgehende rechtliche und bürgerliche Gleichstellung der Jüdinnen und Juden und durch die Aufhebung der Torsperre 1861, die es ermöglichte, auch in Gebiete außerhalb der Stadtbefestigung zu ziehen, setzte ab den 1880er-Jahren eine Bevölkerungsfluktuation von zu Wohlstand gekommenen jüdischen Einwohnerinnen und Einwohnern Hamburgs aus der Neustadt in die neuen, vornehmeren Stadterweiterungen von Harvestehude und Rotherbaum ein,[3] so dass eine neue Synagoge in diesem Teil Hamburgs notwendig wurde.

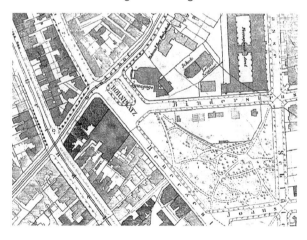

Als größte Hamburger Synagoge bot die Bornplatzsynagoge Platz für etwa 1100 Menschen. Mit 19,5 Metern war die Kuppel im Innern nur etwa halb so hoch wie die auf Fernwirkung angelegte, 39 Meter hohe äußere bauliche Kubatur.[4] Rückwärtig zur Binderstraße hin angegliedert waren eine Wochentagssynagoge, ein Sitzungssaal und Büroräume sowie eine Mikwe im Keller des Gebäudes.

In der Baukonstruktion mit Beton und Eisengerüst durchaus modern, wurde die Synagoge als eine der letzten Großbauten in einer neoromanischen Formensprache mit roten Klinkern, ockerfarbigem Backstein und rotem Mainsandstein

2
Historischer Lageplan: 1921
Historic site plan: 1921
—
1:5000

The Bornplatz Synagogue, built in Hamburg's Grindel district between 1904 and 1906, was the first fully freestanding synagogue in Hamburg,[1] and served the German Israelite community as its primary house of worship. The monumental building—occupying a highly exposed location, crowned with a cupola, and visible from afar—testified to the recognition achieved around the turn of the century by the Jewish community in the Hanseatic city, and was a manifestation of its identification with the German nation. The Talmud Torah School at Grindelhof, in immediate proximity to the synagogue at Bornplatz, was completed in 1911.[2]

During the 1880s, far-reaching legal and civil equality was won by the Jewish people in the wake of the bourgeois revolution of 1848/49, as proclaimed by the Hamburg Constitution of 1860 and through the removal in 1861 of residency restrictions which meant that Jews could now reside beyond the town fortifications. This resulted in Hamburg witnessing a rapid flow of newly prosperous Jewish residents from the Neustadt district into the new, more fashionable urban expansion areas of Harvestehude and Rotherbaum,[3] necessitating the construction of a new synagogue in that part of the city.

As the largest synagogue in Hamburg, the Bornplatz Synagogue could accommodate approximately 1,100 worshipers. With a total height of 19.5 meters, the interior of the cupola rose to only one-half of the height of the external structure, which extended up to 39 meters, and was designed to be visible from afar.[4] At the rear, facing Binderstraße, was a weekday synagogue, a conference room, and offices, as well as a mikveh in the cellar of the building.

A thoroughly modern construction in concrete with iron scaffolding, the synagogue was one of the last major buildings to be erected using a neo-Romanesque form language, with red clinker, ocher-colored brick, and red Main River sandstone. This style, widespread at the time, expressed identification with the German nation, and enjoyed great prestige in late-nineteenth-century architectural theory for sacred and secular buildings alike. This choice also meant avoiding recourse to the Gothic style, so strongly associated with Christian church building and, moreover, widely perceived as "German."[5]

The building, with its precise eastern orientation, was accessed from the west from the intersection of Bornplatz/Grindelhof via a vestibule with a central entrance for the men and lateral entrances to the galleries for the women, which were screened off with latticework. Conceived as a square central space, the prayer room was organized—in conformity with the neo-Orthodox cult—according to the traditional spatial schema, with a central almemar set beneath the cupola.

errichtet. Dieser seinerzeit weit verbreitete Stil brachte eine Identifikation mit der deutschen Nation zum Ausdruck und genoss in der Profan- und Sakralbautheorie des späten 19. Jahrhunderts großes Ansehen. So musste hier nicht auf den ebenfalls als «deutsch» empfundenen, jedoch zu stark mit dem christlichen Kirchenbau verbundenen, gotischen Stil zurückgegriffen werden.[5]

Der exakt geostete Bau wurde von Westen her, von der Kreuzung Bornplatz/Grindelhof, über eine Vorhalle mit mittlerem Eingang für Männer und seitlichen Zugängen zu den vergitterten Frauenemporen betreten. Als quadratischer Zentralraum konzipiert, war der Gebetsraum dem neo-orthodoxen Kultus entsprechend nach traditionellem Raumschema mit zentral unter der Kuppel befindlichem Almemor organisiert. Die mit einem sternförmigen Rippengewölbe artikulierte Kuppel endete in einem zentralen runden Oberlicht. Nach Osten hin in einer Art Apsis erhob sich auf einer Estrade der Thoraschrein als «architektonischer Höhepunkt des Baues»[6] in Form einer Scheinarchitektur aus schwarzem, weißem und rotem Marmor.[7]

Nachdem es bereits seit 1930 im Grindelviertel zu antisemitischen Vorfällen gekommen war, wurde die Bornplatzsynagoge während der Novemberpogrome am 10. November 1938 verwüstet. Mit Verweis auf eine Rückkaufsklausel im Kaufvertrag von 1902 musste die Gemeinde das Grundstück im Mai 1939 zu einem geringen Preis an die Stadt Hamburg zurückverkaufen und bis Mitte 1940 selbst für den Abriss der Synagoge sorgen.[8] Auf dem Gelände wurde Anfang der 40er-Jahre ein Hochbunker errichtet, der, renoviert und umgebaut, heute durch die Universität genutzt wird.

Zum fünfzigsten Jahrestag der Zerstörung erfolgte eine Neugestaltung des heute unbebauten, seit 1989 nach Joseph Carlebach benannten Platzes. Ein Bodenmosaik nach dem Entwurf der Künstlerin Margrit Kahl von 1986 bildet den Grundriss und das Deckengewölbe der Synagoge in dunklen Pflastersteinen und schwarzem polierten Granit auf dem Platz nach.[9]

Als einer der repräsentativsten großstädtischen Synagogenbauten der Jahrhundertwende kommt der Bornplatzsynagoge besondere Bedeutung zu. Zu den größten Synagogen Nordeuropas zählend und freistehend an prominenter Lage im Hamburger Stadtbild errichtet, war sie Ausdruck eines im Laufe des 19. und frühen 20. Jahrhunderts gewandelten Selbstverständnisses jüdischer Gemeinden in Deutschland.

Articulated with star-shaped ribbed vaulting, the cupola terminated in a central, circular top light. Toward the east, the Torah shrine was elevated on a dais in a kind of apse, "the building's architectural highpoint,"[6] in the form of mock architecture in black, white, and red marble.[7]

The Grindelviertel witnessed anti-Semitic attacks as early as 1930, and the Bornplatz Synagogue was ransacked during the pogrom of November 10, 1938. In May of 1939, ostensibly legitimated by reference to a repurchase clause contained in the purchase contract of 1902, the community was compelled to sell the property back to the City of Hamburg for a paltry sum while making arrangements for the demolition of the synagogue by mid-1940.[8] An aboveground bunker was erected on the site in the early 1940s; this was later renovated and converted, and remains in use by the university.

The fiftieth anniversary of the synagogue's destruction was commemorated by a redesign of the site, still unbuilt today, on the square known since 1989 as Joseph-Carlebach-Platz. In 1986 a pavement mosaic based on a design by the artist Margrit Kahl was installed on the square; this reconstructs the ground plan and ceiling vault of the synagogue in dark cobblestones and black polished granite.[9]

One of the most representative turn-of-the-century metropolitan synagogue buildings, the Bornplatz Synagogue is of special significance. Among the largest synagogues of northern Europe, and a freestanding structure at a prominent location within the Hamburg cityscape, it was an expression of the self-image of the Jewish community in Germany, which underwent profound transformation during the nineteenth and early twentieth centuries.

3
Joseph-Carlebach Platz mit Bodenmosaik, Foto: 1988
Joseph-Carlebach-Platz with pavement mosaic, photo: 1988

1 Vgl. Ulrich Bauche (Hg.): *Vierhundert Jahre Juden in Hamburg. Eine Ausstellung des Museums für Hamburgische Geschichte vom 8.11.1991 bis 29.3.1992,* Hamburg 1991, S. 320.
2 Vgl. Museum für Hamburgische Geschichte (Hg.): *Ehemals in Hamburg zu Hause. Jüdisches Leben am Grindel. Bornplatz-Synagoge und Talmud-Tora-Schule,* Hamburg 1991 (Hamburg Porträt, Heft 22), S. 4.
3 Vgl. Harold Hammer-Schenk: *Synagogen in Deutschland. Geschichte einer Baugattung im 19. und 20. Jahrhundert (1780–1933),* Teil 1, Hamburg 1981 (Hamburger Beiträge zur Geschichte der deutschen Juden, Band VIII), S. 412.
4 Vgl. Arno Herzig und Saskia Rohde (Hg.): *Die Juden in Hamburg 1590 bis 1990. Wissenschaftliche Beiträge der Universität Hamburg zu Ausstellung «Vierhundert Jahre Juden in Hamburg»,* Hamburg 1991, S. 159.
5 Vgl. Harold Hammer-Schenk: *Synagogen in Deutschland,* S. 413 f.
6 Arno Herzig und Saskia Rohde (Hg.): *Die Juden in Hamburg 1590 bis 1990,* S. 159.
7 Vgl. Harold Hammer-Schenk: *Synagogen in Deutschland,* S. 413.
8 Vgl. Arno Herzig und Saskia Rohde (Hg.): *Die Juden in Hamburg 1590 bis 1990,* S. 159 f.
9 Vgl. Museum für Hamburgische Geschichte (Hg.): *Ehemals in Hamburg zu Hause. Jüdisches Leben am Grindel,* S. 12.

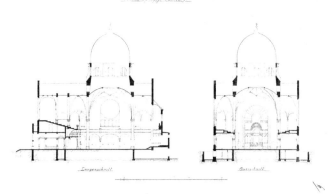

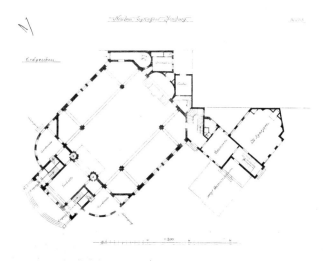

4
Ansicht
Grindelhof
elevation

5
Schnitte durch
Gebetsraum
Sections through
prayer room

6
Erdgeschoss
Ground floor

7
Gebetsraum
Bornplatz-
synagoge,
Foto: um 1906
Prayer hall,
Bornplatz
Synagogue,
photo: ca. 1906

Thomas Jankowski & Hanna Tschierse

HafenCity Universität Hamburg
Prof. Gesine Weinmiller

Bis heute ist der Bunker am Bornplatz ein Symbol für Willkür: Die größte Synagoge Nordeuropas musste weichen, damit an gleicher Stelle ein Gebäude für Kriegszwecke errichtet werden konnte. Um städtebaulich eine Setzung in der ersten Reihe am Platz zu ermöglichen, wird das zur Zeit des Nationalsozialismus errichtete Bunkergebäude zurückgebaut. Auf diese Weise lassen sich die Stadträume klären, die Straßenfluchten der Umgebung fortführen sowie der jüdischen Gemeinde den ihr ursprünglich überlassenen Bauplatz zurückgeben – als erstes Haus am Platz und nicht versteckt in zweiter Reihe, hinter einem Bunker. Der hier vorgeschlagene Neubau mutet trotz der Materialien Stahl und Beton durch und durch zeltartig, textil und leicht an – eine Reminiszenz der Verfasser an den Mischkan, das provisorische Stiftszelt, welches als Leitmotiv bei der Entwurfsarbeit diente. Auch die ineinander gesteckten Bauvolumen folgen diesem Motiv und deuten in Ansicht und Aufsicht ein Flechtwerk an.

Up to the present, the bunker on Bornplatz remains a symbol of tyranny: the largest synagogue in northern Europe had to disappear so that a building serving military purposes could be erected on the same site. In order to make possible an urbanistic situation on the first row of the square, the bunker erected during the National Socialist era must be demolished. This clarifies the urban space, reestablishing the adjacent street alignment while restoring to the Jewish community the building site that was originally granted to it—allowing the synagogue to occupy the premier site on the square rather than being concealed in the second row behind the bunker. Despite the materials used, namely steel and concrete, the proposed new building makes an entirely tent-like, lightweight, textile impression—a reminiscence by the designers of the mishkan, the temporary tabernacle, which served as a leitmotif during the design process. The interpenetrating architectural volumes, too, are consistent with this motif, and are suggestive of wickerwork from both the side and top views.

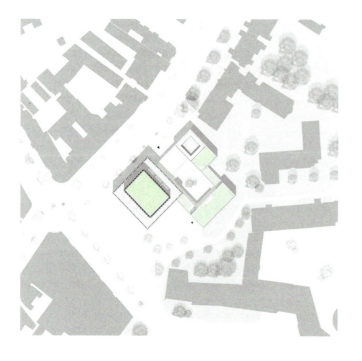

1
Lageplan
Site plan

2
Blick vom
Grindelhof
View from
Grindelhof

—
1:2500

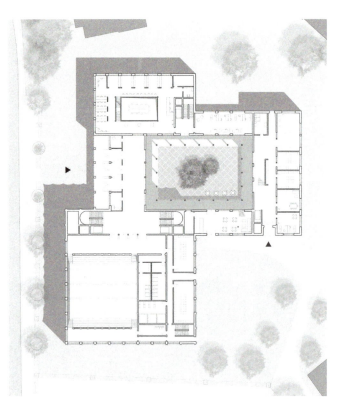

3
Blick vom
Grindelhof
View from
Grindelhof

4
1. Obergeschoss
First floor

5
Erdgeschoss
Ground floor

—
1:1000

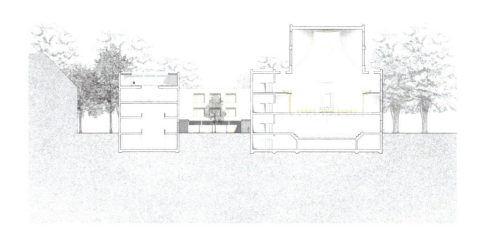

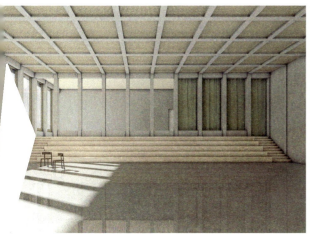

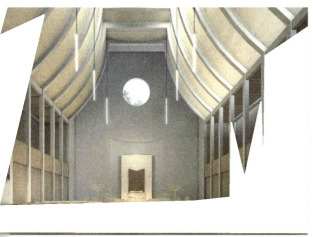

6
Querschnitt
Cross section

7
Festsaal
Banquet hall

8
Gebetsraum
Prayer room

—
1:1000

Nadine Kreth

Technische Universität Darmstadt
Prof. Wolfgang Lorch

Mit einer souveränen städtebaulichen Setzung auf dem Joseph-Carlebach-Platz wird der Konflikt zwischen Öffentlichkeit und Zurückgezogenheit lesbar thematisiert. Trotz der geschlossenen Form setzt die neue Synagoge am Bornplatz auf Integration und bewusste Öffnung statt Distanz oder Abgrenzung und schafft einen niederschwelligen Zugang in die Gebäude. Schwellen und Grenzen, wo sie existieren müssen, sind dezent gehalten. Mit der Inszenierung der Arkaden werden die Talmud-Thora-Schule mit der Universität verbunden und Menschen durch das neue Gemeindezentrum geführt. Die sich öffnenden Bauformen regen zum Eintreten an und geben einen Einblick in die jüdische Kultur. Durch den gezielten Einsatz des zweischaligen Mauerwerks wird die Transparenz des Gemeindezentrums unterstrichen und zugleich die Massivität und Stabilität der Synagoge an diesem Ort betont.

With its confident urbanistic siting on Joseph-Carlebach-Platz, the new synagogue explicitly thematizes the conflict between public presence and reclusiveness. Despite its self-enclosed form, the building on Bornplatz opts for integration and deliberate openness rather than distance or delimitation, generating a low threshold of access to the interior. Wherever unavoidable, thresholds and boundaries remain discreet. With the scenarization of the arcades, the Talmud Torah School is linked to the university, and people are guided through the new community center. The architectural forms, characterized by openness, welcome guests and provide a glimpse of Jewish culture. The purposeful use of double-shell masonry underscores the transparency of the community center while emphasizing the massiveness and stability of the synagogue at this location.

1
Lageplan
Site plan

2
Gebetsraum
Prayer room

—
1:2500

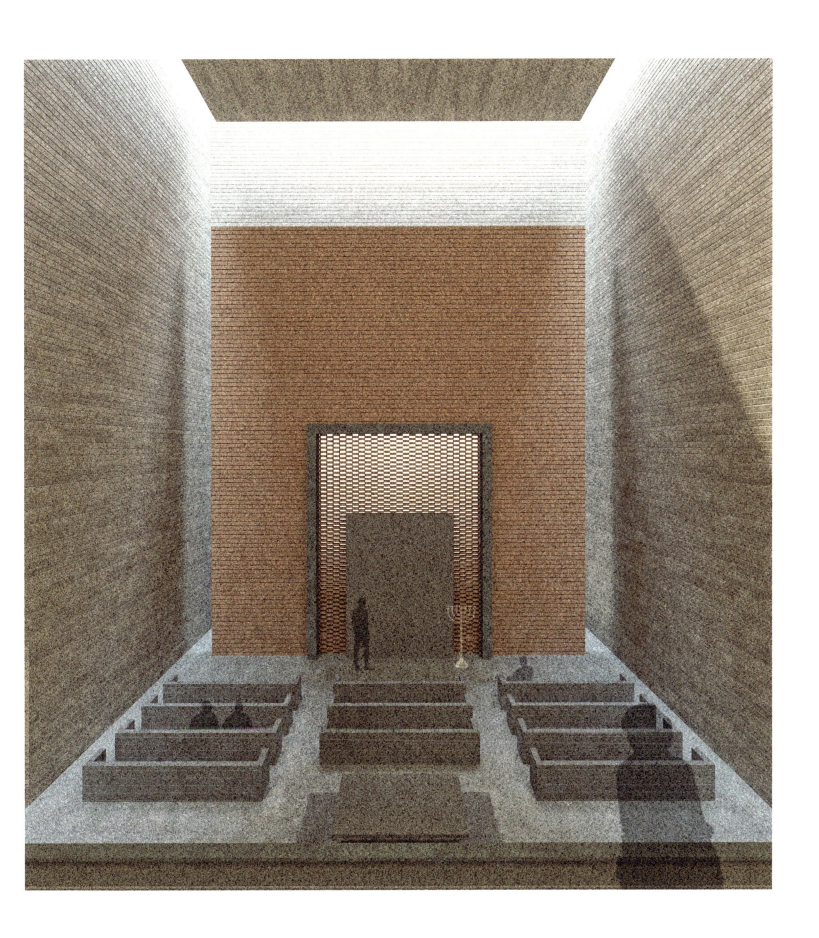

3
Gebäudepaar
Pair of buildings

4
Querschnitt
durch
Gemeindehaus
Cross section
through
community
center

5
Querschnitt
mit Gebetsraum
Cross section
with prayer room

6
Längsschnitt
Longitudinal
section

—
1:1000

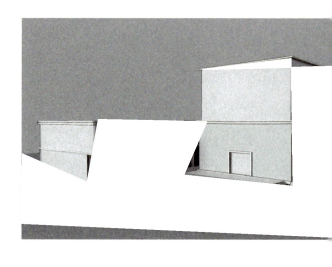

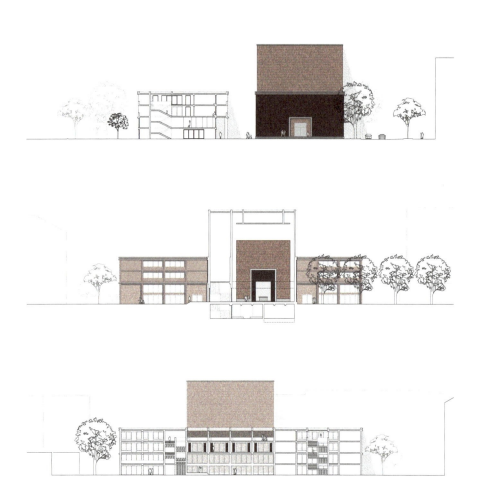

7
1. Obergeschoss
First floor

8
Erdgeschoss
Ground floor

—
1:1000

Mahmoud Ghazala Einieh & Sven Petersen

HafenCity Universität Hamburg
Prof. Gesine Weinmiller

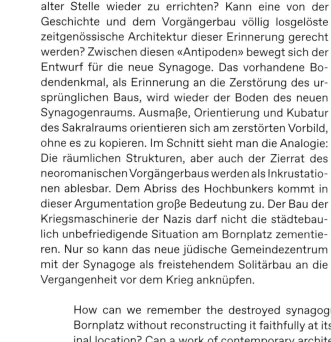

Wie erinnert man an die zerstörte Synagoge am Bornplatz, ohne sie als originalgetreue Rekonstruktion an alter Stelle wieder zu errichten? Kann eine von der Geschichte und dem Vorgängerbau völlig losgelöste zeitgenössische Architektur dieser Erinnerung gerecht werden? Zwischen diesen «Antipoden» bewegt sich der Entwurf für die neue Synagoge. Das vorhandene Bodendenkmal, als Erinnerung an die Zerstörung des ursprünglichen Baus, wird wieder der Boden des neuen Synagogenraums. Ausmaße, Orientierung und Kubatur des Sakralraums orientieren sich am zerstörten Vorbild, ohne es zu kopieren. Im Schnitt sieht man die Analogie: Die räumlichen Strukturen, aber auch der Zierrat des neoromanischen Vorgängerbaus werden als Inkrustationen ablesbar. Dem Abriss des Hochbunkers kommt in dieser Argumentation große Bedeutung zu. Der Bau der Kriegsmaschinerie der Nazis darf nicht die städtebaulich unbefriedigende Situation am Bornplatz zementieren. Nur so kann das neue jüdische Gemeindezentrum mit der Synagoge als freistehendem Solitärbau an die Vergangenheit vor dem Krieg anknüpfen.

How can we remember the destroyed synagogue on Bornplatz without reconstructing it faithfully at its original location? Can a work of contemporary architecture that is utterly dissociated from its predecessor really do justice to memory? The design for the new synagogue oscillates between these "antipodes." The existing pavement mosaic memorial, a reminder of the destruction of the original building, once again becomes the ground level of the new synagogue. Without actually copying it, the dimensions, orientation, and cubature of the sacred space are oriented toward the destroyed model. In section, the analogy becomes clear: the spatial structures, but also the embellishments of the neo-Romanesque predecessor building, become legible as incrustations. With this proposal, the demolition of the aboveground bunker acquires great significance. An element of Nazi war machinery, that building cannot be allowed to reinforce the urbanistically unsatisfactory situation at Bornplatz. Only in this way can the new Jewish community center, with the synagogue as a freestanding solitaire, reconnect with the era that preceded World War II.

1
Lageplan
Site plan

2
Blick in den Gebetsraum
View into the prayer room

1:2500

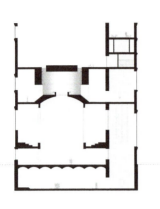

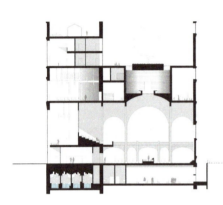

3
Querschnitt
Cross section

4
Längsschnitt
Longitudinal section

5
Blick vom Grindelhof
View from Grindelhof

—
1:1000

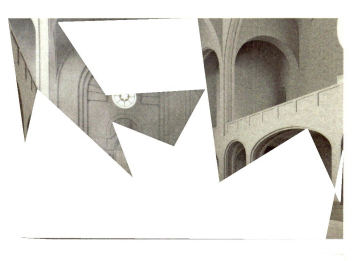
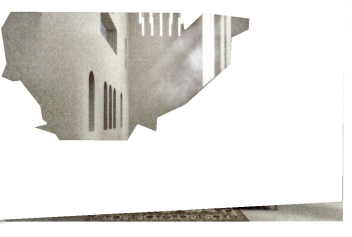

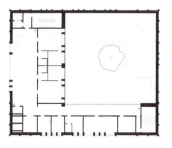

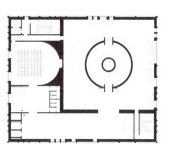

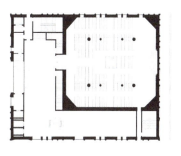

6
Gebetsraum
Prayer room

7
Luftraum Foyer
Air space foyer

8
4. Obergeschoss
Fourth floor

9
2. Obergeschoss
Second floor

10
Erdgeschoss
Ground floor

—
1:1000

Valentin Müller & Malte Wiegand

    Bauhaus-Universität Weimar
    Prof. Jörg Springer

Das Gebäude ist als konglomerates Gebilde aus violettrotem Klinker entwickelt, das in dem an der Platzecke positionierten, überhöhten Gebetsraum gipfelt und so die Präsenz der zerstörten Bornplatzsynagoge im Stadtraum zurückgewinnen will. Die Grundrisskonfiguration wird durch in ihrer Lage verspringende Höfe strukturiert, sodass auch in den oberen Geschossen Außenräume, etwa für die Kindertagesstätte oder für das Laubhüttenfest, zur Verfügung stehen. An den Höfen entlang wird auch die zentrale Treppenanlage bis zum Gebetsraum im dritten Obergeschoss geführt. Außen wie innen entwickelt der Entwurf eine eigenständige Formensprache, die eine gewisse Nähe zu den neoromanischen Formen des Vorgängerbaus sucht, um diese Nähe im gleichen Moment durch Verfremdung und die Hinzugabe nicht-referenzieller Elemente zu hinterfragen. So gelingt es, Kraft im Ausdruck des Gebäudes und eine besondere Präsenz im Stadtraum zu erzeugen.

The building, a conglomerate structure of violet-red clinker brick, culminates in the lofty prayer room, positioned at the corner of the square, and aims to reestablish the presence of the destroyed synagogue on Bornplatz within the urban environment. The floor plan is structured through courtyards that are offset in position in such a way that outdoor spaces are accessible in the upper levels as well, for example for the daycare center or the Feast of Tabernacles. Also running along the courtyards is the central staircase, which ascends to the prayer room on the third floor. Both externally and internally, the design develops an independent formal language, which however pursues a certain proximity to the neo-Romanesque forms of the predecessor building while at the same time interrogating them through defamiliarization and the addition of non-referential elements. This strategy makes it possible to generate the building's powerful expressiveness and its singular presence within the urban context.

1
Lageplan
Site plan

2
Blick vom Grindelhof
View from Grindelhof

—
1:2500

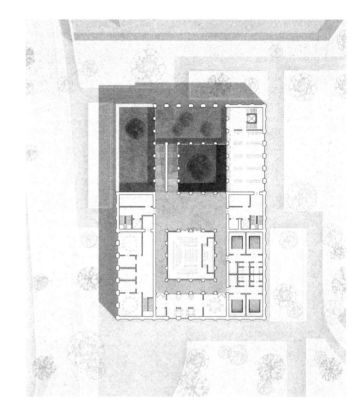
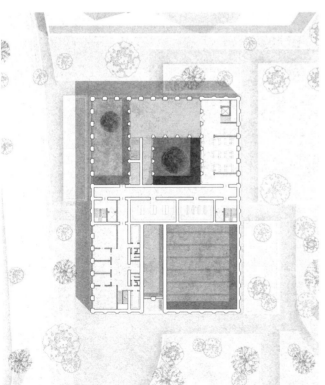
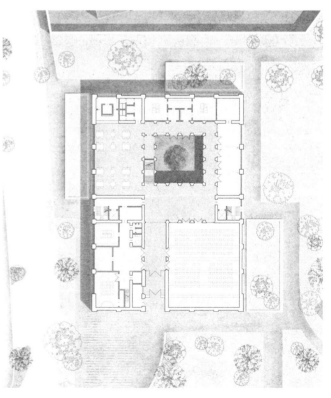

3
3. Obergeschoss
Third floor

4
2. Obergeschoss
Second floor

5
1. Obergeschoss
First floor

6
Erdgeschoss
Ground floor

—
1:1000

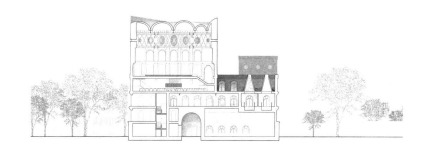

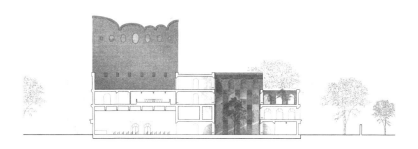

7
Blick in den
Gebetsraum
View into the
prayer room

8
Querschnitt
Cross section

9
Längsschnitt
Longitudinal
section

—
1:1000

10
Aufbau der Synagoge
Structure of the synagogue

11
Ansichten
Elevations
—
1:1000

Clara Poursedighi

Technische Universität Darmstadt
Prof. Wolfgang Lorch

Auf innovative und einzigartige Weise wird mit dem Neubau der Synagoge der Leerraum der zerstörten Bornplatzsynagoge inszeniert. Inmitten der dicht bebauten Struktur ist der Platz freigehalten, um das Verlorene wieder sichtbar zu machen. Der Ort des ehemaligen Innenraums der Bornplatzsynagoge wird zu einer markanten Leerstelle, die in einem Abguss des ehemaligen Thoraschreins aus pigmentiertem Beton ihren Höhepunkt findet. Überlagert wird der Innenraum durch das erhaltene Bodenmosaik, welches die Umrisse der einstigen Synagoge nachzeichnet. Integrierte Messingelemente ermöglichen ein flexibles Öffnen und Schließen der Synagoge sowie des Gemeindezentrums und erlauben gleichzeitig eine permanente Bespielung des neuen Synagogen-Hofs durch die Öffentlichkeit. Der neue Baukörper der Synagoge wird durch eigene Ornamentik zum Stadtraum gegliedert.

In innovative and singular fashion, the new synagogue orchestrates the empty space of the destroyed synagogue on Bornplatz. Within the densely built structure, the plaza remains unobstructed, allowing that which has been lost to become visible again. The location of the former interior of the synagogue on Bornplatz becomes a striking blank space or void whose high point is the cast replica of the former Torah shrine, fashioned in pigmented concrete. Superimposed on the interior space is the preserved pavement mosaic, which traces out the contours of the former synagogue. Integrated brass elements facilitate the flexible opening and closing of the synagogue as well as the community center, while allowing continuous public access to the new synagogue courtyard. Through its characteristic ornamentation, the new building is articulated in relation to the urban space.

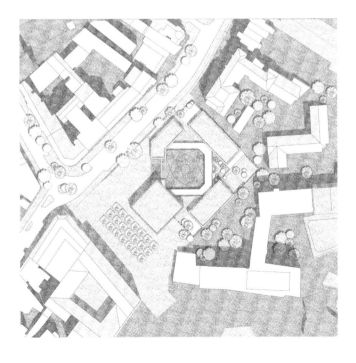

1
Lageplan
Site plan

2
Blick vom Hof
View from
the courtyard

—
1:2500

3
1. Obergeschoss
First floor

4
Erdgeschoss
Ground floor

5
Blick vom Grindelhof
View from Grindelhof

—

1:1000

6
Gebetsraum
Prayer room

7
Ansicht
Grindelhof
elevation

8
Längsschnitt
Longitudinal
section

—
1:1000

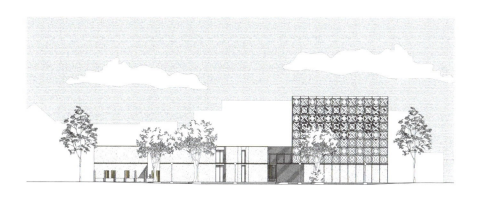

Ria Roberg

Bauhaus-Universität Weimar
Prof. Jörg Springer

Durch die Art der Einbindung des Gebäudekomplexes in die umgebende Stadtstruktur wird ein zurückhaltendes Selbstverständnis vermittelt. Eine ortstypische Materialisierung und die niedrigen, durch eine umfriedende Mauer zusammengefassten Gebäudevolumen bilden eine gleichermaßen standhafte wie bescheidene Erscheinung. Bis auf das Kinderhaus, das als Anbau an die bestehende Talmud-Tora-Schule gedacht ist, werden alle Nutzungen um einen innenliegenden Hof angeordnet. Seitlich über ein zurückliegendes Portal erschlossen, entsteht ein Ort geschützter Zusammenkünfte, der eine vielfältige und lebendige Gemeinschaft von Jüdinnen und Juden in den Blick nimmt. Auf wirksame Präsenz im Stadtraum und öffentlichen Austausch wird zugunsten der inneren Orientierung des Hauses verzichtet. Im Vergleich zur zerstörten, am Bornplatz sehr präsenten Synagoge wird eine gänzlich konträre Strategie verfolgt, die sich auf die innenräumlichen Qualitäten konzentriert – in der Diskussion um einen angemessenen Ausdruck der Synagoge an diesem Ort eine sehr eigenständige Position.

The way in which the architectural complex is integrated into the surrounding urban environment conveys a restrained overall impression. The locally typical materialization and the low architectural volumes, unified by a surrounding wall, create an appearance that is at once steadfast and unassuming. With the exception of the daycare center, conceived as an annex to the existing Talmud Torah School, all utilizations are arranged around an interior courtyard. Accessed laterally via a recessed portal is a place for sheltered gatherings that accommodates the multifarious and lively Jewish community. Any notion of an effective presence within the urban space or of public exchange is renounced in favor of the structure's inward orientation. Pursued here—and contrasting with the once-powerful presence of the destroyed synagogue on Bornplatz—is a radically different strategy, one that focuses on the qualities of the interior: a highly independent stance within the larger discussion of the appropriate approach to expression for a synagogue at this location.

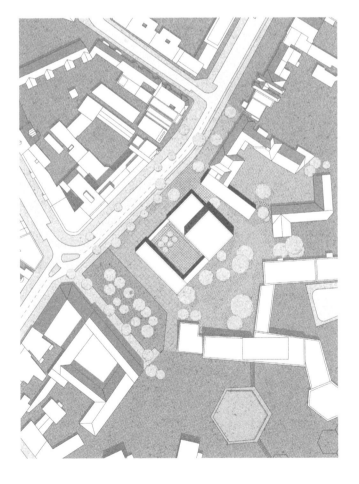

1
Lageplan
Site plan

2
Blick vom Hof
View from the courtyard

—
1:2500

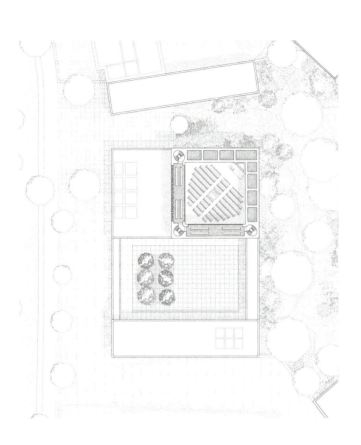

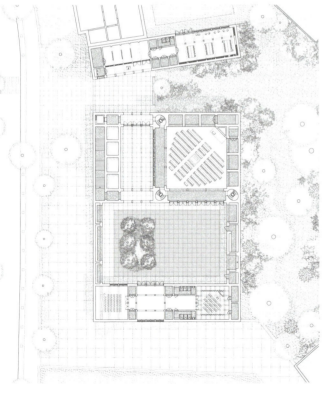

3
Brunnen im Hof
Courtyard fountain

4
1. Obergeschoss
First floor

5
Erdgeschoss
Ground floor

—
1:1000

6
Querschnitt
Cross section

7
Längsschnitt
Longitudinal
section

8
Gebetsraum
Prayer room

—
1:1000

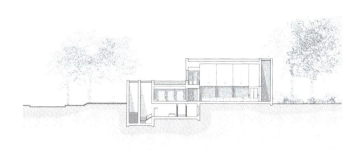

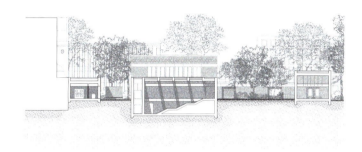

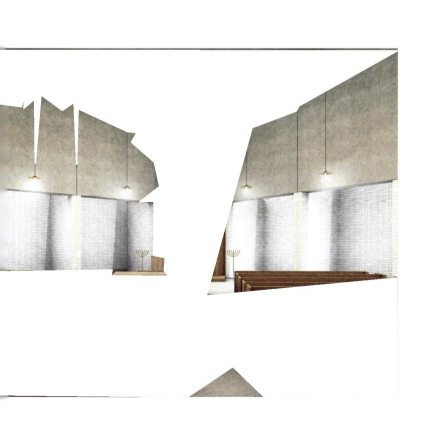

Robin Thomä

Technische Universität Darmstadt
Prof. Wolfgang Lorch

Die Synagoge drückt selbstbewusstes Sichtbarwerden der jüdischen Gemeinde bei gleichzeitiger Bewahrung schützender Distanz aus. Der überhöhte Synagogenbaukörper platziert sich symbolisch in der ehemaligen Raummitte und vermittelt zwischen dem privaten Garten und dem öffentlichen Stadtplatz. Öffnungen, vertikal wie horizontal, entstehen durch Schrägstellung, was Einblicke bei gleichzeitiger Wehrhaftigkeit ermöglicht. Eingänge werden durch ein Portal betont und bilden eine einladende, aber nur teiltransparente Geste. Über die Materialität des Backsteins wird die Synagoge in Hamburg verortet, eine weiße Schlämme im Inneren hebt sakrale Orte hervor. Städtebaulich entsteht auf dem Fußabdruck des ehemaligen Bunkers ein öffentlicher Synagogenvorplatz. Ein von Nationalsozialisten entfremdeter Ort jüdischer Geschichte wird mit diesem Entwurf zum neuen Anknüpfungspunkt für deutsch-jüdische Kultur.

The synagogue expresses the self-confident visibility of the Jewish community while preserving a protective distance. The soaring synagogue building is positioned symbolically at the center of the space, mediating between the private garden and the public urban square. Openings, whether vertical or horizontal, are given inclined positions, allowing views inside while remaining defensive in character. Entrances are emphasized by portals, giving rise to an inviting but only partially transparent gesture. The brick materiality situates the synagogue firmly in Hamburg; the white slurry of the interior emphasizes the building's sacred character. Arising on the footprint of the former bunker in urbanistic terms is a public synagogue forecourt. With this design, a place of Jewish history that was appropriated by the National Socialists becomes a new point of reference for German-Jewish culture.

1
Lageplan
Site plan

2
Zugang
Grindelhof
access

—
1:2500

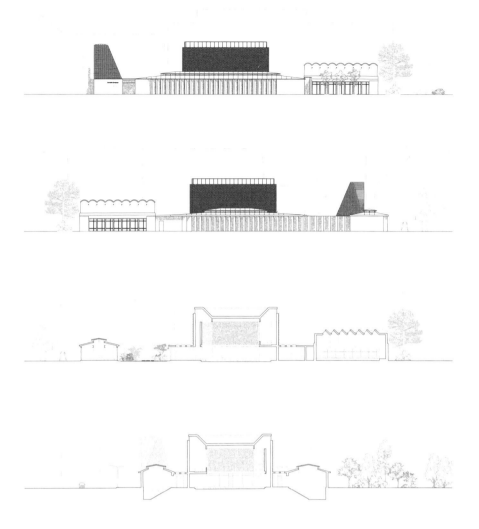

3
Ansicht
Grindelhof
elevation

4
Ansicht
Park
elevation

5
Längsschnitt
Longitudinal
section

6
Querschnitt
Cross section

—
1:1000

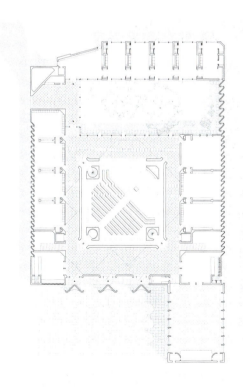
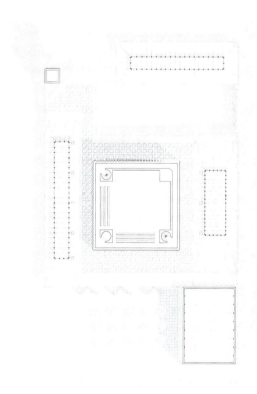

7
Gebetsraum
Prayer room

8
Erdgeschoss
Ground floor

9
1. Obergeschoss
First floor

—
1:1000

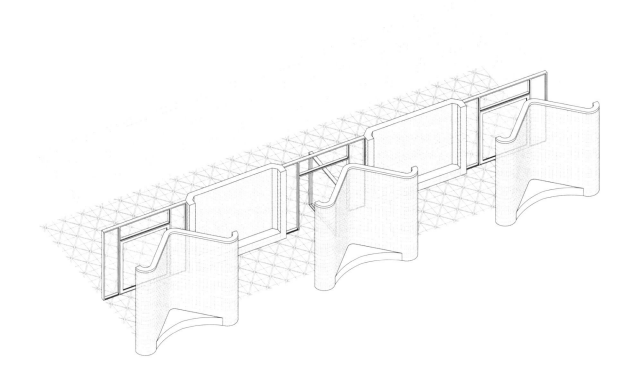

10
Eingangsportale
Entrance portals

11
Blick vom Vorplatz
View from the forecourt

Josefine Wolf

Technische Universität Darmstadt
Prof. Wolfgang Lorch

Individuelle Baukörper bilden städtebaulich ein klares und introvertiertes Ensemble, welches sich schützend und zugleich selbstbewusst im Stadtraum präsentiert. Hierbei wird das alttestamentliche Motiv des Tempels mit aufgegriffen. Raumhaltige Begrenzungen nach außen sowie enge Zwischenräume zum Stadtraum lösen die Anforderungen an die Sicherheit, ohne in den Vordergrund zu treten. Café und Bibliothek fungieren als Schnittstelle zwischen Stadt und Gemeinde und ermöglichen eine kontrollierte Fortsetzung des öffentlichen Raums im Inneren. Mit der Typologie des Hofes werden Übergänge zwischen öffentlichen und internen Nutzungen sowie ein Versammlungsort für das Gemeindeleben geschaffen. Durch die Nutzung der Synergien zwischen den verschiedenen Gebäudeelementen spielt das Ensemble mit der Koexistenz zweier Gegensätze, einer schützenden Hülle und sich öffnender Übergänge zum Stadtraum.

Individual volumes give rise to a lucid and introverted urbanistic ensemble that presents itself in a protective and at the same time self-confident fashion within the urban context. Taken up here, as well, is the Old Testament motif of the temple. Space-containing boundaries toward the outside as well as interspaces toward the urban environment satisfy security requirements without emerging into the foreground. The café and library function as interfaces between the city and the community while making possible a controlled continuation of public space within. Generated through the typology of the courtyard are transitions between public and internal uses, as well as a gathering place for community life. By exploiting synergies between the various elements of the building, the ensemble plays with the coexistence of two opposed elements: a protective shell and a welcoming within the transitional zones that are oriented toward the urban environment.

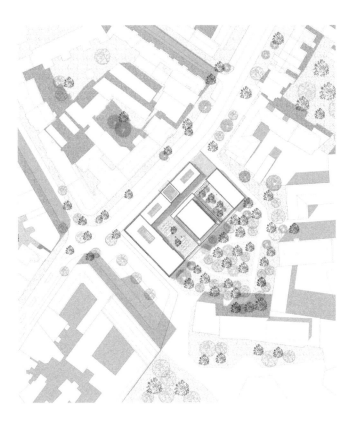

1
Lageplan
Site plan

2
Gebetsraum
Prayer room

—
1:2500

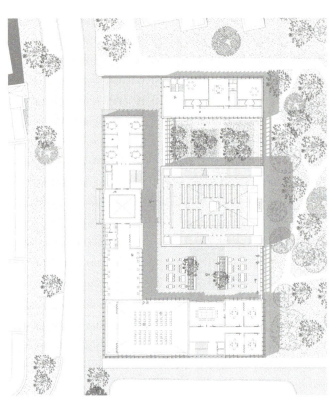

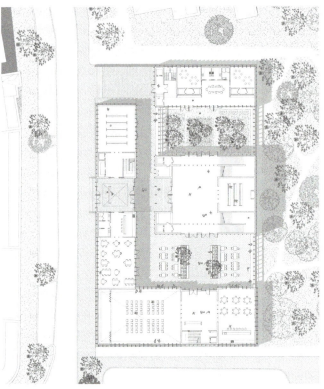

3
Erdgeschoss
Ground floor

4
1. Obergeschoss
First floor

5
Blick vom
Vorplatz
View from
the forecourt

—
1:1000

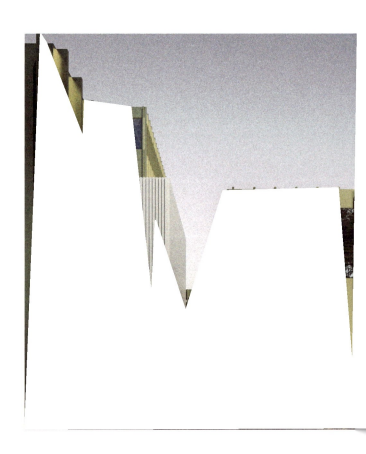

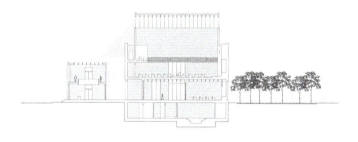

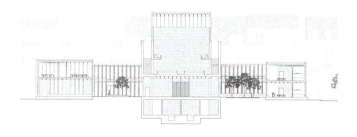

6
Innenhof
Inner courtyard

7
Querschnitt
Cross section

8
Längsschnitt
Longitudinal section

9
Ansicht Grindelhof
elevation

—
1:1000

Grit Farl

Bauhaus-Universität Weimar
Prof. Jörg Springer

Das Projekt nimmt die Rekonstruktion der zerstörten Bornplatzsynagoge zum Ausgangspunkt. Als überkuppelter Zentralraum prägte der große Betsaal auch die äußere Gestalt der alten Synagoge; eine Rekonstruktion der Gebäudehülle ohne die gleichzeitige Rekonstruktion dieses Innenraums erscheint daher kaum denkbar. So werden die Räume der Gemeinde und das Kinderhaus in zwei ergänzenden Bauteilen an der Talmud-Tora-Schule (heute Josef-Carlebach-Bildungshaus) und an der zu rekonstruierenden Synagoge vorgeschlagen. Die Sprache der Anbauten ist eine heutige – dennoch suchen die Ergänzungen einen engen, selbstverständlichen Bezug zu den Architekturen der Synagoge und der alten Schule. In der recht heterogenen Umgebung werden die Bauten der Jüdischen Gemeinde als ein Ensemble mit der Synagoge als natürlichem Mittelpunkt verstanden. Mittels dieser Ergänzungen gelingt es, die rekonstruierte Synagoge in dem inzwischen stark veränderten stadträumlichen Kontext schlüssig zu verankern. Bei aller gebotenen Zurückhaltung zeigt das Gemeindehaus mit dem Baumgarten im Obergeschoss eine der Aufgabe angemessene Eigenständigkeit.

The project takes the historic reconstruction of the destroyed Bornplatz Synagogue as its point of departure. As a domed central space, the large prayer hall also shaped the former synagogue's external form; to reconstruct the building's shell without reconstructing this interior therefore seems almost inconceivable. Also proposed are spaces for the community and daycare center, accommodated in two supplementary structures set alongside the Talmud Torah School (today the Josef-Carlebach-Bildungshaus) and the synagogue. The language of the annexes is contemporary—nonetheless, they seek to establish an intimate and self-evident affinity with the architecture of the synagogue and the old school. As an ensemble, the Jewish community buildings, together with the synagogue, will be comprehensible as a self-evident center of gravity within these highly heterogeneous surroundings. The additional buildings make it possible to anchor the reconstructed synagogue coherently within an urbanistic context that has meanwhile changed drastically. Despite its deliberately restrained character, the community building—with an arboretum in the upper story—displays an independence that is commensurate with its purpose.

1
Lageplan
Site plan

2
Blick von
Südwesten
View from
southwest

—
1:2500

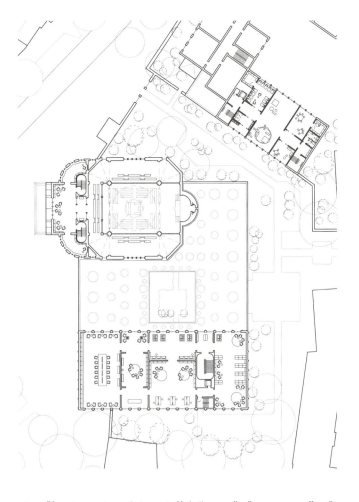

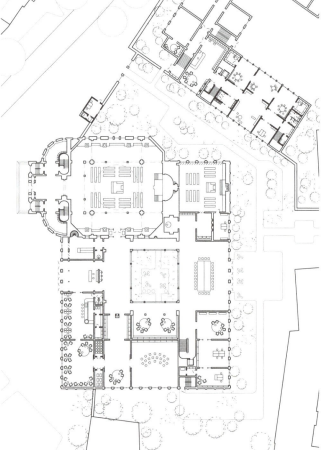

3
1. Obergeschoss
First floor

4
Erdgeschoss
Ground floor

5
Bibliothek
Library

—
1:1000

6
Innenhof
Inner courtyard

7
Ansicht
Allende-Platz
elevation

8
Ansicht
Grindelhof
elevation

9
Querschnitt
Cross section

—
1:1000

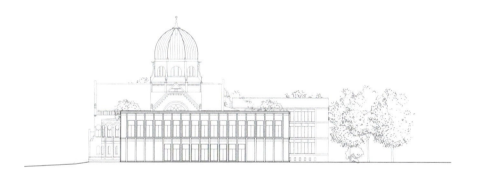

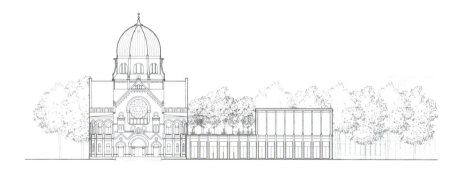

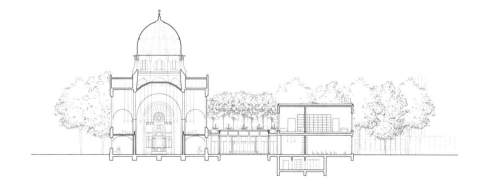

Appendix

Gesamtschau aller Entwürfe
Overview of all projects

Heinrike Aue
Kira Wrigge
Fraenkelufer, Berlin
HafenCity Universität Hamburg
Prof. Gesine Weinmiller

Julian Bäckermann
Daniel Cornelius Holzwarth
Poolstraße, Hamburg
Technische Universität Dresden
Prof. Ivan Reimann
Prof. Thomas Müller

Niko Bakhsh
Bornplatz, Hamburg
HafenCity Universität Hamburg
Prof. Gesine Weinmiller

Melih Baki
Bornplatz, Hamburg
Technische Universität Darmstadt
Prof. Wolfgang Lorch

Merve Bakirci
Bornplatz, Hamburg
Technische Universität Darmstadt
Prof. Wolfgang Lorch

Felix Balling
Poolstraße, Hamburg
Bauhaus-Universität Weimar
Prof. Jörg Springer

Mélanie Bauer
Vincent Nerád
Fraenkelufer, Berlin
Technische Universität Dresden
Prof. Ivan Reimann
Prof. Thomas Müller

Clemens Becker
Bornplatz, Hamburg
Bauhaus-Universität Weimar
Prof. Jörg Springer

Léon Raffael Becker
Moritz Köhler
Fraenkelufer, Berlin
Technische Universität Dresden
Prof. Ivan Reimann
Prof. Thomas Müller

Helen Beckmann
Johanna Bernhard
Poolstraße, Hamburg
Technische Universität Dresden
Prof. Ivan Reimann
Prof. Thomas Müller

Teresa Berg
Lea-Paulin Göhner
Poolstraße, Hamburg
Technische Universität Dresden
Prof. Ivan Reimann
Prof. Thomas Müller

Clara Bergerhoff
Bornplatz, Hamburg
Technische Universität Darmstadt
Prof. Wolfgang Lorch

Marthe Betsch
Leonie Ederer
Fraenkelufer, Berlin
Bauhaus-Universität Weimar
Prof. Jörg Springer

Velat Bilgili
Max Kresse
Poolstraße, Hamburg
Technische Universität Dresden
Prof. Ivan Reimann
Prof. Thomas Müller

Anastasia Blank
Bornplatz, Hamburg
Technische Universität Dresden
Prof. Ivan Reimann
Prof. Thomas Müller

Vivian Bonzel
Bornplatz, Hamburg
Technische Universität Dresden
Prof. Ivan Reimann
Prof. Thomas Müller

Leonie Maria Böttcher
Juline Junge
Poolstraße, Hamburg
Technische Universität Dresden
Prof. Ivan Reimann
Prof. Thomas Müller

Julia Burgdorf
Emilia Dürst
Poolstraße, Hamburg
Technische Universität Dresden
Prof. Ivan Reimann
Prof. Thomas Müller

Leon Bußfeld
Konstantin Heinke
Fraenkelufer, Berlin
Technische Universität Dresden
Prof. Ivan Reimann
Prof. Thomas Müller

Tugba Cakmak
Bornplatz, Hamburg
Technische Universität Darmstadt
Prof. Wolfgang Lorch

Marie Carraux
Fraenkelufer, Berlin
Technische Universität Dresden
Prof. Ivan Reimann
Prof. Thomas Müller

Jessica Michelle Deistler
Bornplatz, Hamburg
Bauhaus-Universität Weimar
Prof. Jörg Springer

Benedict Deutsch
Bornplatz, Hamburg
Bauhaus-Universität Weimar
Prof. Jörg Springer

Dominic Dietrich
Felix Knopf
Fraenkelufer, Berlin
Technische Universität Dresden
Prof. Ivan Reimann
Prof. Thomas Müller

Aymar Dower
Fraenkelufer, Berlin
Technische Universität Dresden
Prof. Ivan Reimann
Prof. Thomas Müller

Anna-Maria Epperlein
Lisa Kriehme
Poolstraße, Hamburg
Technische Universität Dresden
Prof. Ivan Reimann
Prof. Thomas Müller

Grit Farl
Bornplatz, Hamburg
Bauhaus-Universität Weimar
Prof. Jörg Springer

Daria Fedorova
Fraenkelufer, Berlin
Technische Universität Dresden
Prof. Ivan Reimann
Prof. Thomas Müller

Franka Maria Fetzer
Elias Martinez Moreno
Poolstraße, Hamburg
Bauhaus-Universität Weimar
Prof. Jörg Springer

Erland Freiwald
Melanie Mequita de Almeida
Bornplatz, Hamburg
HafenCity Universität Hamburg
Prof. Gesine Weinmiller

Clara Lauren Freyschmidt
Vivien Galdirs
Poolstraße, Hamburg
Technische Universität Dresden
Prof. Ivan Reimann
Prof. Thomas Müller

Daniela Garcia Martinez
Fraenkelufer, Berlin
HafenCity Universität Hamburg
Prof. Gesine Weinmiller

Tim Gebhardt
Maximilian Schmidt
Fraenkelufer, Berlin
Bauhaus-Universität Weimar
Prof. Jörg Springer

Katja Gellentin
Bornplatz, Hamburg
Bauhaus-Universität Weimar
Prof. Jörg Springer

Leoni Gensel
Benjamin Fahnauer
Poolstraße, Hamburg
Technische Universität Dresden
Prof. Ivan Reimann
Prof. Thomas Müller

Mahmoud Ghazala Einieh
Sven Petersen
Bornplatz, Hamburg
HafenCity Universität Hamburg
Prof. Gesine Weinmiller

Marie Göben
Emilia Kuhlendahl
Fraenkelufer, Berlin
HafenCity Universität Hamburg
Prof. Gesine Weinmiller

Eleonore Goldammer
Jonas Rehwagen
Poolstraße, Hamburg
Technische Universität Dresden
Prof. Ivan Reimann
Prof. Thomas Müller

Sema Günbeyi
Bornplatz, Hamburg
Technische Universität Darmstadt
Prof. Wolfgang Lorch

Qingping Guo
Bornplatz, Hamburg
Technische Universität Darmstadt
Prof. Wolfgang Lorch

Florian Gutbier
Florian Häßler
Poolstraße, Hamburg
Technische Universität Dresden
Prof. Ivan Reimann
Prof. Thomas Müller

Hui He
He Liu
Poolstraße, Hamburg
Technische Universität Dresden
Prof. Ivan Reimann
Prof. Thomas Müller

Arthur Helmecke
Poolstraße, Hamburg
Bauhaus-Universität Weimar
Prof. Jörg Springer

Lisa Hendle
Bornplatz, Hamburg
Technische Universität Darmstadt
Prof. Wolfgang Lorch

Max Hoffmann
Chutong Wu
Poolstraße, Hamburg
Technische Universität Dresden
Prof. Ivan Reimann
Prof. Thomas Müller

Philipp Jainz
Poolstraße, Hamburg
Bauhaus-Universität Weimar
Prof. Jörg Springer

Thomas Jankowski
Hanna Tschierse
Bornplatz, Hamburg
HafenCity Universität Hamburg
Prof. Gesine Weinmiller

Franziska Junkes
Johanna Kaifer
Bornplatz, Hamburg
HafenCity Universität Hamburg
Prof. Gesine Weinmiller

Bálint Kemeny
Poolstraße, Hamburg
Bauhaus-Universität Weimar
Prof. Jörg Springer

Martin Knoll
Bornplatz, Hamburg
Technische Universität Darmstadt
Prof. Wolfgang Lorch

Lea Knuth
Maria Thal
Poolstraße, Hamburg
Technische Universität Dresden
Prof. Ivan Reimann
Prof. Thomas Müller

Nadine Kreth
Bornplatz, Hamburg
Technische Universität Darmstadt
Prof. Wolfgang Lorch

Martin Kuhnt
Hannes Mikschofsky
Poolstraße, Hamburg
Technische Universität Dresden
Prof. Ivan Reimann
Prof. Thomas Müller

Janis Kukral
Fraenkelufer, Berlin
Bauhaus-Universität Weimar
Prof. Jörg Springer

Marie Kusche
Bornplatz, Hamburg
Bauhaus-Universität Weimar
Prof. Jörg Springer

Stella Kuzsel
Laura Rzepka
Fraenkelufer, Berlin
Technische Universität Dresden
Prof. Ivan Reimann
Prof. Thomas Müller

Ina Lafrentz
Samuel Pahlke
Bornplatz, Hamburg
HafenCity Universität Hamburg
Prof. Gesine Weinmiller

Sabrina Lange
Bornplatz, Hamburg
Bauhaus-Universität Weimar
Prof. Jörg Springer

Raquel Leal Azevedo
Bornplatz, Hamburg
Technische Universität Darmstadt
Prof. Wolfgang Lorch

Liu Yuwei
Bornplatz, Hamburg
Technische Universität Darmstadt
Prof. Wolfgang Lorch

Fang Li
Tom Stier
Poolstraße, Hamburg
Technische Universität Dresden
Prof. Ivan Reimann
Prof. Thomas Müller

Jakob Lichtblau
Bornplatz, Hamburg
Technische Universität Darmstadt
Prof. Wolfgang Lorch

Maxim Macarov
Bornplatz, Hamburg
HafenCity Universität Hamburg
Prof. Gesine Weinmiller

Ruth März
Felix Tinneberg
Bornplatz, Hamburg
Bauhaus-Universität Weimar
Prof. Jörg Springer

Lea Marzinzik
Leonard Weber
Poolstraße, Hamburg
Bauhaus-Universität Weimar
Prof. Jörg Springer

Tom Meißner
Fraenkelufer, Berlin
Technische Universität Dresden
Prof. Ivan Reimann
Prof. Thomas Müller

Marie Isabel Cara Menninger
Fraenkelufer, Berlin
Technische Universität Dresden
Prof. Ivan Reimann
Prof. Thomas Müller

Jaques Merfort
Bornplatz, Hamburg
HafenCity Universität Hamburg
Prof. Gesine Weinmiller

Paula-Lioba Müller
Clara Prugger
Poolstraße, Hamburg
Technische Universität Dresden
Prof. Ivan Reimann
Prof. Thomas Müller

Valentin Müller
Malte Wiegand
Bornplatz, Hamburg
Bauhaus-Universität Weimar
Prof. Jörg Springer

Mai Anh Nguyen
Fraenkelufer, Berlin
Technische Universität Dresden
Prof. Ivan Reimann
Prof. Thomas Müller

Natalia Elisa Ordóñez Corredor
Fraenkelufer, Berlin
Technische Universität Dresden
Prof. Ivan Reimann
Prof. Thomas Müller

Zoe Pianaro
Fraenkelufer, Berlin
Bauhaus-Universität Weimar
Prof. Jörg Springer

Clara Poursedighi
Bornplatz, Hamburg
Technische Universität Darmstadt
Prof. Wolfgang Lorch

Laura Reichert
Leonie Siebern
Poolstraße, Hamburg
Technische Universität Dresden
Prof. Ivan Reimann
Prof. Thomas Müller

Marlies Richter
Bornplatz, Hamburg
Technische Universität Darmstadt
Prof. Wolfgang Lorch

Philipp Riebel-Vosgerau
Bornplatz, Hamburg
Technische Universität Darmstadt
Prof. Wolfgang Lorch

Ria Roberg
Bornplatz, Hamburg
Bauhaus-Universität Weimar
Prof. Jörg Springer

Lorenzo Scheibner
Josephine Louise Stübinger
Poolstraße, Hamburg
Technische Universität Dresden
Prof. Ivan Reimann
Prof. Thomas Müller

Sabrina Schindling
Bornplatz, Hamburg
Technische Universität Darmstadt
Prof. Wolfgang Lorch

Janna Schmidt
Bornplatz, Hamburg
Technische Universität Dresden
Prof. Ivan Reimann
Prof. Thomas Müller

Jan Schmidt-Schweda
Nils Niklas Schröder
Bornplatz, Hamburg
Bauhaus-Universität Weimar
Prof. Jörg Springer

Clemens Seeger
Bornplatz, Hamburg
Technische Universität Darmstadt
Prof. Wolfgang Lorch

Lisa-Marie Seidel
Poolstraße, Hamburg
Bauhaus-Universität Weimar
Prof. Jörg Springer

Vanessa Seidel
Fraenkelufer, Berlin
Technische Universität Dresden
Prof. Ivan Reimann
Prof. Thomas Müller

Zülal Serbes
Bornplatz, Hamburg
Technische Universität Darmstadt
Prof. Wolfgang Lorch

Michal Stryjski
Poolstraße, Hamburg
Bauhaus-Universität Weimar
Prof. Jörg Springer

Robin Thomä
Bornplatz, Hamburg
Technische Universität Darmstadt
Prof. Wolfgang Lorch

Pia Katherina Thunde
Zimo Wang
Poolstraße, Hamburg
Technische Universität Dresden
Prof. Ivan Reimann
Prof. Thomas Müller

Antigoni Tolgou
Bornplatz, Hamburg
Technische Universität Darmstadt
Prof. Wolfgang Lorch

Cosima Vogel
Fraenkelufer, Berlin
Technische Universität Dresden
Prof. Ivan Reimann
Prof. Thomas Müller

Yijun Wang
Bornplatz, Hamburg
Technische Universität Darmstadt
Prof. Wolfgang Lorch

Robert Wehner
Fraenkelufer, Berlin
Technische Universität Dresden
Prof. Ivan Reimann
Prof. Thomas Müller

Josefine Wolf
Bornplatz, Hamburg
Technische Universität Darmstadt
Prof. Wolfgang Lorch

Rahsan Yilmaz
Houda Zalghout
Fraenkelufer, Berlin
HafenCity Universität Hamburg
Prof. Gesine Weinmiller

Kuanghua Yu
Fraenkelufer, Berlin
Technische Universität Dresden
Prof. Ivan Reimann
Prof. Thomas Müller

Maximilian Zepezauer
Bornplatz, Hamburg
Technische Universität Dresden
Prof. Ivan Reimann
Prof. Thomas Müller

Lei Zhang
Bornplatz, Hamburg
Technische Universität Darmstadt
Prof. Wolfgang Lorch

Yi Zhong
Bornplatz, Hamburg
Technische Universität Darmstadt
Prof. Wolfgang Lorch

Julius Zimmer
Bornplatz, Hamburg
Technische Universität Darmstadt
Prof. Wolfgang Lorch

Kurzbiografien
Biographies

Manuel Aust
studierte Architektur an der FH Erfurt, der TU Eindhoven und der Bauhaus-Universität Weimar. Er arbeitete bei Bekkering Adams Architecten in Rotterdam und Morger Partner Architekten in Basel. Seit 2020 ist er als selbstständiger Architekt und als wissenschaftlicher Mitarbeiter am Lehrstuhl Entwerfen und komplexe Gebäudelehre von Prof. Jörg Springer an der Bauhaus-Universität Weimar aktiv.

Roger Diener
studierte Architektur an der Eidgenössischen Technischen Hochschule (ETH) Zürich, unter anderem bei Luigi Snozzi. 1976 begann er seine Arbeit im Büro seines Vaters, Marcus Diener, welches er seit 1980 weiterführt. Nach Gastprofessuren an der École Polytechnique Fédérale de Lausanne (EPFL), der Harvard University sowie an Hochschulen in Wien, Amsterdam und Kopenhagen war er von 1987 bis 1989 Professor für Entwurf an der EPFL und von 1999 bis 2015 Professor an der ETH Zürich. Von 2005 bis 2013 war Roger Diener Mitglied des Landesdenkmalrats Berlin. Seit 2013 ist er in der Eidgenössischen Kommission für Denkmalpflege tätig und seit 2018 Mitglied der Denkmalpflegekommission der Stadt Zürich. Roger Diener erhielt zahlreiche Auszeichnungen, darunter die französische Grande Médaille d'Or d'Architecture, den Prix Meret Oppenheim, die Heinrich Tessenow-Medaille und den Kulturpreis der Stadt Basel. 2019 ehrte ihn die Bauhaus-Universität Weimar mit der Ehrendoktorwürde.

Andreas Fuchs
studierte Architektur an der TU Dresden und arbeitete anschließend in verschiedenen Architekturbüros, unter anderem bei Adolf Krischanitz in Wien, Müller Reimann Architekten in Berlin und Selldorf Architects in New York. Seit 2018 ist er als freischaffender Architekt in Berlin tätig und unterrichtet als wissenschaftlicher Mitarbeiter am Lehrstuhl Öffentliche Bauten von Prof. Ivan Reimann und Prof. Thomas Müller an der TU Dresden.

Manuel Aust
studied architecture at the FH Erfurt, the TU Eindhoven, and the Bauhaus-Universität Weimar. He has worked at Bekkering Adams Architecten in Rotterdam and Morger Partner Architekten in Basel. Since 2020, he has been an independent architect, and has been active as a research associate with the Chair of Design and Complex Building Theory, headed by Prof. Jörg Springer, at the Bauhaus-Universität Weimar.

Roger Diener
studied architecture at the Eidgenössische Technische Hochschule (ETH) Zürich, with Luigi Snozzi among others. In 1976, he began working in the architectural practice of his father, Marcus Diener, which he has continued to direct since 1980. Following guest professorships at the École Polytechnique Fédérale de Lausanne (EPFL), Harvard University, as well as academies in Vienna, Amsterdam, and Copenhagen, Roger Diener was a professor of design at the EPFL from 1987 until 1989, and a professor at the ETH Zürich from 1999 until 2015. He was a member of the Berlin State Board for the Preservation of Monuments in Berlin from 2005 until 2013. He has been active on the Swiss Federal Commission for Monument Preservation (EKD) since 2013, and has been a member of the Commission for the Preservation of Monuments of the City of Zürich since 2018. Diener has received numerous awards, among them the French Grande Médaille d'Or d'Architecture, the Prix Meret Oppenheim, the Heinrich Tessenow-Medaille, and the Kulturpreis der Stadt Basel. In 2019, he received an honorary doctorate from the Bauhaus-Universität Weimar.

Andreas Fuchs
studied architecture at the TU Dresden and went on to work at various architectural offices, among them Adolf Krischanitz in Vienna, Müller Reimann Architekten in Berlin, and Selldorf Architects in New York. Since 2018, he has been active as a freelance architect in Berlin, and works as a research associate with the Chair for Public Building, headed by Prof. Ivan Reimann and Prof. Thomas Müller, at the TU Dresden.

Franz-Josef Höing
studierte Raumplanung an der Universität Dortmund. Er war wissenschaftlicher Mitarbeiter am Institut für Städtebau und Raumplanung der Technischen Universität Wien und am Lehrstuhl für Städtebau und Landesplanung der Rheinisch-Westfälischen Technischen Hochschule (RWTH) Aachen. Als persönlicher Referent des Oberbaudirektors der Freien und Hansestadt Hamburg von 2000 bis 2004 war er unter anderem für die Leitung der Projektgruppe HafenCity verantwortlich. Von 2004 bis 2008 war er Professor für Städtebau an der Fachhochschule Münster. Bevor er 2012 als Dezernent für Stadtentwicklung, Planen, Bauen und Verkehr der Stadt Köln tätig wurde, war er ab 2008 Senatsbaudirektor beim Senator für Umwelt, Bau und Verkehr der Freien Hansestadt Bremen. Seit November 2017 ist Franz-Josef Höing Oberbaudirektor der Freien und Hansestadt Hamburg.

Monika Grütters
studierte Germanistik, Kunstgeschichte und Politikwissenschaften in Münster und Bonn. Seit 1991 wirkt sie als Honorarprofessorin mit Lehrauftrag, zunächst an der Hochschule für Musik Hanns Eisler Berlin und seit 1999 an der Freien Universität Berlin. Monika Grütters ist seit 2005 Mitglied des Deutschen Bundestages in der CDU/CSU-Bundestagsfraktion. Von 2009 bis 2013 war sie unter anderem Vorsitzende des Ausschusses für Kultur und Medien im Deutschen Bundestag, Mitglied des Ausschusses für Bildung und Forschung und Obfrau im Unterausschuss Auswärtige Kultur- und Bildungspolitik. Von 2013 bis 2021 war Monika Grütters Staatsministerin bei der Bundeskanzlerin als Beauftragte der Bundesregierung für Kultur und Medien.

Dr. Salomon Korn
studierte Architektur an der TU Berlin sowie an der TH Darmstadt, wo er im Nebenfach Soziologie belegte und 1976 promovierte. Er ist seit 1999 Vorsitzender der Jüdischen Gemeinde Frankfurt am Main und war von 2003 bis 2014 Vizepräsident des Zentralrats der Juden. 2006 wurde Salomon Korn zum Ehrensenator der Universität Heidelberg und aufgrund seiner Verdienste zum Thema Erinnerung durch das Land Hessen zum Professor ernannt. Von 2003 bis 2015 war er Kuratoriumsmitglied der Hochschule für Jüdische Studien Heidelberg und Vorsitzender des Zentralarchivs zur Erforschung der Geschichte der Juden in Deutschland. Salomon Korn ist Mitglied des Senats der deutschen Nationalstiftung sowie der Ludwig-Börne-Stiftung und vertritt die Jüdische Gemeinde als Vorstand in der Jehoshua und Hanna Bubis-Stiftung, der Georgina Sara von Rothschild'schen Stiftung, der Moses J. Kirchheim'schen Stiftung, der Eduard und Adelheid Kann-Stiftung und der Georg und Franziska Speyer'sche Hochschulstiftung.

Franz-Josef Höing
studied space planning at Dortmund University. He was an academic associate with the Institute for Urban Planning and Space Planning at the TU Wien, and with the chair of urban design at the RWTH Aachen. As the personal adviser to the chief building director of the Free and Hanseatic City of Hamburg from 2000 until 2004, he was responsible, among other things, for directing the HafenCity project group. From 2004 until 2008, he was a professor of urban planning at the Münster University of Applied Sciences. From 2008, before becoming a department head for Urban Development, Planning, Building, and Traffic for the City of Cologne in 2012, he was senate building director for the Senator for Environment, Building, and Transport for the Free and Hanseatic City of Bremen. Höing has been chief building director of the Free and Hanseatic City of Hamburg since November 2017.

Monika Grütters
studied German philology, art history, and political science in Münster and Bonn. Since 1991, she has been an honorary professor holding teaching appointments, first at the Hanns Eisler School of Music Berlin, and since 1999 at the Freie Universität Berlin. Monika Grütters has been a member of the German Bundestag since 2005 as part of the CDU/CSU parliamentary group. Between 2009 and 2013, she was—among other things—chair of the Committee on Cultural and Media Affairs in the German Bundestag, a member of the Committee for Education and Research, and chair of the Subcommittee on Foreign Culture and Educational Policy. From 2013 until 2021, Monika Grütters was Minister of State to the Federal Chancellor and Federal Government Commissioner for Culture and the Media.

Dr. Salomon Korn
studied architecture at the TU Berlin and at the TH Darmstadt, where he took sociology as a minor and earned a doctorate in 1976. He has been the chief executive of the Jewish community of Frankfurt am Main since 1999, and was vice president of the Central Council of the Jews in Germany between 2003 and 2014. In 2006, Korn became an honorary senator of Heidelberg University, and was appointed professor by the Federal State of Hesse for his accomplishments related to the topic of Memory. Between 2003 and 2015, he was a member of the board of trustees of the Hochschule für Jüdische Studien Heidelberg and chairman of the Zentralarchivs zur Erforschung der Geschichte der Juden in Deutschland (Central Archive for Research into the Jews in Germany). Korn is a member of the senate of the German National Foundation, as well as of the Ludwig Börne Foundation, and represents the Jewish community as chairman in the Jehoshua and Hanna Bubis Foundation, the Georgina Sara von Rothschild'schen Foundation, the Moses J. Kirchheim'schen Foundation, the Eduard and Adelheid Kann Foundation, and the Georg and Franziska Speyer'sche University Foundation.

Wolfgang Lorch
studierte Architektur in Darmstadt und Barcelona. Seit 1990 ist er freier Architekt und führt heute als Partner das international tätige Büro Wandel Lorch Götze Wach. Bekannt ist die Werkgemeinschaft neben einer Vielzahl öffentlicher Gebäude und Wohnhäuser im Besonderen für ihre Sakralbauten. Dazu zählen beispielsweise das Jüdische Zentrum in München sowie die Synagoge in Dresden, die mit dem Deutschen Architekturpreis ausgezeichnet wurde. Nach Lehrtätigkeiten an der Universität Kaiserslautern und der Staatsbauschule Stuttgart ist Wolfgang Lorch seit 2003 Professor für Entwerfen und Baugestaltung an der Technischen Universität Darmstadt. Darüber hinaus ist er seit mehreren Jahren als Gestaltungsbeirat unter anderem in München und Dresden tätig.

Mario Marcus
ist als Kind Berliner Juden im Umfeld der Jüdischen Gemeinde in Berlin aufgewachsen. Seine Familienhistorie, beginnend mit den Urgroßeltern und der Familie seiner Ehefrau, verbindet ihn persönlich mit der Synagoge am Fraenkelufer. Mario Marcus studierte Medizin und war bis zu seinem Ruhestand als Gefäßchirurg tätig. Seit etwa 50 Jahren ist er aktives Mitglied der Jüdischen Gemeinde und Beter in der Synagoge am Fraenkelufer.

Thomas Müller
studierte Architektur in Berlin, New York sowie London und ist seit 1988 als Architekt tätig. Er lehrte als Gastprofessor an der Cooper Union School of Architecture in New York und an der Harvard University Graduate School of Design in Cambridge. Heute führt er zusammen mit Ivan Reimann ein Architekturbüro in Berlin. Zu ihren Entwürfen gehören beispielsweise die Bebauung des Leipziger Platzes und das Innenministerium in Berlin sowie die Neubauten für die Goethe-Universität auf dem Campus Westend in Frankfurt am Main. Thomas Müller war unter anderem Mitglied des Gestaltungsbeirates für Baukultur in Groningen/Niederlande und des Gestaltungsforums der Stadt Leipzig. Seit 2016 lehrt er als Professor für Gebäudelehre und Entwerfen an der Technischen Universität Dresden.

Dr. Dekel Peretz
studierte Geschichte, Philosophie sowie Volkswirtschaft und promovierte im Rahmen des Walther-Rathenau-Kollegs am Moses Mendelssohn Zentrum in Potsdam zum Thema *Zionism and Cosmopolitanism. Franz Oppenheimer and the Dream of a Jewish Future in Germany and Palestine*. Er ist Vorsitzender des Vereins Jüdisches Zentrum Synagoge Fraenkelufer und Gründer des Eruv Hub, Deutschlands erstem Coworking-Space für gemeinnützige jüdische Organisationen und Initiativen, sowie von LABA Berlin, einem Künstler-Stipendienprogramm, dass das Studium jüdischer Texte mit künstlerischer Produktion verbindet. Gegenwärtig ist Dekel Peretz wissenschaftlicher Mitarbeiter am Max-Weber-Institut für Soziologie der Universität Heidelberg und Gastforscher am Max-Planck-Institut zur Erforschung multireligiöser und multiethnischer Gesellschaften.

Wolfgang Lorch
studied architecture in Darmstadt and Barcelona. He has been a freelance architect since 1990 and now heads the internationally active office of Wandel Lorch Götze Wach as a partner. Apart from a number of public and residential projects, the working association is known in particular for its religious buildings. These include the Jewish Center in Munich and the New Synagogue in Dresden, which received the German Architecture Prize. Following teaching activities at the Technische Universität Kaiserslautern and the Hochschule für Technik in Stuttgart, Wolfgang Lorch was appointed to a professorship in design and building design at the Technische Universität Darmstadt in 2003. He has also been active for a number of years on design advisory boards in Munich and Dresden, among others.

Mario Marcus
grew up as the child of Berlin Jews in the milieu of the city's Jewish community. His family history, beginning with his great-grandparents and his wife's family, connect him personally to the Fraenkelufer Synagogue. Marcus studied medicine and was a vascular surgeon until his retirement. He has been an active member of the Jewish community and has worshipped at the Fraenkelufer Synagogue for around fifty years.

Thomas Müller
studied architecture in Berlin, New York, and London, and has been active as an architect since 1988. He was a guest professor at the Cooper Union School of Architecture in New York and the Harvard University Graduate School of Design in Cambridge, Massachusetts. Today, he heads an architectural office in Berlin together with Ivan Reimann. His designs include the development of Leipziger Platz and the Federal Ministry of the Interior in Berlin, as well as new buildings for the Goethe University on the Westend Campus in Frankfurt am Main. Among other projects, Thomas Müller has been a member of the Design Advisory Board for Building Culture in Groningen, the Netherlands, and the Design Forum of the City of Leipzig. He has been a professor of building and design at the Technische Universität Dresden since 2016.

Dr. Dekel Peretz
studied history, philosophy, and economics, and earned a doctorate at the Walther Rathenau College at the Moses Mendelssohn Center in Potsdam on the topic of *Zionism and Cosmopolitanism. Franz Oppenheimer and the Dream of a Jewish Future in Germany and Palestine*. He is the chairman of the Verein Jüdisches Zentrum Synagoge Fraenkelufer and founder of Eruv Hub, Germany's first coworking space for Jewish nonprofit organizations and initiatives, as well as of LABA Berlin, a scholarship program for artists that links the study of Jewish texts with artistic production. Currently, Peretz is a research associate at the Max Weber Institute for Sociology at Heidelberg University, and a guest researcher at the Max Planck Institute for the Study of Religious and Ethnic Diversity.

Ivan Reimann
studierte Architektur in Berlin, Prag und London. Von 1989 bis 1994 war er an der Technischen Universität Berlin Assistent von Prof. Dr. Schmidt-Thomsen und ist seit 1988 als Architekt tätig. Heute führt er zusammen mit Thomas Müller ein Architekturbüro in Berlin. Ihre überwiegend großmaßstäblichen und komplexen Bauwerke, die zumeist im städtischen Kontext verortet sind, verstehen sie als Teil einer gewachsenen Bausubstanz. Zu ihren Entwürfen gehören beispielsweise der Sitz des Auswärtigen Amtes in Berlin und der Marienturm in Frankfurt am Main. Ivan Reimann war unter anderem von 2014 bis 2016 Mitglied des Beratungsgremiums der Stadt Prag sowie von 2015 bis 2017 des Gestaltungsbeirates der Stadt Halle. Seit 1999 ist er Professor für Gebäudelehre und Entwerfen an der Technischen Universität Dresden.

Jörg Springer
studierte Architektur in Berlin und Barcelona. Nach seiner Mitarbeit bei Josep Lluís Mateo gründete er 1995 sein Büro Springer Architekten in Berlin. Seine Arbeiten, die – oft in historischen Kontexten – nach einer selbstverständlichen Einheit aus gewachsenem Bestand und zeitgenössischer Hinzufügung suchen, wurden mit wichtigen Architekturpreisen, darunter zwei Niken des BDA und dem Deutschen Städtebaupreis, ausgezeichnet. Von 2012 bis 2014 lehrte Jörg Springer als Vertretungsprofessor an der Technischen Universität Darmstadt, seit 2014 ist er Professor für Entwerfen und komplexe Gebäudelehre an der Bauhaus-Universität Weimar. Neben zahlreichen Tätigkeiten als Jurymitglied ist er zurzeit unter anderem Vorsitzender des Gestaltungsbeirates der Stadt Leipzig, Mitglied des Baukunstbeirates der Stadt Nürnberg und des Baukollegiums der Stadt Berlin.

Philipp Stricharz
ist Rechtsanwalt und seit 2010 Partner einer internationalen Wirtschaftskanzlei. In den Jahren 2011 bis 2019 war er Mitglied im Direktorium des Zentralrats der Juden. Seit 2011 gehört er zum Vorstand der Jüdischen Gemeinde in Hamburg, die unter anderem die Hamburger Synagoge sowie das Joseph-Carlebach-Bildungshaus mit Kindergarten, Grund- und Stadtteilschule im Grindelviertel betreibt. Philipp Stricharz wurde 2019 zum 1. Vorsitzenden der Jüdischen Gemeinde in Hamburg gewählt.

Ivan Reimann
studied architecture in Berlin, Prague, and London From 1989 until 1994, he was an assistant to Prof. Dr. Schmidt-Thomsen at the Technische Universität Berlin, and has been active as an architect since 1988. He now heads an architectural office in Berlin together with Thomas Müller. They regard their generally large-scale, complex architectural projects, mostly located in urban contexts, as elements of an evolved architectural substance. Among their designs is the headquarters of the German Foreign Office in Berlin and the Marienturm in Frankfurt am Main. Among other distinctions, Reimann was a member of the Advisory Board for the City of Prague from 2014 until 2016 and the Design Advisory Board for the City of Halle from 2015 until 2017. He has been a professor of building theory and design at the Technische Universität Dresden since 1999.

Jörg Springer
studied architecture in Berlin and Barcelona. In 1995, after working with Josep Lluís Mateo, he founded the office of Springer Architekten in Berlin. His works strive to achieve a self-evident unity—often in historical contexts—between evolved architectural substance and contemporary additions. He has received major architectural prizes, among them two Nikes from the BDA and the Deutscher Städtebaupreis. From 2012 until 2014, Jörg Springer was a temporary professor at the Technische Universität Darmstadt, and has been a professor of design and complex building theory at the Bauhaus-Universität Weimar since 2014. Alongside numerous jury memberships, he is currently Chair of the Design Advisory Board for the City of Leipzig, a member of the Architectural Advisory Board of the City of Nuremberg and the City of Berlin.

Philipp Stricharz
is an attorney, and has been a partner in an international corporate law firm since 2010. From 2011 until 2019, he was a member of the directorate of the Central Council of Jews in Germany. Since 2011, he has been a member of the governing board of the Hamburg Jewish Community, which operates the city's synagogues, along with the Joseph-Carlebach-Bildungshaus, with a kindergarten, elementary school, and district school, located in the Grindel district. In 2019, Stricharz was elected first chair of the Hamburg Jewish community.

Drs. Edward van Voolen
studierte Kunstgeschichte und Geschichte an der Universität Amsterdam. Er wurde am Leo Baeck College in London und am Hebrew Union College in New York als Rabbiner ausgebildet und 1978 in London ordiniert. Von 1978 bis 2013 war er Kurator und Kustos am Joods Museum in Amsterdam. Er war als Rabbiner in den Niederlanden und Deutschland tätig, heute wirkt er in Göttingen. Er ist Direktoriumsmitglied des Abraham Geiger Kollegs an der Universität Potsdam, Mitglied der Central Conference of American Rabbis (CCAR) und Kuratoriumsmitglied der Freunde des Tel Aviv Museum of Art Deutschland (TAMAD). Edward van Voolen war als Jurymitglied beim Architekturwettbewerb für das Jüdische Museum Berlin, das Felix-Nussbaum-Haus in Osnabrück und das Polin, Museum für polnisch-jüdische Geschichte, Warschau und als Beiratsmitglied für die Jüdischen Museen in Wien, Chicago, Paris und Brüssel aktiv. Er ist Gründungsmitglied der Association of European Jewish Museums und Verfasser zahlreicher Bücher und Aufsätze über jüdische Religion, Kultur, Architektur und Geschichte in niederländischer, deutscher und englischer Sprache.

Gesine Weinmiller
studierte Architektur in München. Nach anschließender Mitarbeit im Büro von Prof. Hans Kollhoff gründete sie 1992 ihr Architekturbüro in Berlin und war von 1992 bis 1994 als Assistentin von Flora Ruchat Roncati an der ETH Zürich tätig. Zusammen mit Michael Großmann führt Gesine Weinmiller seit 1999 ein Architekturbüro mit Standorten in Hamburg und Berlin. Das Werk des Büros umfasst zahlreiche großmaßstäbliche öffentliche Gebäude und Sakralbauten, wie die mehrfach ausgezeichnete Genezareth-Kirche mit Gemeindezentrum in Aachen. Gesine Weinmiller war Mitglied des Architekturbeirates des Auswärtigen Amtes und ist Mitglied des Gestaltungsbeirates der Stadt Regensburg. Seit 2000 ist sie Professorin für Entwerfen und Gebäudelehre an der HafenCity Universität Hamburg.

Dr. Mirjam Wenzel
studierte Allgemeine und Vergleichende Literaturwissenschaft, Theater-, Film- und Fernsehwissenschaft sowie Politikwissenschaft an der Freien Universität Berlin. Von 2001 bis 2007 war sie wissenschaftliche Mitarbeiterin am Institut für Deutsche Philologie der Ludwig-Maximilians-Universität München, wo sie 2009 zum Dr. phil. promovierte. In den Jahren 2007 bis 2015 war Mirjam Wenzel Leiterin der Medienabteilung des Jüdischen Museum Berlin. Seit 2016 ist sie Direktorin des Jüdischen Museums Frankfurt. Ihre Arbeit am neuen Corporate Design des Jüdischen Museums Frankfurt wurde 2018 mit dem Red Dot Design Award ausgezeichnet. Der grundlegend erneuerte und von Staab Architekten erweiterte Museumskomplex am Bertha-Pappenheim-Platz 1 erhielt 2022 die Große Nike des Bunds deutscher Architektinnen und Architekten. Mirjam Wenzel wurde 2019 zur Honorarprofessorin an der Goethe-Universität Frankfurt ernannt, wo sie seitdem am Seminar für Judaistik lehrt.

Drs. Edward van Voolen
studied art history and history at Amsterdam University. He was trained as a rabbi at the Leo Baeck College in London and the Hebrew Union College in New York, and was ordained in London in 1978. He was a curator and custodian at the Joods Museum in Amsterdam from 1978 to 2013, and has been a practising rabbi in the Netherlands and Germany, most recently in Göttingen. He is a member of the board of directors of the Abraham Geiger College at Potsdam University, a member of the Central Conference of American Rabbis (CCAR), and part of the curatorial board of the Friends of the Tel Aviv Museum of Art in Germany (TAMAD). Edward van Voolen has been a jury member for the architectural competition for the Jewish Museum in Berlin, the Felix-Nussbaum-Haus in Osnabrück, and the Polin, Museum of the History of Polish Jews in Warsaw. He has also been on the advisory boards for the Jewish museums in Chicago, Paris, and Brussels. He is a founding member of the Association of European Jewish Museums, and the author of numerous books and essays on Jewish religion, culture, architecture, and history, published in Dutch, German, and English.

Gesine Weinmiller
studied architecture in Munich. In 1992, after working in the office of Prof. Hans Kollhoff, she founded an architectural office in Berlin, and worked as an assistant to Flora Ruchat Roncati at the ETH Zürich from 1992 until 1994. Together with Michael Großmann, Gesine Weinmiller has headed an architectural office with branches in Hamburg and Berlin since 1999. The practice's activities encompass numerous large-scale public and sacred buildings, among them the Genezareth-Kirche and Community Center in Aachen, which has received multiple awards. Gesine Weinmiller was a member of the Architectural Advisory Board of the Federal Foreign Office, as well as the chair of the Design Advisory Board for the City of Wiesbaden, and has been a professor of design and building theory at HafenCity University Hamburg since 2000.

Dr. Mirjam Wenzel
studied general and comparative literature, theater, film, and television studies, as well as political science, at the Freie Universität Berlin. From 2001 until 2007, she was a research associate at the Institute for German Philology at the Ludwig-Maximilians-Universität in Munich, where she earned a doctorate in 2009. From 2007 until 2015, Wenzel was head of the media department at the Jewish Museum in Berlin. She has been the director of the Jewish Museum in Frankfurt since 2016. In 2018, her work on the new corporate design of the Jewish Museum in Frankfurt received the Red Dot Design Award. In 2022, the new Jewish museum complex, restored and enlarged by Staab Architects, was awarded with the Big Nike by the Association of German Architects. In 2019, Wenzel was named an honorary professor at the Goethe University Frankfurt, and has been an instructor with the Department of Jewish Studies there ever since.

Danksagung
Acknowledgements

Wir danken

der Bundesbeauftragten der Bundesregierung für Kultur und Medien und dem Kreativfonds der Bauhaus-Universität Weimar für die großzügige Förderung des Synagogen-Projekts;

den Kollegen und Kolleginnen
Wolfgang Lorch und Dana Pretzsch von der Technischen Universität Darmstadt,
Ivan Reimann, Thomas Müller, Andreas Fuchs, Patrick Gründel und Henrike Schoper von der Technischen Universität Dresden,
Gesine Weinmiller, Lena Ehringhaus und Roland Unterbusch von der HafenCity-Universität Hamburg sowie
Martin Pasztori und Sebastian Schröter
für die Anregungen, die das Synagogen-Projekt überhaupt erst möglich gemacht haben, für die intensive Betreuung der studentischen Projekte, für die zahlreichen inhaltlichen Beiträge und für die engagiert geführten Gespräche mit unseren Gästen;

allen Studierenden in Darmstadt, Dresden, Hamburg und in Weimar für ihre beeindruckenden Beiträge;

unseren Gesprächspartnern
Roger Diener, Franz-Josef Höing, Salomon Korn, Mario Marcus, Dekel Peretz, Philipp Stricharz, Mirjam Wenzel und Edward van Voolen für die wertvollen, offenen Gespräche;

Grit Farl für die nicht immer ganz einfache Transkription der Gespräche sowie für ihre kompetente Mitwirkung bei der Redaktion der Textbeiträge und Nils Niklas Schröder für die Bildrecherchen;

Bucharchitektur \ Kathrin Schmuck für die wunderbare Konzeption und Gestaltung (und für ihre Geduld);

Thomas Kramer und dem Verlag Park Books für die engagierte Betreuung, Inka Humann und Colette Forder für das Lektorat und Ian Pepper und Lisa Schons für die Übersetzungen ins Englische;

der Druckerei zu Altenburg für die Lithografie und Herstellung.

Our thanks to

the Federal Government Commissioner for Cultural and Media and the Kreativfonds of the Bauhaus-Universität Weimar for their generous sponsorship of the Synagogue Project;

our colleagues
Wolfgang Lorch and Dana Pretzsch from the Technische Universität Darmstadt,
Ivan Reimann, Thomas Müller, Andreas Fuchs, Patrick Gründel, and Henrike Schoper from the Technische Universität Dresden,
Gesine Weinmiller, Lena Ehringhaus, and Roland Unterbusch from HafenCity-University Hamburg, as well as
Martin Pasztori and Sebastian Schröter
for ideas and stimuli that made the Synagogue Project possible in the first place, for the intensive mentoring of student projects, for numerous thematic contributions, and for their enthusiastic participation in discussions with our guests;

all of the students in Darmstadt, Dresden, Hamburg, and Weimar for their remarkable contributions;

our discussion partners
Roger Diener, Franz-Josef Höing, Salomon Korn, Mario Marcus, Dekel Peretz, Philipp Stricharz, Mirjam Wenzel, and Edward van Voolen for their invaluable and open-minded exchange of ideas;

Grit Farl for transcribing the discussions (not always an easy task), and for her competent assistance in editing the text contributions, as well as to Nils Schröder for image research;

Bucharchitektur \ Kathrin Schmuck for the marvelous conception and design of this volume (and for her patience);

Thomas Kramer and Park Books for their dedicated support; to Inka Humann and Colette Forder for editing; and to Ian Pepper and Lisa Schons for the English translations;

Druckerei zu Altenburg GmbH for lithography and production.

Bildnachweis
Illustration credits

Neue Synagogen
New synagogues in Hamburg & Berlin
Jörg Springer

1 unbekannter Fotograf / Initiative Wiederaufbau Bornplatz
2 Kurt Hamann / ullstein bild
3 unbekannter Fotograf; Verlag M. Glückstadt & Münden / William L. Gross
4 unbekannter Künstler / The College of Charleston Library
5 Robert Arnauld d'Andilly, Philon von Alexandria: The works of Josephus, London 1683, S. 82 / University of Pittsburgh Library

Salomon Korn im Gespräch mit
in conversation with
Jörg Springer

1 unbekannter Fotograf / Leo Baeck Institute, F 17963
2 unbekannter Fotograf / Leo Baeck Institute, F 17965
3 Waltraud Krase / Deutsches Dokumentationszentrum für Kunstgeschichte / Bildarchiv Foto Marburg
4 Marko Priske / Stiftung Denkmal für die ermordeten Juden Europas
5 Sigrid Schütze-Rodemann & Gert Schütze / akg-images

Mario Marcus & Dekel Peretz im Gespräch mit
in conversation with
Andreas Fuchs & Ivan Reimann

1 Waldemar Titzenthaler / Landesarchiv Berlin, F Rep. 290 Nr. II12109
2 Abraham Pisarek / akg-images
3 unbekannter Fotograf / akg-images
4 unbekannter Fotograf / Kedem Auction House Ltd.
5 unbekannter Fotograf / Leo Baeck Institute, F 129
6 Abraham Pisarek / akg-images
7 Jürgen Henschel / FHXB Friedrichshain-Kreuzberg Museum, K03.0561 31-34

Synagoge Fraenkelufer
Fraenkelufer Synagogue

1 unbekannter Fotograf / Deutsche Bauzeitung, Bd. 63, Berlin 1916, S. 339
2 Walter Mittelholzer / ETH-Bibliothek Zürich, Bildarchiv / Stiftung Luftbild Schweiz, LBS_MH02-15-0024
3 unbekannter Fotograf / Deutsche Bauzeitung, Bd. 63, Berlin 1916, S. 329
4 Lutz Röhrig / www.zeit-fuer-berlin.de
5 Alexander Beer / Ralf Bothe: Synagogen in Berlin. Zur Geschichte einer zerstörten Architektur, Bd. 1, Berlin 1983, S. 144
6–7 Alexander Beer / Ralf Bothe: Synagogen in Berlin. Zur Geschichte einer zerstörten Architektur, Bd. 1, Berlin 1983, S. 145
8 Curt Leschnitzer / Daniela Gauding, Christine Zahn: Die Synagoge Fraenkelufer, Jüdische Miniaturen, Bd. 40, Berlin 2009, S. 24

Edward van Voolen im Gespräch mit
in conversation with
Ivan Reimann & Gesine Weinmiller

1 Bernard Picart / Leo Baeck Institute, 78.65a-l
2 unbekannter Fotograf / bpk / Kunstbibliothek, SMB
3 Erich Mendelsohn / bpk / Kunstbibliothek, SMB / Dietmar Katz
4 Genaro Perez de Villa-Amil / Patricio de la Escosura, Genaro Perez de Villa-Amil: España artística y monumental. Vistas y descripción de los sitios y monumentos más notables de españa, Bd. 1, Paris 1842, S. 44
5 unbekannter Fotograf; Verlag Jurany & Hensel / StadtA WI F000, 3174

Roger Diener im Gespräch mit
in conversation with
Jörg Springer

1–3 Diener & Diener Architekten
4 Sigrid Schütze-Rodemann & Gert Schütze /
 akg-images
5 Hufton+Crow / Studio Libeskind
6 Hélène Binet
7 Valentin Müller & Malte Wiegand

Tempel Poolstraße
Temple Poolstraße

1 unbekannter Künstler / Leo Baeck Institute, F 3248
2 Vermessungskarten 1:4000 1880 bis 1925 Hamburg /
 Freie und Hansestadt Hamburg / Kulturbehörde
3–4 Dorfmüller Klier
5–7 Bàlint Kemeny
10 Heinrich Jessen / Wikimedia Commons / gemeinfrei

Franz-Josef Höing & Philipp Stricharz im Gespräch mit
in conversation with
Wolfgang Lorch, Ivan Reimann,
Jörg Springer & Gesine Weinmiller

1 An-d / Wikimedia Commons / gemeinfrei
2 Ina Lafrentz & Samuel Pahlke
3 unbekannter Fotograf / Architekten- und Ingenieur-
 Verein zu Hamburg: Hamburg und seine Bauten unter
 Berücksichtigung der Nachbarstädte Altona und
 Wandsbek 1914, Hamburg 1914, S. 142
4 Architekten- und Ingenieur-Verein zu Hamburg:
 Hamburg und seine Bauten unter Berücksichtigung der
 Nachbarstädte Altona und Wandsbek 1914, Hamburg
 1914, S. 203
5 unbekannter Fotograf / Initiative Wiederaufbau
 Bornplatz

Mirjam Wenzel im Gespräch mit
in conversation with
Wolfgang Lorch & Jörg Springer

1 J. Kolb / akg-images
2 Uwe Dettmar
3 unbekannter Fotograf; Verlag Zedler & Vogel /
 Wikimedia Commons / gemeinfrei
4 Hervé Champollion / akg-images
5 Ria Roberg
6 Norbert Miguletz
7 Florian Mohnheim / Bildarchiv Mohnheim

Synagoge Bornplatz
Synagogue Bornplatz

1 unbekannter Fotograf; Verlag Knackstedt & Nähter /
 SHMH / Museum für Hamburgische Geschichte,
 Inv.-Nr.: 2008-1015
2 Vermessungskarten 1:4000 1880 bis 1925 Hamburg /
 Freie und Hansestadt Hamburg / Kulturbehörde
3 Margrit Kahl / Forum für Künstlernachlässe
4–6 Semmy Engel & Ernst Friedheim / Staatsarchiv
 Hamburg, 522-1 / Jüdische Gemeinden, Nr. 447
7 unbekannter Fotograf / Central Archives for the History
 of the Jewish People (CAHJP), D-Ph-127

Impressum
Imprint

Projektträger
Project partners

Bauhaus-Universität Weimar
Professur für Entwerfen und komplexe Gebäudelehre
Prof. Jörg Springer
Manuel Aust
Martin Pasztori
Sebastian Schröter

HafenCity Universität Hamburg
Professur Entwerfen und Gebäudelehre
Prof. Gesine Weinmiller
Lena Ehringhaus
Roland Unterbusch

Technische Universität Dresden
Professur Öffentliche Bauten
Prof. Ivan Reimann
Prof. Thomas Müller
Dr. Henrike Schoper
Andreas Fuchs
Patrick Gründel

Technische Universität Darmstadt
Fachgebiet Entwerfen und Baugestaltung
Prof. Wolfgang Lorch
Dana Pretzsch

Herausgeber
Edited by
Jörg Springer, Manuel Aust

Redaktion
Content editing
Manuel Aust
Martin Pasztori
Grit Farl
Arthur Helmecke
Nils Niklas Schröder

Konzept & Gestaltung
Visual concept and book design
Bucharchitektur \ Kathrin Schmuck

Übersetzung
Translation
Ian Pepper

Lektorat / Korrektorat
Copy editing / Proofreading
Inka Humann / Colette Forder

Schrift
Font
ABC Dinamo

Papier und Bucheinband
Paper and cover material
Pergraphica Classic Rough, 120 g/qm
Duoleinen Bamberger Kaliko, kalkstein

Lithografie, Druck und Bindung
Image processing, printing, and binding
DZA Druckerei zu Altenburg GmbH, Thüringen

Förderung
With support from
Die Beauftragte der Bundesregierung
für Kultur und Medien
Kreativfonds der Bauhaus-Universität Weimar

© 2022 Park Books AG, Zürich
© für die Texte: die Autorinnen und Autoren
for the texts: the authors
© für die Bilder: siehe Bildnachweis
for the images: see image credits

Park Books
Niederdorfstrasse 54
8001 Zürich
Schweiz / Switzerland
www.park-books.com

Park Books wird vom Bundesamt für Kultur mit einem Strukturbeitrag für die Jahre 2021–2024 unterstützt.
Park Books is being supported by the Federal Office of Culture with a general subsidy for the years 2021–2024.

Alle Rechte vorbehalten; kein Teil dieses Werks darf in irgendeiner Form ohne vorherige schriftliche Genehmigung des Verlags reproduziert oder unter Verwendung elektronischer Systeme verarbeitet, vervielfältigt oder verbreitet werden.
All rights reserved; no part of this publication may be reproduced, stored in a retrieval system or transmitted in any form or by any means, electronic, mechanical, photocopying, recording, or otherwise, without the prior written consent of the publisher.

ISBN 978-3-03860-300-9

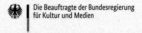